Metini Village

An Archaeological Study of Sustained Colonialism in Northern California

Kent G. Lightfoot and Sara L. Gonzalez

With Contributions by Fanya Becks, Elliot H. Blair,
and Thomas A. Wake

Foreword by Reno Keoni Franklin

Published by eScholarship, Berkeley, CA
1st edition
Ebook: ISBN 978-0-9890022-6-4
POD: ISBN 978-0-9890022-7-1

Available open access at: www.escholarship.org/uc/item/2zn2c26r
Publication of this book was made possible by funding from
UC Berkeley Library and Berkeley Research Impact Initiative Funds.

Front cover image: Darren Modzelewski
Back cover image: Lee Panich

Design and Production: Lisa Devenish, Detta Penna, Ronel Alberts

Contents

List of Figures

List of Tables

Acknowledgments

The investigation of the Metini Village site (CA-SON-175) would not have been possible without the assistance and support of many people and institutions. We begin by thanking members of the Kashia Band of Pomo Indians who worked on all aspects of the fieldwork and made the study a successful collaborative project. We are particularly indebted to Otis Parrish, whose participation was crucial in directing, facilitating, and implementing the survey and excavation components of the project; to Violet Parrish Chappell and Vivian Wilder, who spent many hours teaching students and faculty about the history and culture of the Kashaya people, as well as creating some of the most delicious meals ever served in a field camp; to Warren Parrish, Mary Anne Parrish, and Shawn Marrufo, who were indispensable in undertaking the surface investigation of the site, tirelessly completing many surface collection units; and to Eric Wilder, Violet Wilder, Duke Marrufo, Paul Chappell, and Jack Wilder, along with many others, who made us feel welcome in their beautiful ancestral homeland. We are most grateful for the continued advice, guidance, and friendship of Reno Keoni Franklin, who served as Tribal Historic Preservation Officer and now as Tribal Chairman, during the time when the Metini materials were being analyzed and written up.

We are most appreciative for the continued support of our archaeological investigations by the California Department of Parks and Recreation. We have been blessed to work with a number of fine people in the Sonoma-Mendocino Coast District Office and at Fort Ross State Historic Park (FRSHP). Breck Parkman has been instrumental in providing leadership, moral support, and assistance for most of the archaeological projects initiated by UC Berkeley in California, and the Metini Village project is no exception. The work would not have taken place without his guidance, advice, and foresight. Daniel Murley worked diligently in the field with us and was crucial for the completion of the geophysical survey, including working under a tarp in the field to fix software problems. Bill Walton, as always, was on hand to provide logistical support and a calming influence during any crisis. Glenn Farris was available night and day to provide logistical advice in the field and for answering questions about the history of Colony Ross. The Fort Ross Interpretive Association, now the Fort Ross Conservancy, continues to be a strong supporter of archaeology at FRSHP. We thank the former director, Lyn Kalani, and the current director, Sarah Sweedler, for their generosity, as well as their assistance in using the amazing research facilities and library at Fort Ross. The interpretive staff at FRSHP, particularly Robin Joy and Hank Birnbaum, are also strong supporters of archaeology and incorporate many of the findings from our projects into the interpretive programs of the park, for which we are deeply grateful.

We are also thankful for the leadership and backing of the Anthropology Department and Archaeological Research Facility (ARF) at UC Berkley for continuing to support our field and laboratory research in California archaeology. The past Directors of ARF, Professor Margaret Conkey and Professor Laurie Wilkie, and current Director, Professor Christine Hastorf, helped us greatly in completing the analysis of the Metini materials and in producing this volume. The former ARF administrator, Sherry Pierce Parrish, worked long hours in the field with us, assisted us in obtaining grant funding, and managed the expenditure of these funds during the field and laboratory components of the project. Tomeko Wyrick and Nicholas Tripcevich continue this fine tradition today.

It is crucial to recognize the wonderful archaeological staff and students who worked on the Metini Village project. While Kent Lightfoot managed the overall project, Roberta A. Jewett and Otis Parish served as Field Directors, and they were assisted by Daniel Murley, Stephen Silliman, Barbara Voss, Breck Parkman, James Allan, Bob Orlins, Warren Parrish, Mary Anne Parrish, Shawn Marrufo, and Anna Naruta. Field work during the summer of 1998 was greatly facilitated by a UC Berkeley summer field class (Anthro 133) that provided the opportunity for students to work not only at the Metini Village site, but also at the Petaluma Adobe (with Stephen Silliman) and El Presidio de San Francisco (with Barbara Voss). The super group of students included Colin Bailey, Dale Beevers, Carmen Brown, Lindsay Brustin, Trent Ernst, Julie Federico, Amanda Garbe, Robert Kobald, Renate Massing, Michael Miller, Victoria Morgan, Heather Mozdem, Tamina Isolani-Nagrula, Anne Olney, Elyka Perez, Belinda Perez, Elizabeth Salsedo, Gaurau Singh, Amy Carol Smith, Sean Stasio, Erin Walters, and David Weinreich. Fieldwork conducted in spring 1999 involved Otis Parrish, Roberta A. Jewett, Kent Lightfoot, Daniel Murley, Breck Parkman, Sherry Pierce Parrish, Stephen Silliman, Anna Naruta, Heather Price, Erika Waldenwagen, Kathy Dowdall, Scotty Thompson, and Augustine Diez, who were assisted by UC Berkeley student volunteers—Erin Walters, Lindsay Brustin, Rebecca Graff, Autumn Payne, Anne Olney, Julie Federico, and Sean Stasio.

Laboratory analysis of the Metini Village assemblage in the California Archaeology Laboratory in Kroeber Hall at UC Berkeley was greatly facilitated by Roberta A. Jewett, Kevin Sinats, Elizabeth Campos, Fanya Becks, and Brandon Patterson. Specialized analyses were conducted by Fanya Becks (shell beads), Elliot Blair (glass beads), David Palmer (ceramic, metal, glass artifacts), Allison Leigh Milner (lithic artifacts), Emily Darko (worked glass artifacts), Steven Shackley (geochemical sourcing of obsidian artifacts), Thomas M. Origer (obsidian hydration), Thomas A. Wake (vertebrate faunal assemblage), and Virginia S. Popper (ethnobotanical remains). The cataloguing, photography, and preparation of the Metini materials for long-term curation by the California Department of Parks and Recreation has been carefully managed by Elizabeth Campos. All artifact photos in this volume are courtesy of Elizabeth Campos and we thank her for her time and effort on our behalf.

We are most grateful for the financial assistance from several institutions to undertake the field and laboratory work and to complete this monograph on the Metini Village site. Funding for the project has been generously provided by a grant from the National Science Foundation (SBR-9806901), the Fort Ross Global Village Project grant from the California Department of Parks and Recreation, a Stahl Endowment grant from the Archaeological Research Facility at UC Berkeley, the Salmon Fund Faculty Research grant from Vassar College, and the munificent endowment from the Class of 1960 Chair in Undergraduate Education at UC Berkeley.

We are further indebted to Glenn Farris and Seth Mallios for their insightful, constructive, and extremely helpful peer review comments on an earlier draft of this manuscript. We appreciate greatly the editorial assistance and production expertise of Detta Penna, Lisa Devenish, and Ronel Alberts in the creation of this beautiful monograph for the ARF Contributions Series. Publication for this monograph was made possible by funding from the Collins Faculty Research Grant, UC Berkeley, and Berkeley Research Impact Initiative Funds.

Foreword to This Volume

For thousands of years our Kashaya people enjoyed the land and all that it offered to us. Prior to stepping onto the earth, we made agreements in the before-world, agreements to honor the land and all living things within it through ceremony. Kashaya people continue to honor those agreements today, and despite efforts to remove us from the cultural practices that make us Kashaya, we have persevered and remain steadfast in our commitment to the promotion and preservation of our culture, language, and history.

Metini is alive. To understand what Metini means to us, you must understand and respect the history of this place. You must acknowledge the good and bad history that exists. You must know that the Kashaya at Metini shared our precious resources with other tribes who crossed the river at "Sea View Crossing" to trade with us, there were exchanges of culture with native peoples from foreign lands, a treaty was signed between us and the "undersea" people, Metini was a safe haven for other tribes who were trying to escape the evils of the era, and finally you must celebrate the relationships that have withstood the test of time between the Kashaya and the Siberians, Hawaiians, Russians, Alaska Natives, the Benitz family and the Call family. Knowledge of history, especially a shared history, is the first step in respecting it.

Kashaya is fortunate that our history at Metini is a well-documented one. For nearly two centuries, historical accounts have been written about our village of Metini. These accounts or stories have aided Kashaya's entry into an era of healing. They contributed to a reconciliation of past wrongs, wrongs evidenced by the historic, archaeological, and anthropological records meticulously kept by those who perpetrated these wrongs on our people, wrongs whose gruesome details have been passed down orally through generations of Kashaya families. Along with that history comes a path to heal the wrongs. If you respect it, you will see it. Kashaya has begun our journey on that path.

Over a period of one year, the healing started with Russia returning four seeds that had been hiding in a Kashaya basket taken from Metini nearly 200 years ago. These seeds slowly and deliberately made their way back home to our Kashaya hands once again. Next was the greeting of the Siberian people and a celebration of our welcoming them back into our lands. Soon after, we began to write the next chapter of the history of Kashaya and the Alaska Native people, a welcoming of their people to our shores was completed with a show of gratitude and an acceptance of apologies from the Alaskan Natives. Finally, a reconnection with the Benitz family whose patriarch William Benitz had risked his life all those years ago to rescue 40 Kashaya women and children from Mexican slave traders.

We come to this place in our history at Metini where we can look back and feel no anger, no sadness, no fear. We can teach our next generation what really happened. We can show them how to respect the history of this place, those peoples who are a part of it and most importantly, what their place is in it. We will always remember what was done at Metini and more importantly, we will make sure to recognize the sacrifices that were made.

In honor of the people who worked to make this book happen, I will close the foreword to this book, this opening of a dialogue of our shared history, with a reminder of why we are still here. A tribute to the strong Kashaya men and women who sacrificed in a changing time, so that we could remain Kashaya. This is a firsthand account of four days of raping and murder at the hands of Mexican, white and valley Indian slave traders. It finished with two horrible days at the village of Metini:

> The Raid on Metini, July, 1845, taken from court transcripts (August 1845) and translated by our friends Peter Benitz and Glenn Farris: "...*they headed to Ross: their goal was to take some people as workers, and some lepe or orphans. When they arrived, the Indians ran into the woods and the only ones left in the villages next to the plaza were two Chiefs who were tied up, the first by Rafael Garcia who struck him many times with the stock of his rifle; and the second ran and Don Antonio Castro told the witness to chase and catch him, which he did. With the violent charge of his horse he grabbed him by the top-knot of hair on his head. Upon reaching him, the beast ran him over and the Indian fell. Then Don Antonio Castro arrived and hit him several times with the sword he carried on his belt. Then the two Chiefs were tied together and Don Antonio Castro told them, that if they handed over their people he would let them go, otherwise he would take them prisoner to Monterey for being brazen. Then the Indians basically promised they would bring the village and they were let loose not returning.*"

These two Kashaya Chiefs stood tall in the village of Metini, waiting for the savage rancheros to come. They were beaten and almost killed, but were smart enough to get away. They knew what would happen, but they sacrificed themselves to protect their people. We do not know exactly which of these four Chiefs it was, but we know it is likely two of these four; Chief Tojon, Chief Noportegi, Chief Kolo-biscau, and Chief Cojoto. More importantly, we know their heroic actions saved many people. Eventually William Benitz was able to have our women and children returned to Metini, but the end of an era had signaled its nearing, and soon we would leave Metini.

Yahwee to all of you who have worked on this project. Yahwee for playing your part in helping to tell the history of this special place. Yahwee to our ancestors, elders, and our youth. Yawee Metini.

Chairman Reno Keoni Franklin
Kashia Band of Pomo Indians

Chapter 1

Introduction

This volume, the third in a series on the *Archaeology and Ethnohistory of Fort Ross, California*, describes the results of archaeological investigations during the summer of 1998 and spring of 1999 at the Metini Village site (CA-SON-175) located in Fort Ross State Historic Park in northern California. Recognized as an ancestral place by the Kashia Band of Pomo Indians today, the study of Metini affords an exceptional opportunity to examine how local Native populations negotiated and survived the onslaught of sustained settler colonialism. The Kashaya Pomo people witnessed firsthand the transition from one distinctive colonial regime to another—Russian, Mexican, and American—over the course of more than six decades. The Kashaya commenced their colonial entanglements with Russian merchants who founded a fur trade/agrarian colony in their homeland from 1812–1841. Following this experience, they became immersed in a successful rancho enterprise that spanned almost three decades during the Mexican (1841–1846) and American periods (1846–current). The purpose of the archaeological study of Metini is to examine the consequences of these later manifestations of sustained colonialism on the lifeways, cultural practices, and world views of the Kashaya Pomo people.

Metini Village is situated a short distance north of the imposing stockade walls that the Russian-American Company first erected in 1812 as an integral component of *Selenie Ross* (the Ross Settlement) (Figure 1). For the next 29 years, this place served as the administrative hub for the broader mercantile enterprise of Colony Ross in northern California where Kashaya Pomo men and women, along with other Native Californian people (Coast Miwok, Southern Pomo), labored for and interacted with Russian, Creole (people of mixed Russian and Native heritage), and Native Alaskan (Alutiiq, Unangan, Tlingit, and Tanaina) employees of the mercantile company. When the Russian managers and most of their non-local workers departed Kashaya country in 1841, the indigenous population faced a new intrusion of strangers who soon established a Mexican-style rancho in the place of the old mercantile colony. Wilhelm (William) Benitz and his family eventually took over the Russian holdings where they engineered an agrarian business from the early 1840s to 1867, which depended largely on Kashaya Pomo laborers for its financial viability.

The archaeological investigation of Metini Village involved the collaboration of indigenous scholars and elders from the Kashaya Pomo tribe with archaeologists and resource specialists from the California Department of

1

Figure 1. Location of Metini Village
(CA-SON-175).

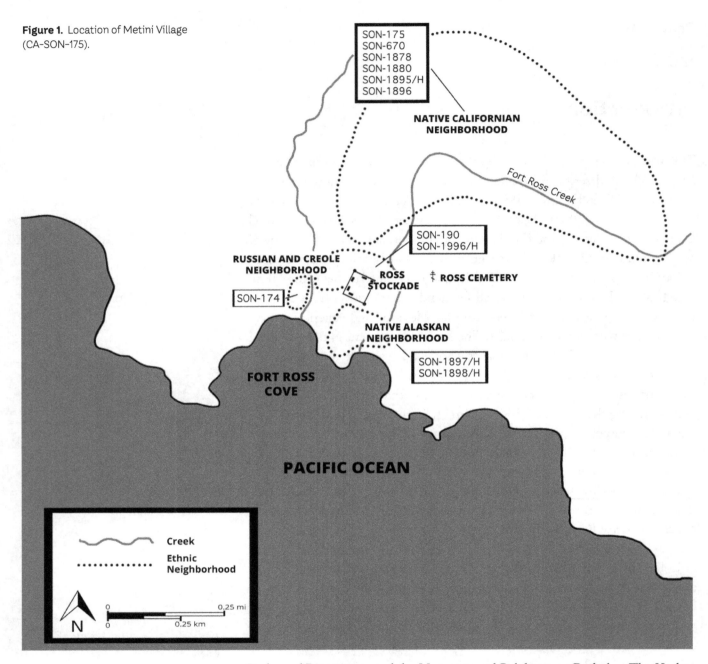

Parks and Recreation and the University of California at Berkeley. The Kashia
Band of Pomo Indians obtained their trust lands at Stewart's Point Rancheria
in 1914 when it was purchased by the federal government (Kennedy 1955:96).
Most tribal members today reside either at the Rancheria, which is situated a
short distance north of Fort Ross State Historic Park, or in nearby towns and
cities in Sonoma County. A major objective of this project, in working closely
with the tribe and state parks, was to create a detailed map and recording of the
site that could be employed by managers at the Fort Ross State Historic Park
and would also aid tribal officials in the further protection and preservation of

this important place. Another primary objective of the collaborative research team was to enhance the interpretative program at the park by highlighting the significance of Metini Village in the history of the region and the important role it played in colonial entanglements in northern California. Specifically, the archaeological investigation addressed four research issues:

1. Chronology of Metini Village: When was it first occupied, and to what degree did its occupation overlap with Russian colonization of Kashaya lands and the later development of the Benitz Rancho?

2. How was Metini Village spatially organized? What kinds of daily practices did residents perform at the village?

3. How were the Kashaya Pomo treated as laborers for the colonial enterprises at the Ross settlement and the Benitz Rancho? Local Indians provided a critical labor source for ranching and other endeavors, but little is known about their treatment and compensation as agrarian and industrial workers.

4. What kinds of cultural transformations are evident at Metini Village? How did the residents maintain their Indian ethos and community while laboring and living a short distance from the Ross settlement and the Benitz Rancho?

It is important to recognize that the Kashaya Pomo today refer to the area encompassing the Fort Ross State Historic Park as *Metini*, the Kashaya word for "this place," their ancestral homeland; this designation should not be confused with that of the specific site of Metini Village, CA-SON-175, that is the focus of this volume. Although other iterations have been used in the past to refer to the archaeological remains of the village, including May-Tee-Nee, Mad-shui-nee, and Me tini, we remain consistent in this volume by referring to the site as Metini Village. As a former village, the Metini Village site (CA-SON-175) is considered a sacred place by the contemporary Kashaya Pomo, and as such it has been off-limits to archaeologists working in the Fort Ross State Historic Park for many years. Our collaborative project with the tribe represents the first detailed investigation of the site since its initial recording by archaeologists in 1935 and 1949. The field strategy employed at Metini was planned in accordance with Kashaya values and cultural protocols for dealing with sacred sites and was consequently designed to be as non-intrusive as possible by maximizing information about the spatial organization of the site based on surface and near-surface investigations. The goals of the field program were to obtain a sample of archaeological materials from across the site and to document its spatial structure by producing a series of overlapping topographic, geophysical, and artifact isopleth maps. The spatial structure of the site, constructed from both surface and near surface investigations, was then evaluated by limited subsurface testing.

Chapter 2

Research Agenda

The Archaeology of Sustained Colonialism

The study of Metini Village marks a major shift in the objectives of our research program at Fort Ross State Historic Park. Our previous work exemplified culture contact research that examined how the Kashaya Pomo responded to initial Russian colonization, and how these early encounters affected the magnitude, direction, and meaning of culture change among various indigenous and pluralistic foreign populations. The methodology involved the construction of a comparative baseline for measuring the material culture, subsistence, settlement patterns, and other cultural practices of the diverse participants prior to their colonial encounters. This baseline was derived from the combination of findings of archaeological investigations of late prehistoric sites in the region, as well as the earliest observations of indigenous men and women by European explorers. To measure the degree of cultural change that had taken place among the Kashaya Pomo during the first decade or two of their encounters with Russian, Native Alaskan, and Creole workers, we compared this late prehistoric/protohistoric baseline to archaeological discoveries from sites associated with Colony Ross and to accounts of the Native population in the nearby region penned by the Russian merchants after 1812 (see Lightfoot et al. 1998; Lightfoot 1995; Lightfoot, Schiff, and Wake 1997).

The study of the Metini Village transports our archaeological investigation of Colony Ross beyond the processes and consequences of initial culture contact. We are now examining how the Kashaya Pomo sustained and nurtured their Indian community after several decades of prolonged entanglements with successive waves of foreigners from distant lands. This extended view of Native and foreign interactions at Colony Ross dovetails nicely with a new emphasis in the archaeology of colonialism today—examining the long-term consequences of sustained, settler colonialism. Earlier studies of colonial encounters in North American archaeology, similar to our original work at Colony Ross, often focused on initial contact situations—colonial settings where early contacts took place between indigenous populations and foreigners. While these culture contact studies remain a critical component of archaeological research today, it is equally important to develop a long-term, diachronic perspective that allows researchers to examine the full continuum of colonial encounters—from initial contacts through later historical times, and continuing up to the present (see Silliman 2005a).

Unfortunately, archaeologists in North America have tended to ignore colonial contexts of the nineteenth and early twentieth century, where sustained later colonial entanglements between native and various foreign and settler populations have been ongoing for centuries. There are multiple reasons for the neglect of later episodes of colonialism. One reason is that scholars are relatively comfortable in examining the material remains of first contacts that can be compared directly to the pre-contact archaeological records of local regions. Much work has been devoted to the study of late pre-contact archaeology across North America. The investigation of first contacts represents, in many respects, a continuation of this research trajectory that provides a fairly clear-cut linkage to previous archaeological research.

A second reason is that the archaeology of colonialism in North America cut its teeth addressing research questions pertaining to first encounters. This is exemplified by the considerable research undertaken as part of the Columbus Quincentenary in the 1990s, which solidified the first contact perspective (Thomas 1989, 1990, 1991). These ground breaking works examined the archaeological signatures of the encampments of early European explorers, and asked various questions about how indigenous peoples first responded to various kinds of European colonial programs (missions, fur trade outposts, settler colonies), and their material culture, trade connections, labor practices, etc. A major component of this research focused on the implications of alien, communicable diseases and the mortality rates of Indian groups first exposed to these lethal pathogens (Dobyns 1983, 1991; Dunnell 1991; Verano and Ubelaker 1992).

A third reason is the innate difficulty of undertaking many archaeological investigations of later episodes of colonialism. The archaeological record of indigenous people in California, and indeed in the rest of North America, tends to become more difficult to detect and study in the decades following initial contact and settlement by foreign nations (Lightfoot 2006; Silliman 2009). The material remains of Native groups are less obvious and more muted, while their archaeological sites become more fragmented and less distinctive. These material patterns correlate with strategies of persistence and survival that resulted in Native communities "hiding in plain site" by downplaying outward and public displays of their community traditions and identities (Sleeper-Smith 2001). For example, many Native communities in California were forced to disperse, hide, or even change their outward identities in order to survive, especially in the early decades of American occupation (Lightfoot 2006:281–284; Lindsay 2012). Consequently, the detection and study of archaeological remains of indigenous people, who may have been intentionally trying to blend in with other ethnic groups or with the dominant population, may be challenging to identify solely on the basis of material remains.

However, despite these difficulties, we now recognize that it is crucial to undertake studies of indigenous people who were experiencing the impact of full-blown and sustained colonialism in the nineteenth century and onwards. In forging collaborative partnerships with Indians and other stakeholders in California, archaeologists are finding that it is the study of the recent past that is often of most pressing concern to many descendant communities. Native Californian groups grappling with issues of federal recognition, repatriation of ancestral remains (e.g., NAGPRA), and legal definitions of tribal territories must demonstrate cultural connections and continuities in tribal organizations between the present and the ancient past. The dark perilous days of the mid-to-late 1800s and early 1900s are among the most problematic for many California tribes, when many of these indigenous communities faced forced removal from tribal lands, legal slavery, bounty hunters, and death squads (often disguised as state or local militias) (Castillo 1978; Cook 1976; Heizer and Almquist 1971; Lightfoot 2005:210–233). During this period of California history, many Native groups who faced explicit brutality and extermination found it best to disappear into the colonial landscape and to leave few explicit signs of their presence.

Archaeological investigations can play a significant role in developing a better understanding of what happened to Native peoples during these later episodes of colonialism (Hart 2012; Lightfoot et al. 2013; Mrozowski et al. 2009). In moving beyond culture contact research, archaeologists can assist in reexamining or rewriting the histories of Native Californian groups who are enmeshed in legal battles concerning their cultural legitimacy or rights to territorial claims. We can employ empirically based lines of evidence (archaeological, documentary, oral traditions, ecological) to trace and evaluate historical developments of tribal nations that transcends from the contemporary through the bleak days of the nineteenth and twentieth centuries, back to initial culture contact episodes and beyond to ancient times. Archaeological studies of nineteenth and early twentieth century colonialism have the potential to make important contributions to our understanding of Native cultural transformations and the survival and persistence of these communities into the present.

The examination of later entanglements can also provide new theoretical and methodological approaches for archaeological studies of colonialism. Previous research on culture contact tended to emphasize the degree to which Native communities were impacted by and changed in relation to colonial encounters. Archaeologists measured the degree of cultural change among indigenous populations by comparing transformations from a late prehistoric/early contact baseline with those from early colonial contexts, typically by calculating the ratios or percentages of foreign, hybrid, and indigenous materials found in the archaeological record (Lightfoot 1995). While the study of cultural change and the long-term impacts of colonial encounters remains important in the archaeology of colonialism, there is a growing concern to document and study continuities in cultural practices. In creating collaborative programs with tribal groups who have a vested interest in demonstrating direct and unbroken connections with the past over time, archaeologists can no longer ignore periods of cultural continuity as insignificant and not requiring explanation.

In no longer taking cultural continuity for granted, Ann Stahl (2012) and others argue we need to develop theoretical approaches and methods to account for pulses of both stasis and change. As Silliman (2009:211) notes, archaeologists no longer perceive change and continuity as diametrically opposed responses to foreign entanglements, but rather as two different sides of the same process that unfold during colonial interactions. Diachronic perspectives of colonialism provide an excellent venue for experimenting with approaches that examine cultural trajectories that involve the continual interplay of change and continuity over the course of long-term colonial entanglements, what Lee Panich refers to as the archaeology of persistence (Panich 2010, 2013). When we view the history of communities in terms of cultural transformation, resistance, and survival, or what Vizenor (2008) refers to as survivance, what emerges is a more nuanced view of the multiple entanglements, outcomes, and routes that Native communities have experienced through their histories.

Sustained Colonialism at Colony Ross

The study of Metini Village presents an excellent opportunity to explore the later episodes of colonialism at Colony Ross. During the early-to-mid 1800s, the Kashaya Pomo people encountered two distinctive colonial ventures in relatively rapid succession—the mercantile enterprise of the Russian-American Company during the period of 1812 to 1841, and the subsequent Benitz Rancho during the 1840s, 1850s, and 1860s.

The Russians established the Ross settlement, which would become the administrative center of their northern California colony, on a windswept marine terrace overlooking what is now known as the Fort Ross Cove. Here they built a mercantile village, the Ross Settlement, with a palisade complex for protecting its managers and economic goods, nearby houses for their workers, shops for the many industrial and manufacturing activities at the settlement, and outlying buildings and features associated with agricultural lands, orchards, and free-range livestock grazing. During its early years, the primary economic enterprise of the Russian colony was the commercial harvesting of sea otter and fur seal pelts and other marine products for which they imported hundreds of Native Alaskan hunters to scour the nearby waters for sea mammals. When local populations of sea otters plummeted from over-exploitation in the late 1810s and 1820s, the Ross managers intensified agrarian productivity by expanding farming land around the Ross Settlement and by establishing several outlying ranches. They also enhanced industrial productivity at the Ross Settlement through the construction of a shipyard where they attempted to build a small fleet of ships, as well as producing, repairing, and trading goods for and with the Spanish California missions (see Farris 1989, 2012a; Gibson 1976; Lightfoot 2005 for a more detailed discussion of the Russian-American Company colony).

The Russian merchants imported not only Native Alaskan hunters to the Colony Ross, but also lower class Russian and Eastern European men, along with Creole workers who became integral members of the colonial labor force. The Russians also relied upon local Native Californians as seasonal laborers who performed difficult, and sometimes dangerous, back breaking work, such as hauling clay to make bricks, cutting timber in nearby forests, working in the shipyard, and toiling in agricultural production. The latter involving tilling the soil, harvesting crops by hand, and threshing and grinding wheat and barley into flour. As outlined elsewhere (Lightfoot 2005:137–140), it appears the Ross managers contracted for the employment of these seasonal laborers primarily in the late 1820s and 1830s, when agricultural intensification was at its peak in Russian California. Although Coast Miwok and Southern Pomo Indians were prominently represented in the Ross Colony labor pool, the majority of the workers appear to have been Kashaya Pomo men and women.

Previous archival and archaeological research suggests that many of the Californian Indians who served as seasonal workers for the Russians resided a short distance north of the Ross stockade in a series of Indian villages comprising what is now referred to as the Native Californian Neighborhood (Lightfoot et al. 1991:24–26). Metini Village (CA-SON-175) is one of the six archaeological sites that have been mapped and surface collected within the Native Californian Neighborhood (Figure 1). One of the questions we evaluate in this volume is whether Metini Village was actually part of this colonial neighborhood and contemporaneous with the Russian-American Company occupation of the *Metini* region.

When the Russian-American Company, after struggling for many years to make their colony economically viable, sold the land and extant structures and assets to John Augustus Sutter in 1841, the Kashaya Pomo witnessed the founding of a new colonial institution on their ancestral lands—the rancho: livestock and agricultural operations that individuals established through land grants from the Spanish and Mexican governments in California. In 1843, Wilhelm (William) Benitz was appointed as the overseer of Sutter's newly acquired property and later became lessee of the property in 1845, an action that was contested by the Mexican government and subsequently led to the creation of the Muñiz Rancho, which was claimed by Manuel Torres and included the coastal lands of the old Ross Settlement. Benitz eventually paid $5000 to Torres in 1849 to obtain legal claim to the Muñiz Rancho and during the succeeding years he built up a successful ranching enterprise (first with Ernest Rufus, and later with Charles Meyer). Using the former buildings of the Russian-American Company as his headquarters and home, Benitz established a rancho where he raised livestock and crops, maintained a commercial timber operation, a ferryboat across the Russian River, and a brewery, and even signed leases with mining companies and established a fishery with the help of Italian fishermen from San Francisco (see Tomlin 1993:6–10; Kalani and Sweedler 2004:35–41; Lightfoot et al. 1991:122). Similar to the Russian-American Company, the principal laborers for undertaking agrarian and other physical work at the Benitz Rancho were local California Indians, primarily the Kashaya Pomo, with a few additional Mexican vaqueros.

In summary, previous archival and archaeological research, along with Kashaya Pomo oral traditions, indicate that the Metini Village played a critical role in the history of local Indian encounters with the Russian-American Company and the Benitz Rancho. Given its prominence in local tribal history, the study of Metini Village offers an exceptional opportunity to examine the following four issues concerning colonial and Native entanglements in northern California.

Research Issues

Issue 1: Chronology

A significant goal of our archaeological investigations involved resolving the chronology of Metini Village. While there is convincing archival evidence that the Metini Village was associated with the Benitz Rancho and occupied during the Mexican and early American periods, when Metini Village was first established is unknown. As first reported by Glenn Farris (1986:16), the site is marked as an Indian Rancheria on the 1859 Plan map of the Muñiz rancho (Matthewson 1859). Based upon archival sources and oral histories, the terminal occupation of Metini Village probably does not date much later than the late 1860s–1870, which corresponds to the time period during which the Kashaya Pomo were largely removed from the *Metini* region by the current owners of the Muñiz Rancho, James Dixon and Lord Charles Fairfax (Kennedy 1955:83).

As for the founding of the village, in our collaboration with members of the Kashaya Pomo on this project, several tribal elders and scholars noted that tribal oral traditions indicated the site has considerable antiquity—possibly spanning back to ancient historical times. These traditions suggest the possibility that Metini Village may have been inhabited at points before, or even perhaps during the settlement of Colony Ross. The degree to which the village was contemporaneous with the construction and use of the Ross settlement, however, is not clear. For example, although records from the 1820s and 1830s document Russian managers' intensification of the colony's agricultural operations and indicate that these pursuits involved the active recruitment of Native Californian laborers, Company documents do not clearly illustrate where these laborers lived, either in close proximity to the stockade or further afield in a discrete residential location such as at Metini Village.

Issue 2: Spatial Organization

Our investigation of Metini Village will evaluate aspects of spatial organization for the purpose of contributing to a detailed understanding of daily lifeways within each of the ethnic neighborhoods of Colony Ross. Previous studies of the Native Alaskan Village site and survey of archaeological resources within FRSHP revealed the variability in how the neighborhoods were spatially structured and used by people. The goals of this investigation are to determine how the settlement of Metini Village was laid out, where domestic and religious structures were situated, where food processing and consumption took place, and where different kinds of activities occurred. This information provides a critical window for examining the ways in which daily practices within the Native Californian Neighborhood may have been materially distinct from other colonial and indigenous spaces (i.e., Kashaya settlements beyond the Ross Settlement).

Little is known about the California Indian communities where Native laborers resided a short distance from the Ross Settlement or Benitz Rancho. A number of observations about the local California Indians were made by Russian managers and visitors to Colony Ross, but many of these accounts describe indigenous communities located at Bodega Bay, near the Russian settlement of Port Ruminatsev, or in the outlying hinterland of Colony Ross, such as along the Russian River (Corney 1896:33–34; Golovnin 1979:168–169; Kostromitinov 1974:8–13; Kotzebue 1830:126–127; Lütke 1989:275–278; Wrangell 1974:3–6). Few of these descriptions are specific to the villages in the Native California Neighborhood or to the Indians living near the Ross Settlement, either during the Russian period or at later points in time. Beyond the historical references synthesized in Mary Jean Kennedy's (1955) pioneering work, for example, we have found no other references to the Indian villages associated with Benitz Rancho.

The most detailed account of an Indian village near the Ross Settlement, recently translated and annotated by Glenn Farris, was penned by the French naval officer, Captain Cyrille Théodore Laplace, who visited the Ross Settlement and nearby Port Rumiantsev on Bodega Bay in August, 1839. His observations are particularly pertinent for this study because he made them at the end of the Russian occupation and not long before the incorporation of the Benitz Rancho. Laplace's tour of the Ross facilities included traveling to one of the nearby Indian villages near the Ross Settlement, which may have been the Metini Village or one of the other five known sites comprising the Native Californian Neighborhood.

Therefore, I accepted with enthusiasm the proposition made by my host [Rotchev] to visit one afternoon before sunset an example of a hamlet that the natives and their families employed in agricultural work, had established in the vicinity of the fort.

Its population was rather considerable and was composed of some several hundred individuals. During this visit and another that I made the next day, I was able to study these singular beings in more detail; although following the counsel of my guide [Rotchev], I only dared to wander among them in his company, so as to not to raise their distrust, always dangerous for a stranger.

I understood this precaution in seeing the suspicious looks that followed my least movement, until the governor [Rotchev] having explained to my new hosts the motive of my visit, I distributed to the notables among them some glass trinkets, some little copper ornaments, and some cigars, to all of which both sexes seemed to attach a very high value. From this moment I could move freely in the huts and admit myself thus to the secrets of their interior.

This interior was hardly secluded, it is true, because the habitations of these poor people consisted without exception of miserable huts formed of branches through which the rain and wind passed without difficulty. It was there that all the family, father, mother, and children spent the nights lying pell-mell around the fire, some on cattle hides, the majority on the bare ground, and each one enveloped in a coverlet of wool that served him also as a mantle during the day when the weather was cold or wet.

Such was the costume of the men that all of them who surrounded me seemed to me nearly nude, except the chief and several young men who, only due to the presence of the governor for whom they showed profound respect, had decided to wear European shirts and pants.

I was disappointed. I would have much preferred to see them in their native ceremonial costume, more picturesque, more in harmony with their martial spirit and their truly dignified air, which I was later able to verify when this same chief who welcomed me at his house came to visit me the next day.

Although taken by surprise by the visit, these men seemed to me handsome, tall, robust, and perfectly well-built. Their smouldering black eyes, an aquiline nose rising to a high forehead, rounded cheekbones, and strong lips showing white, well-spaced teeth, symmetrically traced tattooing on their copper skin, a vigorous neck supported by large shoulders; in all, an air at once intelligent and dignified, all reminded me perfectly of the descriptions made by [Captain James] Cook and our Lapérouse, of the indigenous natives of the northwest coast of America, of which they were, if not the first, the most distinguished explorers...

In vain I sought to discover among the females some analogous advantages. I found all the women horribly ugly, having a stupid air, glum, their health broken by misery and hard work. If some young women showed in her figure or in the features of her face some vestiges of the charms that in the bosom of civilized societies the women are so generously endowed by nature, they were so dirty, the hide or wool skirt that composed nearly their only garment so filthy, their hair was so disheveled, that they could only inspire pity and disgust.

The majority were busy with the housekeeping, preparing meals for their husbands and children. Some were spreading out on the embers some pieces of beef given as rations, or shell-fish, or even fish which these unhappy creatures came to catch either at the nearby river [Fort Ross Creek?] or from the sea; while the others heated the [wheat] grain in a willow basket before grinding it between two stones. In the middle of this basket they shook constantly some live coals on which each grain passed rapidly by an ever more accelerated rotating movement until they were soon parched, without letting the inner side of the basket be burned by the fire. Some of these baskets [*paniers*], or more accurately, these deep baskets [*vases*] seemed to me true models of basketmaking, not only by their decoration but by the finishing touches of the work. They are made of shoots of straw or compact gorse so solidly held together by the thread [sic, coiling] that the fabric was water resistant, as efficiently as baked clay and earthernware. But, more behind in the material civilization than the Kaloches [Russian term used for native of Alaska], my savages [at

Fort Ross] did not know how to construct wooden bowls in which
the Indian housekeepers of the northwest came to boil liquids by
immersing some stones red-hot from the fire.

Mr. Rotchev, noting my astonishment that contact with his compatriots
had not modified more the ways and habits of the natives assured me
that these people, just like their counterparts in New Archangel [Sitka],
obstinately refused to exchange their customs for ours.

"However," he added, "thanks to a great deal of perseverance
and enticements, I have succeeded somewhat in diminishing this
adverse sentiment to whites among the natives of the tribes that
frequent Bodega Bay; several chiefs and a good number of young
people, encouraged by the bounty and generosity with which
they were treated by the Russian agents, and finding, with reason,
horribly miserable the life which they led during the winter in the
woods where they had no other protection against the cold and the
snow than the caves or the shelter of trees, and no other means of
subsistence than the unreliable products of the hunt, remain near
the fort during the bad season, working with our colonists and are
nourished like them. So, one sees their tastes change more each day
to the varied articles of adornment, dress and other things that are
used to pay for the services that they provide to the colony. Thus
one could hope that if the company retains this establishment for
long enough, the natives will be led little by little to submit to the
yoke of civilization. Seeing their labors generously paid for, their
freedom and religious beliefs, absurd as they are, respected; the most
indulgent principle of justice exercised to the point that deportation
to one of our other establishments is the most severe punishment
that I may inflict on those among them who have committed the
worst derelictions against our properties. Seeing, I say, the interest
that the public functionaries take in their well-being, they return
each spring in larger number than the year before, to cultivate our
fields and attach themselves to us, to the degree that in their desire to
remain always in good stead with the colonists, they are generally the
first to denounce the troublemakers who, for vengeance or by love of
disorder, kill the beasts in the fields or even destroy our crops." (Farris
2012b:250–253)

Laplace's descriptions of the village he visited—which may or may not be
Metini Village—add important historical detail to the settlements of Native
Californians at Colony Ross. The archaeological investigation of Metini Vil-
lage may thus complement and enhance our current historical and material

understanding of the Indian villages situated near the Ross Settlement and Benitz Rancho. Our goal is to examine the spatial layout of the residential site to better understand the organization of space involving public architecture (religious or non-domestic structures), domestic architecture, and adjacent work and recreational areas. Our investigation, following those conducted elsewhere within the colony, will examine the diversity and kinds of daily practices undertaken at Metini, how they were spatially organized across the village, and how materials were deposited within the broader community. These analyses have the potential to reveal the variability of indigenous colonial experiences at the colony, and those of the Kashaya Pomo specifically, at different points in time—from the Russian occupation to the present.

Issue 3: Colonial Laborers

Since little is known about the laboring conditions of Native Californian workers at either Colony Ross or the Benitz Rancho, we believe the study of Metini Village may possibly provide important perspectives about the laboring processes and compensation for Native Californian laborers. Silliman (2004) demonstrated the important role that archaeology can play in better understanding the indigenous experiences of colonial labor and laborers in the nearby Petaluma Adobe in the 1830s and 1840s.

Russian-American Company. Russian accounts of Indian laborers at Colony Ross are sparse and lacking in detail. The merchants noted that the Indians were used for "reaping and hauling sheaves to the threshing floors, hauling clay for bricks," along with other demanding chores such as cutting and hauling timber for shipbuilding (Lightfoot, et al. 1991:16–20; Wrangell 1969:211). The best account of the kind of agrarian work performed by Indian workers derives from the oral tradition of the Kashaya Pomo tribe, which vividly describes how they raised, harvested, and processed wheat crops using sea lion skin sacks, horses, and a windmill (see Oswalt 1964:267–269, Herman James' story of "Grain Foods").

Unlike other Russian-American Company workers who were paid salaries in script that could be redeemed in the company store, California Indian laborers were paid "in kind" for specific tasks performed. Payment might include food, clothing, tobacco, beads, and other goods negotiated with the Ross managers (Khlebnikov 1990:193–194; Kostromitinov 1974:8–9; Laplace 2006:58; Wrangell 1969:211). In bargaining directly with Indian workers or their leaders, Peter Kostromitinov (the manager of the Ross settlement from 1830–1838) noted "they sometimes demand a great deal for work performed by them, sometimes, on the other hand, very little" (Kostromitinov 1974:8).

By one Russian manager's own admission, however, it appears that seasonal laborers often worked long hours for very little pay. In his tour of the Ross colony in 1833, the Chief Manager of the Russian-American Company, Ferdinand Petrovich Wrangell, wrote a searing critique about its management and treatment of its lower ranking Russian, Creole, and Native Alaskan (referred to as Aleuts) laborers, noting that many of them were poorly paid and in debt to the company. He also observed the mistreatment of the seasonal Indian workers who were also poorly compensated for their work, with some forcibly relocated to the Ross colony to work in the fields.

> In the aforementioned proposal I have authorized providing the Indians and Aleuts the best food, as against formerly, and especially paying the Indians somewhat more generously for work. Not only humanity but also wisdom demand that the Indians be encouraged more: from the bad food and the negligible pay the Indians have stopped coming to the settlement for work, from which the Factory found itself forced to seek them in the tundra, attack by surprise, tie their hands, and drive them to the settlement like cattle to work: such a party of 75 men, wives, and children was brought to the settlement during my presence from a distance of about 65 verstas (43 miles) from here, where they had to leave their belongings without any attention for two months. It goes without saying what consequences there must be in due course from such actions with the Indians, and will we make them our friends? I hope that the Factory, having received permission from me to provide the Indians decent food and satisfactory pay, will soon see a change in their disposition toward us, and the Main Administration will of course recognize these increased expenses, justifiable and useful, as against the former expense (Wrangell 1969:211).

A recent study suggests that working conditions may have improved for California Indians at Colony Ross following Wrangell's 1833 visit (see Lightfoot 2005:139–140). With the establishment of outlying ranches in the late 1830s, for example, people were hired to cook and help provision the agrarian laborers. Furthermore, with the secularization of the Franciscan mission in Spanish California in the mid-1830s, a new source of labor became available to the Russian managers and there is some evidence that ex-Indian neophytes from some of the northern missions moved in substantial numbers to the Ross colony to work for the Russians (Jackson 1984:228–231).

Benitz Rancho. With the establishment of his rancho in 1843, William Benitz recruited local Native Californians to serve as his primary workers. Metini Village appears to have served as one of the primary residences for Benitz's workers as noted on the 1859 Plat Map. Another Native settlement that probably housed Native people working on the Benitz Rancho is CA-SON-174, located a short distance west of the Russian stockade complex (Farris 1983; Newquist 2002). It appears that many of the difficult and back breaking tasks that Indian laborers had originally performed for the Russian-American Company—the cultivation and harvesting of wheat, barley, and potato crops, tending orchards, working with livestock, and hauling and cutting wood—continued during this time.

Benitz created a successful enterprise that at its height supported over a thousand head of cattle, about one thousand sheep, two hundred horses, numerous pigs, in addition to many hectares of potatoes, wheat, barley, peas, beans, and other vegetable crops. Benitz and his workers also maintained and expanded the former Russian orchards by planting another 1700 trees of apples, peaches, pears, quince, and cherries. In correspondence with family members, his brother Anthony Benitz (1852) noted the rancho in 1852 "had sold 400,000 pounds of potatoes for 5 cents a pound." William Benitz (1856) wrote in 1856 that there were 70 acres of wheat, 70 of oats, 30 of barley, 60 of potatoes and 20 of peas, beans and other vegetables under cultivation. In his 1856 letter, Benitz also noted that he had sold 20,000 pounds of apples at 12 cents a pound. In addition to these agricultural activities, the timber operation at nearby Timber Cove involved the construction of a sawmill and a chute for loading and unloading schooners that plied the north coast of California (Tomlin 1993:9). Employing the schooners to take his goods to markets, Benitz reportedly supplied timber, potatoes, grain, building stones, deer hides, eggs, butter, apples, live ducks and pigeons, and other goods to markets in Sonoma, Sacramento, and San Francisco (Kalani and Sweedler 2004:41; Tomlin 1993:9).

The number of local Indians involved as laborers at the rancho was impressive. In January 8, 1848, a census of the rancho indicated that 161 Indians lived and worked here, including 62 men, 53 women counted as wives, and 47 children. The census listed four Indian men as "chiefs" (Chief Tojon, Chief Noportegi, Chief Cojoto , and Chief Kolo-biscau) (Presidio Ross Census 1848). In Anthony Benitz's letter dated March 14, 1852, he wrote that William Benitz had communicated to him that he was raising "about 1000 head of cattle, 200 mares and horses. We also plant a lot and have done well. Our work is all done by Indians, of which we have about 100 families" (Kalani and Sweedler 2004:26).

It is reported that Benitz provided his Indian laborers with board and lodging and $8 per month for plowing, planting, and harvesting crops, working in the kitchen, milking cows, and taming horses, among other activities. Non-Indian workers were hired for other tasks such as hunting, surveying, carpentry, and blacksmithing, receiving between $35 and $60 per month for their labors (Kalani and Sweedler 2004:36–44; Tomlin 1993:8). Mary Jean Kennedy's (1955) historical treatment of the Kashaya Pomo is especially insightful about their life on the Benitz Rancho. She quoted from an anonymous 1880 account on the history of Sonoma County:

> Benitz continued to reside here for a number of years. He had a large band of well-trained Indians, and it is said that he could get more work out of them and managed them more systematically than any other rancher in the State. He had a large bell which was rung at six in the morning. The Indians all arose at the sound of the bell, and having dressed, they formed in a line and marched up to the commissariat when the rations for breakfast and a drink of whiskey were issued to each man. At seven they had their breakfast and were in the field at work. At half-past eleven the bell rang again and all marched up again and received their allowances, whiskey included. Work was resumed at one in the afternoon. At six the bell called them in from the labors of the day and rations and whiskey were again issued (Kennedy 1955:77).

Kennedy questioned the liberal rationing of whiskey to the Indian workers, as well as their regimented schedule.

Benitz employed some of the Indian women to winnow the barley in baskets, not unlike what they did with wild seeds. Kennedy noted that Benitz "gave sacks of barley and peas to the families of men who worked for him" (ibid:77). Alice Meyers and other Indian consultants informed Kennedy that they had been told that the Benitz family taught the Kashaya Pomo to cook "white foods," and to prepare coffee. A few of the Indian workers appear to have been baptized Catholic, and many learned to speak Spanish. It is unclear from the records how many women who were baptized in the Orthodox faith remained at the rancho, and whether they continued in the faith during this period. Oswalt (1964:4) noted that the Kashaya language contained about 150 Spanish loanwords from this time, more than five times the number of Russian loanwords. From the Mexican workers, the Kashaya supposedly learned to make flour tortillas. Some of the families ate clabbered milk with potatoes, but many are reported to have continued to eat wild foods such as acorns, shellfish, sea grass, and kelp (Kennedy 1955:77–78).

Several Kashaya Pomo consultants confided to Kennedy that their oral traditions stated that Indian women avoided the Mexican vaqueros on the Benitz Rancho because they often abused them, physically and sexually (Kennedy 1955:78). Historic accounts point to specific acts of violence perpetrated upon Native Californians by vaqueros. In 1845, Benitz's Rancho, along with a number of nearby Indian rancherias, was raided by Mexican Californian marauders intent on capturing Indians for use as servants and laborers. A letter of complaint of the incident written by Benitz indicates that they broke into his home while he was gone, stealing "a number of things" and then plundered the "Indian Village." The raiding party captured two of the Indian "captains or chiefs" and tried to force them to reveal where the Indian population was hidden. Members of the raiding party, upon finding several Indian women in Benitz's house, brutally assaulted and raped them (Kennedy 1955:78, also see Reno Keoni Franklin's foreword to this volume).

In sum, the archaeological investigation of Metini Village may provide an opportunity to examine the laboring practices of California Indians involved in ranching and other commercial enterprises. The materiality of these laboring practices may include the kinds of tools and techniques employed by Native workers, as well as the kinds and quality of goods that they may have received in compensation for laboring tasks. Ultimately, the study of Metini may afford a unique situation to compare the processes and outcomes of two different nineteenth century colonial enterprises in which Indian people were employed as agrarian laborers. If possible, we will examine the treatment, welfare, and cultural practices of the Kashaya Pomo people who resided at Metini Village during their earlier encounters with the Russian-American Company in comparison to their later employment at Benitz Rancho.

Issue 4: Maintaining an Indian Community in the Face of Sustained Colonialism

The fourth issue considers the degree to which the Kashaya Pomo, while laboring for both the Russian-American Company and the Benitz Rancho, were able to maintain a distinctive Indian community after decades of settler colonialism. How successful were they in retaining their basic life ways and core beliefs while residing in the midst of subsequent colonial enclaves? And how might the strategies of persistence, or what Gerald Vizenor (2008:19) terms "survivance," that they developed during this critical period inform later negotiations and decisions related to the maintenance of their community after forced removal from the *Metini* homeland? Survivance refers to "an active sense of presence" that shaped the decisions and strategies Native individuals and communities pursued in relation to colonial and imperial policies and relations. Both concepts reject situating Native experiences exclusively within frameworks of tragedy or victimhood and instead focus on the ways in which Native people responded with purpose in the face of ongoing and persistent colonial and imperial oppression by European and American governments and settlers.

There is some documentary evidence that suggests the Kashaya Pomo and other nearby Indian groups maintained many of their traditional spiritual and economic practices in post-Russian times. William Benitz made the following observation in 1856 to Thomas J. Henley, Superintendent of Indian Affairs about the state of affairs among Indians in the area.

> They have some confused ideas of an existence after death, and burn their dead instead of burying them. They also burn the clothing, beads, arms, provisions, &c., of the deceased, so that he may not be in want of anything; they are also believers in witchcraft, believing that a man who has come in possession of this terrible gift can transform himself into a bear to do mischief to his enemies. The condition in which the Indians find themselves in parts where there is plenty of game, fish and shell-fish, is not bad at all—apparently they are the happiest people on the globe; they never get tired of a life that alternates in eating and sleeping only. The Indians here live together in rancherias, subsisting on acorns, wild oats, manzanitas, different roots, herbs, game, fish, shell-fish, sea grass, berries, &c. Those Indians that live in the vicinity of the ocean consider themselves the best off—the beach supplying them continually with shell-fish and sea grass. If I should give my opinion in regard to ameliorating the condition of the Indians, I would suggest to remove all the tribes that live on lands, the occupants of which are in favor of removal to the reserves; have overseers there that compel them to cultivate the ground, in order to raise sufficient produce to supply them (Henley 1857:242–243).

In evaluating the degree to which the Kashaya Pomo sustained an active Indian community after experiencing many years of settler colonialism, we will compare the results of our archaeological investigation at Metini with those from other nearby colonial-period sites in the Ross region. Previous archaeological studies at these sites provide an excellent opportunity to compare the material remains and cultural practices of the Metini residents with indigenous populations who resided in the divergent colonial contexts associated primarily with the Russian-American Company. These sites, most of which date to earlier colonial occupations than Metini Village, offer a window for examining Native engagements during the initial culture contact phase at Colony Ross up through later, sustained colonial entanglements. Our comparison involves the diachronic analysis of various cultural practices involving the use of space, foodways, craft production, trade relationships, and religious organizations and how they may have been transformed in the face of sustained, continuous colonialism over more than a half century. Specifically, we will compare the archaeological remains from Metini Village with those unearthed at five nearby sites: the North Wall Community (NWC), the Native Alaskan Village Site (NAVS), the Tomato Patch site, CA-SON-670, and CA-SON-174.

North Wall Community. Considerable archaeological work has been undertaken in the area along and to the north of the north stockade wall. This area extends at least 50 meters north of the wall. This extensive zone of archaeological material will be referred to as the North Wall Community (CA-SON-190) throughout the rest of this volume. It has also been designated as "Metini" in some earlier archaeological publications (Ballard 1997), but we prefer to define it as the North Wall Community to distinguish this area from that of the specific site of Metini Village and the broader *Metini* region.

Adan Treganza's (1954) initial field work at Fort Ross in 1953 involved archaeological investigations to the north of the stockade in the vicinity of what he defined as "Indian Site No. 1." The first major excavation north of the stockade wall following the 1950s was undertaken by Donald Wood as part of a Sonoma State University field course in 1970. Two trenches, divided into twelve 5-by-5 feet (1.5-by-1.5 m) units (A through L), were laid out and excavated about 20 feet (6.10 m) and 120 feet (36.58 m) north of the wall, respectively. No report was written on this excavation, but Hannah Ballard later examined the field notes and analyzed the artifacts housed in the DPR Archaeological Laboratory in Sacramento as part of her Senior Honors Thesis written for the Department of Anthropology at the University of California, Berkeley in 1995.

In 1971 and 1972, Eric Ritter directed the primary field investigation for the realignment of Highway 1. A series of 5-by-5 feet (1.5-by-1.5 m) units were placed along the highway right-of-way. Additional work north of the stockade wall has taken place since the realignment of Highway 1, including a trench (3.85 m long and 0.5 m wide) in 1975 by Karl Gurke and Paul Nesbitt (see Ballard 1995:20). In 1983, Glenn Farris and Waltraud Taugher excavated a 3-by-3 feet (.914-by-.914 m) unit directly outside the north stockade wall to mitigate the effects of the Continental Telephone (Contel) Undergrounding that routed telephone and power lines outside the complex. In 1995, Kent Lightfoot directed the excavation of the north wall area where the California Department of Parks and Recreation replaced the damaged reconstructed stockade wall with a new one (Lightfoot 1999). Sara Gonzalez recently directed several years of mapping, geophysical, surface, and subsurface investigations of the North Wall Community as part of her dissertation research (Gonzalez 2011).

The comparison of Metini Village with the North Wall Community will focus on the information synthesized by Ballard (1995, 1997) and Gonzalez (2011). Ballard's synthesis focuses on the two trenches excavated by Donald Wood in 1970. These analyses indicate that chronologically sensitive artifacts run the spectrum from a few late prehistoric lithic objects to materials dating to the Russian-American Company, Benitz Rancho, and well into the later American ranching period. However, most of the dateable materials believed to have been worked by Native people in the North Wall Community (e.g., ceramics, glass) suggest an occupation primarily during Russian colonial times (Ballard 1995:167–176). Ballard believes the Native Californian occupation of this area is related to multiethnic households composed of Native women and Creole or Russian men, and/or Native Californian laborers who may have resided in a nearby barracks. Images of this area depicted during the tenure of the Russian-American Company by Duhaut-Cilly in 1828 and Voznesenskii in 1841 indicate this area was populated by Russian-style plank houses with small gardens.

Gonzalez' (2011) research revealed rock cobble foundations that appear to be the remains of Russian period structures. In direct association with these foundations was a rich shell midden matrix composed of shellfish and other faunal remains and a variety of artifacts including eighteenth and early nineteenth century glass and ceramic tablewares, modified (ground and flaked) glass and ceramics, chipped and groundstone tools, both shell and glass beads, porcelain buttons, fire-cracked rock, and Russian-period building materials. While the nature of the deposit is such that we cannot confirm whether the households were comprised of Native Californian-only households vs. multi--ethnic families, the intact portions of this deposit indicate that Native Californians were using this residential space throughout the Russian period and into the subsequent Mexican and American periods. This finding is significant in that it challenges Treganza's (1954) assertion that the deposits along the north wall were related to an ancient Native Californian habitation of the coastal terrace.

Native Alaskan Village Site. Archaeological investigations at the Native Alaskan Village Site (CA-SON-1897/H) in the late 1980s and early 1990s revealed an incredibly rich archaeological record south of the Russian stockade complex (Lightfoot, Schiff, and Wake 1997). These remains are related to residences established by the Native Alaskan workers of Colony Ross and their families. Many of these households were interethnic, comprised of Native Californian women and Native Alaskan men. The study involved geophysical survey, intensive surface collection, and trench excavations, as well as areal excavations that unearthed features detected in the hand-dug trenches. The investigation unearthed sealed deposits dating to the 1820s and 1830s that included diagnostic artifacts of both Native Alaskan and Native Californian manufacture.

Tomato Patch. Situated on the coastal ridge about 4.5 km east of the Russian stockade complex, this Kashaya Pomo village site was investigated by Antoinette Martinez in the mid-1990s (Martinez 1997, 1998). Her investigation revealed a discretely structured site with surface pit features and a well-demarcated midden deposit. The field investigation involved geophysical survey, intensive surface collection, the testing of the pit features, and excavations in the midden deposit. Diagnostic artifacts suggest an occupation that spanned from late prehistoric times through the Russian colonial period. A few later ceramics from the surface also indicate that people during the American ranching period also visited and/or lived at Tomato Patch. Martinez interprets the site as a village site employed by the Kashaya Pomo people during late pre-contact and early historical times, and that during the colonial occupation some of the people may have served as laborers for the Russian-American Company.

CA-SON-670. This extensive site, covering an estimated 3759 m² area in a small, protected valley overlooking Fort Ross Creek, was initially investigated by a Sonoma State University field class directed by David Fredrickson in 1971, prior to the construction of a state park group campground (Stillinger 1975). Later investigations were conducted by California State Park archaeologists in 1979 and 1985. The 1985 study by Breck Parkman and Glenn Farris considered the impacts of placing a septic tank in the campground (Farris 1986). In 1988, UC Berkeley students recorded a small locus 30 m south of the main site area (Lightfoot et al. 1991:79–81). Further work was undertaken in 1990 by a Santa Rosa Junior College field class directed by Thomas Origer to evaluate the possible impacts of expanding the campground facilities. Fieldwork at CA-SON-670 suggests the site has an extensive occupation, spanning pre-contact times and into the period of Russian colonization and probably when the Benitz Rancho was operating (Farris 1986; Fenner 2002; Stillinger 1975). There is also some evidence to suggest the site was used as part of the James Dixon and Charles Fairfax logging operation in the late 1860s and 1870s (Stillinger 1975).

The comparison of CA-SON-670 with Metini Village will focus on the findings from the 1971 excavation that were summarized by Morgan Fenner (2002). Ten 2-by-2 m units were systematically placed across the site area and excavated by field crews to a maximum depth of 50 cm. The entire assemblage of archaeological materials from these units was catalogued, analyzed, and interpreted by Fenner at UC Berkeley as part of her Anthropology Senior Honors Thesis with assistance from Glenn Farris with the California State Parks.

CA-SON-174. This extensive site, situated near the Call House in the Fort Ross State Historic Park, was investigated by Glenn Farris in 1983 as part of the construction of a leach-field system for the construction of the new Fort Ross Visitors Center. Field investigations on the northeast side of Old Highway 1 involved the excavation of 46 units, most measuring 5-by-5 feet in size. The excavations tended to be relatively shallow with the deepest measuring 28 inches in depth and most no more than 8 inches. Field crews unearthed evidence of the foreman's residence for the Call Ranch built in the early 1870s, which was later occupied by Carlos Call beginning in 1902. The structure burned down in the mid-twentieth century.

In addition to the vestiges of Carlos Call's house, outbuildings, and garden, CA-SON-174 also contains the remains of an historic Indian settlement that is believed to be associated with the Benitz Rancho. The first component of this village site is located in the area of the leach-field excavation. A second component of the site extends to the southwest of old Highway 1. It was mapped, recorded, and surface collected by UC Berkeley field crews in 1988. This 346 m² area contains three large depressions, scattered shellfish remains, and sandstone blocks from the first Fort Ross schoolhouse built in 1884. The comparison of CA-SON-174 with Metini Village will be based primarily on the Ingrid Newquist's (2002) detailed study of the archaeological materials from the 1983 leach-field excavation. This work was undertaken with the assistance of Glenn Farris from California State Parks as part of her UC Berkeley Anthropology Senior Honors Thesis.

In sum, the results of the Metini Village investigation will be compared with those from other nearby sites (North Wall Complex, Native Alaskan Village Site, Tomato Patch, CA-SON-670, and CA-SON-174) in a diachronic analysis that will critically evaluate the degree to which various cultural practices were undergoing significant transformations during the later phases of sustained colonialism.

Chapter 3

Previous Field Work at Metini Village

Samuel Barrett was the first anthropologist to describe and locate the historic village of "Metini" on his regional map of "Old Villages" and "Old Campsites" in Kashaya Pomo tribal lands (Barrett 1908:230–231). Omer Stewart designated it as Site 37 on his regional map in 1935 (Stewart 1943:28) though Arnold Pilling and Clement Meighan only first recorded the site for the University of California Archaeological Survey in 1949. Pilling and Meighan estimated that the site covered about 18,241 m², including a large pit depression and possible smaller house pits, but the latter had been largely obliterated by plowing. In 1950, Edward Gifford visited the village site with John McKenzie, the ranger in charge of the Fort Ross State Historic Park, and Herman James, a tribal elder of the Kashaya Pomo. Gifford's firsthand account is as follows:

> Metini [mé-ti?ni]: the village on the inland (northeast) side of Fort Ross. At the site, no longer occupied, we saw one dance-house pit and ten to twelve or possibly fifteen house pits. Plowing had pretty well obliterated the house pits but not the dance-house pit. There were many glass fragments on the site, which lies chiefly in the V-shaped area formed by the junction of the road from Seaview with Highway 1. Midden material extended across the junction of these two roads.

> About 680 feet north of the main Metini site was another, just on the western edge of the gulch of Fort Ross Creek. Mr. John C. McKenzie, Curator of the Fort Ross Museum, showed us several grooved stone sinkers from this second site. We found no sinkers but did find a round-tipped chert arrowpoint, which Mr. McKenzie kept for the Museum. We also found a ring made of the periphery of a limpet shell; Herman James thought this was not an artifact (Gifford 1967:9).

Gifford's description raises the possibility that the original site area may have been quite extensive. The former juncture of Seaview Road (now known as Fort Ross Road) and Highway 1, when Gifford viewed it in 1950, was located about 50 meters north of the reconstructed stockade complex in the archaeological zone now known as the North Wall Community (CA-SON-190).

However, the known location of Metini Village today encompasses a relatively discrete site area (CA-SON-175), situated some distance north of the stockade wall. Gifford's observation raises the possibility that the impressive surface depression and midden deposits that comprise CA-SON-175 may have been part of a larger archaeological manifestation that extended to the area immediate to the north wall of the stockade complex, where he noted high densities of worked glass artifacts.

Evaluating the possibility that Metini Village and the North Wall Community are part of a continuous archaeological manifestation is complicated by the reconfiguration of Highway 1 and Seaview Road in the 1970s. At this time Highway 1, which once passed through the stockade complex, was rerouted to the north around the reconstructed Russian compound. What is today Fort Ross Road was redirected to enter Highway 1 farther to the west, where the entrance to the Fort Ross State Historic Park is now located. The construction work in the 1970s involving the realignment of Highway 1 essentially separated the archaeological remains of CA-SON-175 from those directly north of the stockade wall (CA-SON-190).

It is interesting to note that Ballard's (1995:142) analysis of the materials excavated by Donald Wood and crew in 1970 showed that the density of remains increased from south (Trench 1, Units A-F) to north (Trench 2, units G-L). Gonzalez's (2011:161) surface survey and excavations of the North Wall Community revealed the opposite pattern with artifact densities highest in the southern portions of the site. An analysis of the archaeological investigations conducted by Eric Ritter as part of the highway realignment in 1971 and 1972 might provide the key for evaluating whether Metini Village may have been tied into the North Wall Community. The excavations took place in the area separating CA-SON-175 and CA-SON-190. The 5-by-5 feet (1.5-by-1.5 m) units, placed along the highway right-of-way, were excavated in arbitrary 6 inch (15.24 cm) levels with material passed through 3 mm (1/8 inch) mesh. A final report has not yet been produced, but in a preliminary paper, Ritter indicates that they had found a Russian burial, the remains of a flume, an earth-packed floor or surface, redwood posts, hearths, and a diverse range of faunal remains (shellfish, deer, pig, etc.) and artifacts (lithics, ceramic, glass, and metal). Ritter (1972:4–5) notes that "most of the occupational material derived from Pomo settlement" and "the Russians apparently made little use of this area except for inhumation of at least one individual and as an infrequent depository of discarded goods which may in fact have been trade items to the Indians."

At this time, it is not clear whether Metini Village (CA-SON-175) and the North Wall Community (CA-SON-190) were part of a larger, contiguous archaeological manifestation before the division created by the realignment of Highway 1, or whether these are two separate and discrete archaeological deposits. Further work needs to be done to evaluate how the features and artifacts excavated by Ritter and crew during the reconfiguration of Highway 1 are related to Metini Village (CA-SON-175) and the North Wall Community. However, field observations suggest that archaeological remains were not distributed continuously between the two areas. During the 1998 field season, pedestrian survey transects walked to determine the boundaries of CA-SON-175 indicated that the density of artifacts declined substantially along the southern border of the site area. This interpretation is supported by Gonzalez's (2011:160–162) investigations at the North Wall Community, which revealed that the density of artifacts is highest closest to the north stockade wall and declines substantially 20 m north of it. At this time, it appears that CA-SON-175 may represent a discrete cluster of features and artifacts within a broader distribution of archaeological remains that extends unevenly to the north wall of the stockade, an observation that we will return to later in this volume.

Chapter 4

Field Work at a Sacred Site

There is considerable interest among archaeologists, state and federal agencies, and various stakeholders, especially Native American tribes, in developing low-impact field strategies that minimize impacts to archaeological places. This was certainly the case for the work conducted at Metini Village. To the best of our knowledge, no formal archaeological work has taken place at CA-SON-175 since 1949–1950.

Viewed as a sacred place to the Kashaya Pomo, members of the tribe advocated to the California Department of Parks and Recreation a policy of non-disturbance to their ancestral village, and it has been off-limits to archaeological investigations due to these concerns. Development of the collaborative partnership between members of the Kashaya Pomo tribe, California Department of Parks and Recreation, and UC Berkeley created a pathway for using low-impact archaeological methods to document Kashaya history at Metini Village. Investigations of this area occurred over the course of two field seasons from 1998 to 1999 and were dependent upon the project's use of Kashaya cultural protocols to guide our research.

In recognizing Metini Village as a sacred place with a possible round house (or dance house) and/or sweat house, our Kashaya collaborators made it very clear from the outset that they wanted to minimize subsurface disturbances caused by excavations or any other archaeological intrusions. This perspective was also emphasized by the California Department of Parks and Recreation, which is legally mandated to oversee the protection and conservation of archaeological remains in Fort Ross State Historic Park. Since Metini is preserved in the park lands, there is also an ethical obligation by archaeologists to minimize adverse impacts at the site so that as much of the site as possible is left intact for future generations.

In recognizing the ethical reasons and necessity for developing low-impact field strategies, we also acknowledge the conundrum that these field methods represent for contemporary archaeologists. Low-impact field programs typically involve minimal subsurface testing or areal exposure of archaeological deposits. Yet many theoretical perspectives (e.g., landscape approaches, practice theory, historical ecology) now employed in archaeology are predicated upon developing a sophisticated understanding of the broader spatial dimensions of the archaeological record. Our own interest in the study of daily practices through detailed analyses of the spatial distribution of materials in residential structures, work areas, and communal places exemplifies this point (Lightfoot, et al. 1998). These kinds of studies are ideally implemented using field strategies designed to detect intact archaeological deposits through areal exposures that allow investigators to record stratigraphic relationships and the three dimensional proveniences of artifacts, ecofacts, features, and other remains.

It was clear from the outset of our investigation of CA-SON-175 that we would not be employing some of the time-tested field methods in North American archaeology for locating features (e.g., house structures, hearths, earth ovens, etc.) in village sites. For example, trenching (by hand or by backhoe), the placement of multiple test units across the site (as small excavation units, shovel probes, auger holes, etc.), or the stripping of large areal units by hand or machine were all out of the question at Metini. While these detection and excavation methods can be quite effective for locating features and intact deposits, especially in buried or deeply stratified sites, and provide an excellent methodology for understanding three dimensional site structures, they typically result in heavy impacts to archaeological places. We recognize that these field methods still have an important place in contemporary North American archaeology, but they are not appropriate on sites that are protected and preserved for the future, and which tribal descendants define as sacred, such as is the case for Metini Village (Lightfoot 2008:218–221).

The low-impact field strategy that we employed at Metini was greatly influenced by working with California State Park archaeologists, and especially by conversations with Kashaya elders and scholars. It was during this investigation that they introduced one of us (Lightfoot) to their philosophy of how to care for and treat ancestral sites in Kashaya Pomo country, which has become our model, as outlined below, for working on sacred and protected indigenous sites.

> I have been touched by several Kashaya elders who spoke passionately about their ancestral sites. They view these as living organisms that will feel pain when any subsurface intrusion—such as shovel probes or 1 x 1 m excavation units—penetrate into them. Consequently, I now employ a medical analogy model in working with archaeological remains within the Kashaya Pomo territory. Before implementing any subsurface excavation that may "hurt" an archaeological site, I try to undertake a full evaluation of the surface and near-surface materials in designing specific, low-impact "surgical" (excavation) strategies. In other words, rather than conducting full-scale exploratory surgery on a site at the outset, I now take the time to undertake a comprehensive diagnosis of surface and near-surface conditions before employing any surgical techniques.

In developing this low-impact methodology within a collaborative research design, I advocate a multistage approach that begins with the least intrusive methods and proceeds to increasingly intrusive and destructive techniques. The research design is structured so that after each stage the collaborators' feedback is incorporated into subsequent stages of fieldwork. In order to operationalize a reflexive methodology, field options need to be spelled out at each stage of "intrusiveness" so that changes or modifications in techniques can be implemented quickly depending on the materials and contexts uncovered. This series of planned contingencies is important since some tribal elders may not be physically able to participate directly in the fieldwork, let alone visit the site if they are not feeling well. This empowers the excavators, specialists, and tribal scholars working at the site with the ability to make rapid decisions (Lightfoot 2008:218–219).

This model of employing a multi-phased field strategy that begins with very low-impact methods and proceeds with successively more intrusive field techniques was first formally implemented during our field study of Metini Village. Consultation and collaboration is central to this low-impact methodology. After each phase of research was completed, members of the research team evaluated the results and decided upon whether to implement the next phase of the research design, and if the decision was made to proceed, how it should be undertaken. Our research design outlined four phases of field work: topographic mapping, geophysical survey, intensive surface collection, and the excavation of several units. Since the development of this methodology in our investigations of Metini Village it has been adopted and elaborated upon in the study of other Kashaya sacred sites within FRSHP and elsewhere in California (e.g., Cuthrell 2013; Gonzalez et al. 2006; Gonzalez 2011, 2016; Nelson 2015; Schneider 2010).

Mapping Metini

The Metini Village site area measures about 90 m (north/south) by 65 m (east/west). We began our fieldwork by establishing the site datum five meters west of the large circular pit feature that dominated the site landscape. A 10-by-10 m grid system was laid out 50 m north, 50 m south, 30 m west, and 50 m east. Using an optical transit and metric tape we produced a topographic map of the site (Figure 2). Topographic points were taken from all grid corners, as well as at additional points along the margins of the site and at areas of extreme changes in elevation. The topography of the site area slopes from north to

Figure 2. Roberta Jewett directing the mapping of Metini Village.

south, with a relatively dramatic drop off along the eastern edge that is the upper embankment of Fort Ross Creek and Highway 1 (see Figure 3).

The site today consists primarily of mixed grasslands with some encroaching bishop pines and coyote bush—the latter of which is rapidly expanding across the site area. A substantial surface feature is located in the center of the site area (Figure 4). It appears to be the remains of an impressive semi-subterranean structure—possibly a dance house or assembly house (round house), a sweat house, or large semi-subterranean lodge, as will be discussed later. Because of its potential ritual significance, archaeological investigations were restricted to only mapping and geophysical work within the pit feature.

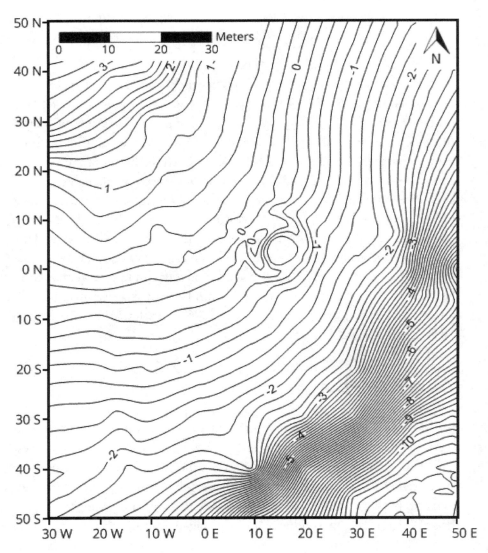

Figure 3. Detailed view of Metini Village topography (20 cm contour interval).

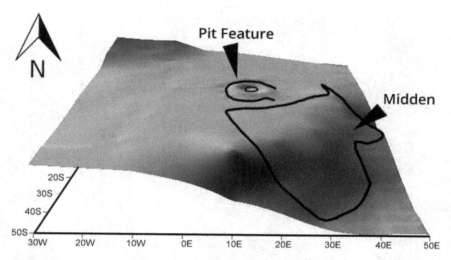

Figure 4. Three-dimensional topographic map of Metini Village. Note the surface depression and outline of midden area.

Geophysical Survey

We undertook an intensive survey of the site area using two different geophysical techniques: magnetometry and electromagnetic conductivity. The former is a passive method for measuring the local magnetic field of an area in gammas or nanotesla (nT). The objective is to search for anomalies that are created by higher or lower than normal magnetic readings that might be created by objects, features, or deposits with induced or remnant magnetism. Natural features, such as rocks with high iron content, may create magnetic anomalies while cultural materials and features such as ferrous metals, ceramics, and fire-cracked rock (with iron oxide) produce high magnetic anomalies. House pits, middens, underground ovens, and areas where the matrix of the site has been altered with the addition of new materials and the mixing of stratigraphic deposits, can also result in magnetic anomalies.

We employed a Geometrics G-858 Cesium Gradiometer in undertaking the magnetometer survey (Figure 5), which was employed as part of a pedestrian survey where the operator carried the bar holding the sensors, positioned 1.4 m apart, parallel to the ground surface. The site area was divided into a series of 20-by-20 m grids. The grid boundaries were staked out in 1 m intervals and nylon guide ropes were employed so that the operator walked a series of one meter transects north/south across the 20-by-20 m grid square. The G-858 Cesium Gradiometer took readings automatically every 0.05 m, which was achieved with the continuous sensor cycling set at 0.1 seconds. The resulting gradiometer map is illustrated in Figure 6.

Figure 5. Belinda Perez and Dan Murley undertaking gradiometer survey at Metini.

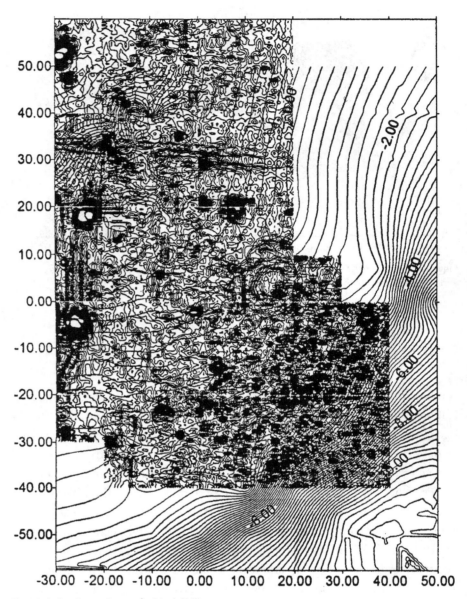

Figure 6. Gradiometer map for Metini Village.

The electromagnetic conductivity survey, an active method of survey, measures differences in the electrical conductivity of near surface deposits. The instrument measures how well the introduced electrical current is conducted through the upper sediments of the site. Anomalies are produced when readings of the electrical current deviate from the normal range for the sediments under investigation. Some natural or cultural features such as rocks, hearths, and walls impede or slow down conductivity. Other cultural features tend to be good electrical conductors, such as midden deposits with lots of organic materials, or clay features, such as house floors, which maintain high soil moisture that can facilitate the flow of the electrical current.

The same grid system and system of marked ropes used in the magnetometer survey were employed in the electromagnetic conductivity survey. We used a Geonics EM-38 electromagnetic conductivity instrument to walk a series of one-meter transects and readings were taken at every one-meter interval along each transect (Figure 7). The resulting electromagnetic conductivity map is depicted in Figure 8.

Figure 7. Bill Walton and Dan Murley working on the electromagnetic conductivity survey.

Figure 8. Electromagnetic conductivity map for Metini Village.

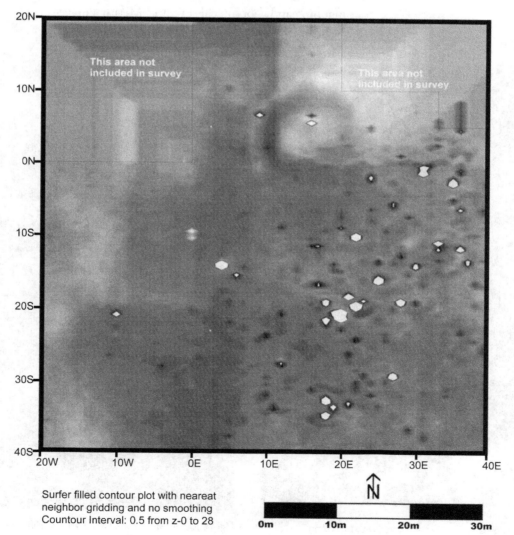

Surfer filled contour plot with neareat neighbor gridding and no smoothing
Countour Interval: 0.5 from z-0 to 28

Surface Collection of Archaeological Materials

We undertook the intensive surface collection of archaeological materials from across the site area using a systematic, unaligned sampling strategy. Using the 10-by-10 m grid system established in our topographic mapping survey, we divided the research area into a series of 5-by-5 meter survey blocks. Within each 5-by-5 m square we randomly chose one 1-by-1 m unit for intensive collection. In each 1-by-1 m surface collection unit, we removed the overlying grass turf (about 8-10 cm in depth) so that a clear view of the ground surface was made (Figures 9, 10). All artifacts and faunal remains were collected within this zone and provenienced by surface collection unit. A total of 183 surface collection units were collected, representing a 4% sample fraction of the site area (Figure 11). No surface collection or subsurface testing was permitted inside the berm area of the semi-subterranean feature documented in our mapping and geophysical survey of Metini Village.

Figure 9. Warren Parrish removing grass turf with Mary Anne Parrish looking on.

Figure 10. Bill Walton and Otis Parrish surface collecting artifacts.

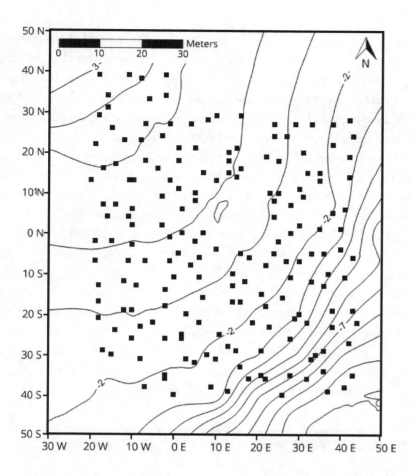

Figure 11. Spatial distribution of 183 surface collection units.

In the field we sorted the surface materials into broad artifact categories (e.g., chipped stone, ground stone, glass, metal, ceramic, etc.) and faunal categories (e.g., shellfish, mammal bone), calculated density figures, and used a spatial mapping program (SURFER) to create isopleth maps based on the density of artifacts and faunal remains collected from the sample of 183 surface units. These artifact and faunal isopleth maps were instrumental in developing our subsurface excavation strategy as outlined below. A dense midden area was identified south and east of the pit feature. Consisting of dark soil, mollusk remains, animal bones, and artifacts, the midden deposit extends along the eastern edge of the site (Figure 4). A more detailed discussion about the spatial distribution of surface materials will be presented later in the volume.

Subsurface Sampling

The initial surface and near surface investigations from our topographic mapping, geophysical surveys, and surface collection provided considerable information on the spatial structure of the Metini Village site. Significantly, the circular topographic feature (possible dance house) was clearly outlined in both geophysical surveys (Figures 6, 8). Additionally, most of the magnetic and conductivity anomalies were detected in the southeastern quad of the site. Isopleth maps of surface artifacts and faunal remains correspond with the geophysical data, as the majority of surface collected remains are distributed in the southeastern quad of the site, primarily in the area of the observed midden deposit. Interestingly, the area north and west of the circular surface feature was relatively clean of geophysical anomalies, as well as artifact and faunal remains.

Employing this information, the archaeologists and Kashaya Pomo tribal elders worked together in selecting the placement of three excavation units (each 1-by-1 m in size) to evaluate specific magnetic anomalies and artifact spatial patterns (Figure 12). These units were excavated in natural or cultural levels when possible; thick deposits or difficult to define stratigraphic deposits were divided into 10 cm arbitrary levels (Figure 13). Each excavation unit was dug to sterile with all sediments dry screened through 3mm (1/8") mesh. Artifacts and faunal remains were either point plotted or provenienced by level (lot provenience) for each unit. We recorded depths from the southwest corner of the units, which served as the unit datum. Sediment samples were collected from each level for flotation analysis and the recovery of ethnobotanical remains and micro-artifacts. A brief description of each excavation unit follows:

Figure 12. Location of 1-by-1 meter excavation units.

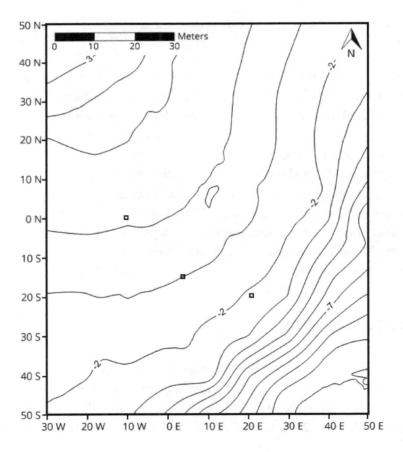

Figure 13. Otis Parrish showing local school children excavation unit 20S 21E. Note the hopper mortar recovered from the unit.

0N 10W. This unit was placed in the western section of the site that was characterized by low magnetic and conductivity readings from the geophysical survey and few to no surface artifacts or faunal remains. The 1-by-1 meter unit was excavated to a depth of about 50 cm below datum. Field crews defined three stratigraphic deposits that graded into each other (Figure 14). The upper deposit, defined as the A horizon, is characterized by a dark brown sandy loam containing grass roots and other organic remains. It extends about 10 cm below datum. This deposit makes a gradual transition into a dark brown sandy loam, which is mottled with pieces of yellowish/brown clay. This deposit extends about 10–25 cm below datum. The third deposit is a highly compact yellowish/brown clay stratum that extends from circa 25 cm below datum to the bottom of the excavation unit, about 45–50 cm below surface. Few artifacts or faunal remains were recovered in this unit, and no features were observed.

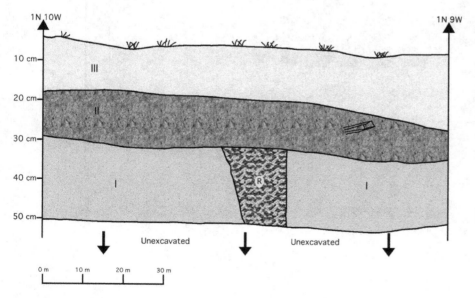

Figure 14. Stratigraphic profile of unit 0N 10W (North Wall).

Key:

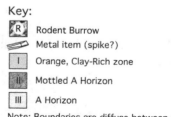

| R | Rodent Burrow |
| Metal item (spike?) |
I	Orange, Clay-Rich zone
II	Mottled A Horizon
III	A Horizon

Note: Boundaries are diffuse between strata.

39

15S 4E. We placed this unit on the western edge of the midden over a significant magnetic anomaly near a cluster of hemlock trees. This area of the site contains only a moderate density of surface artifacts. Field crews observed three major stratigraphic deposits (Figure 15). The A horizon consists of a 20–25 cm thick deposit of light grayish brown sandy loam infused with charcoal, artifacts, and faunal remains. This deposit comprises the western edge of the midden zone. Below the midden material is a distinct deposit of dark brown sandy loam, not unlike what is found in the upper two levels of 0N 10W. This deposit is about 15–25 cm thick. Underlying the dark brown sandy loam is the yellowish-brown clay horizon. It extends about 45–60 cm below datum, the latter being the maximum depth of the unit.

Figure 15. Stratigraphic profile of unit 15S 4E (West Wall). Note the location of the shovel head in the wall profile.

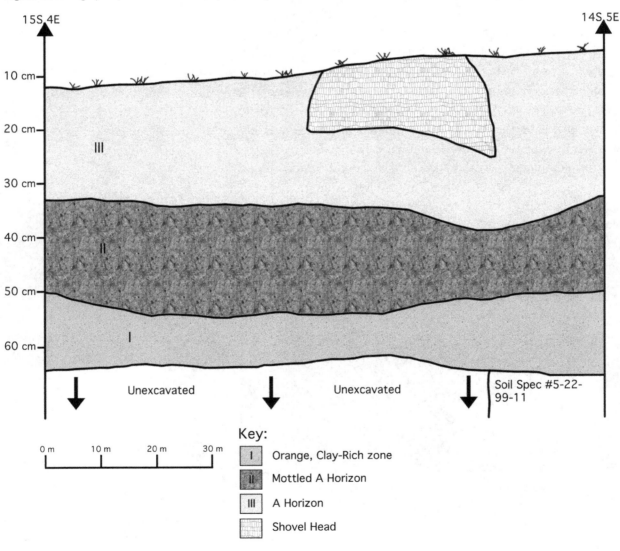

One feature was defined for the unit. It consisted of a 40 cm wide pit running along the western edge of the unit to a depth of about 20 to 27 cm below datum. The pit stratum consisted of a mixture of midden and dark brown sandy loam. In the northwest corner of the unit, at a depth of about 11 to 16 cm below datum, we unearthed a shovel head and shovel handle in association with groundstone, glass, and metal artifacts, along with fire cracked rock, charcoal and wood fragments (Figure 16). It appears that this shovel head/handle created the magnetic anomaly picked up in the geophysical survey. Although the meaning of this pit is still unclear, it is possible that it is the remains of a relic hunter's pit.

Figure 16. Pit feature with shovel head and handle in unit 15S 4E.

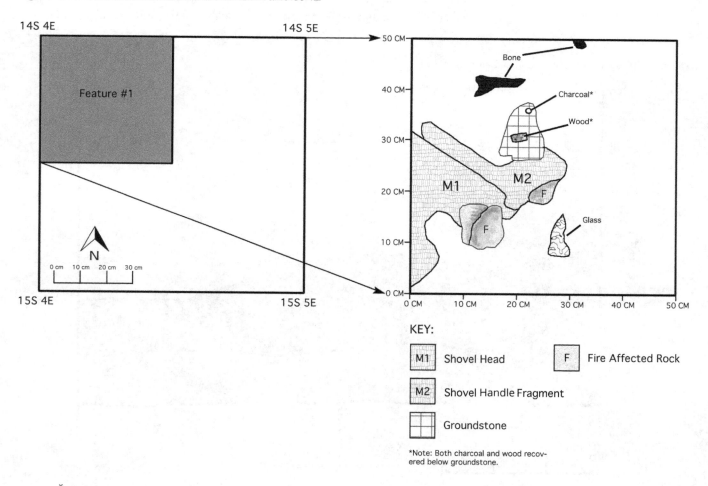

20S 21E. Field crews located and excavated this unit within the midden zone in a place that was distinctive for its high magnetic readings and high surface artifact densities. The unit, excavated to a depth of about 50–60 cm below datum, contained a diverse range of artifacts and faunal remains. We detected three stratigraphic deposits (Figure 17). The upper 25 to 30 cm is the midden zone characterized by a light grayish brown sandy loam containing abundant charcoal particles and artifacts. The upper stratigraphic layer grades into another deposit, which is characterized by light brown sediments and inclusions of yellowish-brown clay. This second deposit, defined as the mottled loamy sand level, is about 10–15 cm thick. Underlying the mottled sandy loam is the yellowish-brown clay, which appears to be mostly sterile except in areas of rodent burrows. The depth below surface of the clay level is 40–45 cm, and this deposit extends to the bottom of the excavation unit. While no features were observed for 20S 21E, a large groundstone slab, probably a hopper mortar, was detected about 14 cm below datum in the northeastern quadrant of the unit (see Figure 13).

Figure 17. Stratigraphic profile of unit 20S 21E (North Wall).

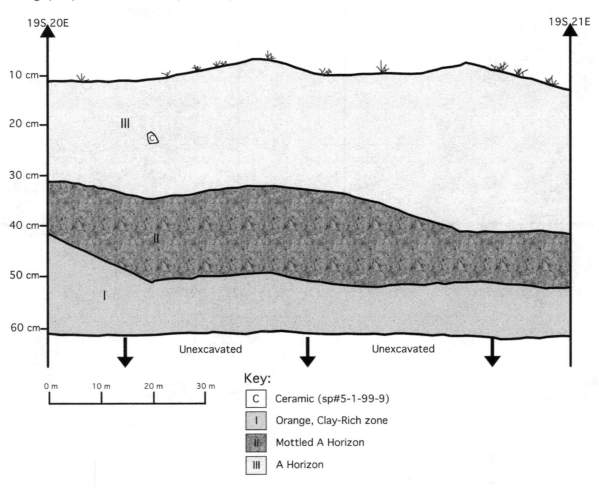

Key:

C	Ceramic (sp#5-1-99-9)
I	Orange, Clay-Rich zone
II	Mottled A Horizon
III	A Horizon

Chapter 5

A Spatial Perspective of Metini Village

The topographic mapping, geophysical surveys, and surface collection focused on a relatively large site area, measuring 5850 square meters, which comprises CA-SON-175.

The topographic map revealed a relatively flat terrain to the north and west of the prominent circular pit feature, but a sharp drop-off to the south and east where the terrain descends rapidly to Fort Ross Creek. Metini Village sits on a relatively level terrace overlooking Fort Ross Creek, which flows in a steep escarpment to the east of the site. In the area mapped, the topographic decline was fairly significant, about a 10 m drop in elevation over about 40 m. In the remainder of this monograph, we will refer to the area of steep topographic descent as the "terrace slope," and the relatively flat places (with some slight, but distinctive knobs) running along this slope as the "terrace edge" (see Figure 4, the red line marks the distribution of the midden that includes both the terrace edge and terrace slope).

The substantial circular pit feature, measuring about 13 m in diameter, was located near the center of the site area (Figure 18). The feature contained a prominent berm that rose about 0.3 to 0.5 meters above the ground surface (Figure 4). Tribal scholars and elders working on the project identified this

Figure 18. Circular pit feature at Metini Village.

feature as a ceremonial structure (discussed below), thus no surface collection or subsurface testing was permitted inside the berm area and archaeological investigations were restricted to only surficial mapping and geophysical survey within the surface feature. In undertaking the detailed topographic mapping of the site area, a slight depression was recorded in a linear configuration that ran almost due north/south across the entire site area, about 15 m west of the pit feature (see Figure 3). The gradiometer survey also recorded minor anomalies along this linear depression. What caused this slight depression is unknown, but we suspect it is the remains of an old ranch road that once connected to Seaview Road or a segment of Seaview Road before it was rerouted.

No other clearly demarcated surface depressions were observed in the site area. Furthermore, visits to the site during different seasons of the year did not reveal any other surface features that might be the remains of visible house structures. Analysis of aerial photos and infrared images also did not reveal any such features in the vicinity of the large pit structure. Thus, despite our best efforts, we were unable to observe the location of the "house pits" initially observed by Pilling and Meighan in 1949 and Gifford in 1950. It is very possible that these surface features have been obliterated over time due to plowing, as suggested by Pilling, Meighan, and Gifford, along with other surface modifications that have taken place over the last half-century since the site was first recorded. Another alternative is that at least some of the "house pits" may have been located farther south in the area modified by the rerouting of Highway 1 in the 1970s.

Archaeological investigations conducted around the large pit feature, along the terrace edge, and down the terrace slope revealed an intriguing pattern of geophysical anomalies and artifact and faunal spatial distributions. The gradiometer and EM-38 electromagnetic conductivity surveys revealed few geophysical anomalies to the west of the large surface feature (see Figures 6, 8). The few large anomalies observed in this area of the site appear to be major spikes caused by metal objects that were located not far from the current roadside of Highway 1. In contrast, the eastern half of the site, specifically the southeastern quadrant south of the pit structure, revealed many significant magnetic and conductivity anomalies. The geophysical anomalies are distributed primarily along the terrace edge and down the terrace slope. Although specific anomaly signatures have not yet been associated with particular near surface and subsurface archaeological remains, they appear to be closely associated with domestic refuse from Kashaya Pomo daily practices at the site.

The intensive surface collection of CA-SON-175 exposed an extensive midden deposit characterized by anthropogenic soils that ranged from grey to black in color, loaded with charcoal, artifacts, and faunal remains (Figure 19). The midden deposit was defined along most of the terrace edge and terrace slope (see Figure 4 with midden area marked by red line). Excavations of units 15S 4E and

Figure 19. Surface collection of the midden zone with Sherry Pierce Parrish, Julie Federico, Otis Parrish, and Roberta Jewett.

20S 21E revealed subsurface samples of this midden deposit. In stark contrast, surface units placed in the western half of the site produced few or no artifacts. Of the 183 units that were surface collected, 80 units (approximately 44%) located mostly in the western half of the site contained no artifactual or faunal materials. The excavation of 0N 10W offers a subsurface window into this area of the site.

In sum, the spatial structure of CA-SON-175 is highly patterned. The large pit feature, recognized by tribal scholars and elders as a ceremonial structure, sits in the center of the site area. The area to the west of the pit feature is distinctive for its paucity of artifactual remains. It appears to have been left intentionally clean of artifacts and faunal remains. In stark contrast, the area south and east of the pit feature contains an extensive midden deposit, which runs along the terrace edge and down the terrace slope. The contents of the midden will be explored in detail in subsequent pages, but suffice it to say for now that this area encompasses a diverse range of ground stone, chipped stone, glass, ceramic, and metal artifacts, along with various shellfish and terrestrial mammal remains, and some fish and sea mammals. There is a very strong correlation between the majority of the observed magnetic and conductivity anomalies and the area identified as a midden deposit.

Chapter 6

Archaeological Materials

The Metini archaeological assemblage is divided into the following basic categories: lithics (chipped stone, ground stone, other lithic artifacts), glass objects (vessel glass, flat glass, glass beads), ceramics, and metal objects. Faunal remains are separated into shellfish and vertebrate faunal specimens (primarily fish and mammal), followed by a discussion of the ethnobotanical remains. We present descriptions for each major category and then discuss the findings from the surface collection units and each excavation unit (0N 10S, 15S 4E, 20S 21E) separately.

Lithic Materials

Flaked Stone Artifacts

The flaked stone artifacts were classified by artifact class and by raw material type. The artifact classes employed here are the same as those employed by Sara Gonzalez (2011) in the recent archaeological investigation of the North Wall Community (CA-SON-190). Allyson Leigh Milner (2009) completed the analysis of the chipped stone materials as part of her Senior Honors Thesis in Anthropology at UC Berkeley. Following Andrefsky (1998), chipped stone was classified according to morphological characteristics and sorted into the Tool and Debitage classes. Tools were classified according to type and, deviating from Andrefsky, debitage was further classified according to Flake type (see below) (see Silliman 2000 and Gonzalez 2011 for a complete description of the lithic classification system). Tools are classified as biface or nonbiface and types include core (CO), biface (BI), projectile point (PP), projectile point fragment (PF), uniface (UN), and flake tools. Flaked stone specimens were examined under a lower power microscope for evidence of edge-modification (use-wear or retouch). Flake tools were analyzed as debitage for the purposes of understanding the technological aspects of lithic reduction and are further categorized as edge-modified (EM). Core fragments are chunks of raw material, often derived from cobbles, from which flakes have been removed. Unifaces are formal tools that have been symmetrically formed on one side by flake removal, while bifaces are symmetrically shaped on both sides. Projectile points are specific kinds of bifaces that may have been used as dart or arrow points.

Debitage types include complete flake (CP), proximal flake (PX), flake shatter (FS), and angular shatter (SH). A complete flake exhibited an intact striking platform and intact termination point for the flake. A proximal flake features an intact striking platform, a bulb of percussion and exhibits a step fracture on the distal end. Flake shatter includes some diagnostic characteristics of a flake (e.g., identifiable ventral and dorsal surfaces as identified by visible lances and/or undulations and dorsal flake scars), but no striking platform or termination point. Angular shatter consists primarily of angular chunks from chipped stone production that did not feature diagnostic characteristics of flakes (e.g., ventral or dorsal surfaces, termination point, striking platform, bulb of percussion). The primary raw materials employed in the production of chipped stone tools at Metini village included chert (CH), obsidian (OB), basalt (BA), quartzite (QZ), chalcedony (CA), and sandstone (SA). Details of the Metini Village chipped stone artifact assemblage are provided in Appendix 1.

Surface Collection Units

As can be seen in Table 1, a total of 77 chipped stone artifacts were recovered and analyzed from the 183 surface collection units. The majority of these artifacts were classified as angular shatter (n=40; 52%), flake shatter (n=15; 19%), and complete flakes (n=11; 14%), along with the finding of a relatively few proximal flakes, core fragments ,and formal tools. No diagnostic projectile points were recovered. Twenty-two (28%) lithic artifacts, including debitage classed as angular shatter and flake shatter, exhibited evidence of edge modification. The majority of the surface chipped stone artifacts were identified as chert (n=62; 80%), followed by obsidian (n=12; 16%), with lesser amounts of chalcedony and quartzite (Table 2).

Table 1.   Counts of Chipped Stone Artifacts.

Chipped Stone	Surface Collection	ON 10W Excavation	15S 4E Excavation	20S 21 E Excavation	SUM
SH	40	4	10	14	**68**
FS	15	1	2	8	**26**
PX	3	0	1	0	**4**
CP	11	0	1	1	**13**
CF	4	0	1	0	**5**
UF	1	0	0	0	**1**
UN	0	0	0	1	**1**
BF	3	1	0	1	**5**
SUM	**77**	**6**	**15**	**25**	**123**

Table 2. Counts of Chipped Stone Raw Material Types.

Chipped Stone Raw Material	Surface Collection	0N 10W Excavation	15S 4E Excavation	20S 21E Excavation	SUM
CH	62	4	12	21	99
OB	12	2	2	2	18
CA	2	0	0	1	3
BA	0	0	0	0	0
QZ	1	0	1	1	3
SA	0	0	0	0	0
SUM	77	6	15	25	123

We produced density maps for the spatial distribution of chipped stone materials across Metini Village. Using SURFER 9, the spatial mapping program, we calculated isopleths of expected artifact densities (per m²) across the entire site area based on the chipped stone counts for the 183 surface units. The results indicate chipped stone artifacts are distributed in two main clusters east of the pit feature along the terrace edge. These two clusters continued down the terrace slope within the midden area (Figure 20). A few lithic artifacts were also collected from the western section of the site. Interestingly, most of the obsidian artifacts were found in the southernmost cluster within the midden deposit (Figure 21).

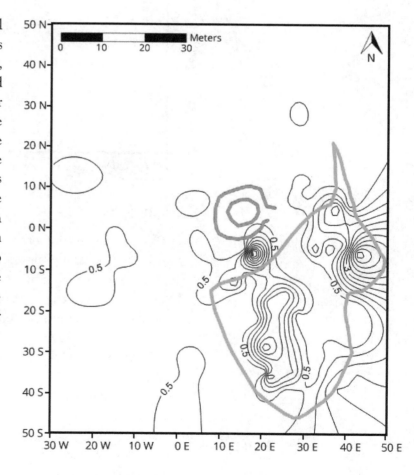

Figure 20. Surface distribution of chipped stone artifacts (0.5 artifact per m² contour interval). Pit depression outlined in red, midden in green.

Figure 21. Surface distribution of obsidian artifacts (0.5 artifact per m² contour interval). Pit depression outlined in red, midden in green.

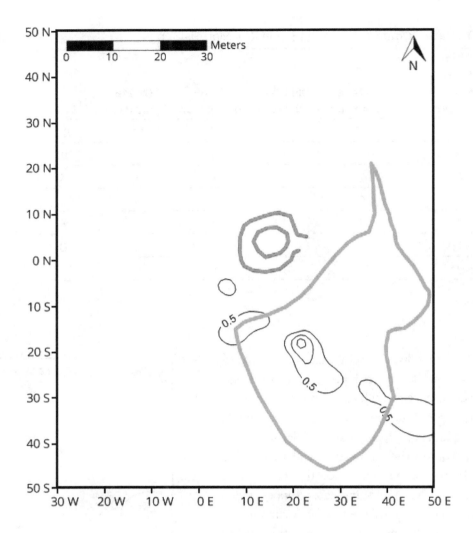

Excavation Units

0N 10W. The excavation of the 1-by-1 m unit yielded a total of six chipped stone artifacts, including four pieces of angular shatter, one flake shatter, and a biface fragment. The latter may be a fragment of a projectile point (too small to be diagnostic). The edges of the biface fragment and flake shatter exhibited signs of edge modification. Two of the pieces of angular shatter were manufactured from obsidian, the rest from local chert raw material. The chipped stone material was unearthed 0–30 cm below unit datum.

15S 4E. Field crews recovered a total of 15 chipped stone specimens from this unit, including 10 pieces of angular shatter, two flake shatter specimens, and one each of a complete flake, proximal flake, and core fragment. Laboratory analysis indicates that the edges of the complete flake, flake shatter, and three pieces of angular shatter have been modified. The majority of the chipped stone materials from 15S 4E were produced from chert (n=12), followed by obsidian (n=2) and quartz (n=1). The chipped stone artifacts were found in the midden deposit (light grayish brown sandy loam) or in the transitional zone in the first few centimeters of the underlying dark brown sandy loam stratum.

20S 21E. The field investigation of this unit yielded a total of 25 chipped stone artifacts. Of these artifacts, the majority were angular shatter (n=14), followed by flake shatter (n=8), and a complete flake, a complete uniface, and a biface fragment. Only the uniface and biface fragment exhibited evidence of edge modification. The majority of the artifacts were produced from local chert (n=21), along with obsidian (n=2), quartz (n=1), and chalcedony (n=1). Twenty-two of the chipped stone artifacts were recovered in the midden deposit, while the remaining three were uncovered in the underlying transitional mottled loamy sandy stratum.

Summary: Chipped Stone Assemblage

The entire chipped stone artifact assemblage from Metini totaled 123 specimens, of which 77 (63%) were recovered from surface collection units, and the remaining 46 (37%) from the three excavation units. For the entire assemblage, debitage consisting of angular shatter (n=68; 55%), of flake shatter (n=26; 21%), and of complete flakes (n=13; 11%; Figure 22) are the most common artifact classes. Other artifact classes include core fragments (n=5; 4%), biface fragments (n=5; 4%; Figure 23), proximal flakes (n=4; 3%), and a uniface tool and uniface fragment (Figure 24). The vast majority of the chipped stone artifacts were produced from local Franciscan chert (n=99;

Figure 22. Example of a complete flake, lithic (6S 6E, Surface, ME-6/18/98-07-LI-01).

Figure 23. Example of a biface fragment, lithic (6S 43E, Surface, ME-4/29/99-01-LI-02A).

Figure 24. Example of a uniface fragment, lithic (13S 14E, Surface, ME-6/20/98-02-LI-01).

80%), followed by obsidian (n=18; 15%). Chalcedony (n=3; 2.5%) and quartzite (n=3; 2.5%) are also present. Thirty-one (25%) chipped stone artifacts exhibited evidence of edge modification. These included 20 of the 99 chert artifacts (20%) 10 of the 18 obsidian specimens (55.6%), and one of the three chalcedony objects (33%). On examination, the lithic knappers at Metini were involved primarily in the expedient production of flake tools. This interpretation is based on the preponderance of debitage artifacts, the existence of few formal tools (including broken fragments), and 25% of the assemblage exhibiting evidence of edge modification, probably from people retouching and reusing flakes for various purposes that necessitated sharpened cutting surfaces.

Obsidian Sourcing and Hydration Research

The obsidian artifacts underwent further analysis to determine their geochemical sources and hydration measurements (Appendix 2). The geochemical sourcing was undertaken by M. Steven Shackley when he served as Director of the Archaeological X-Ray Fluorescence Spectrometry Laboratory at the University of California, Berkeley. The obsidian artifacts were analyzed with a Philips PW2400 sequential wavelength dispersive x-ray spectrometer. This crystal spectrometer uses specific software written by Philips (SuperQ/quantitative) and modifies the instrument settings between elements of interest. Sample selection was automated and controlled by the Philips software. The RGM-1 standard analyzed in this sample and reported in Appendix 2 indicates the analysis is within acceptable limits. Further information on this instrument and obsidian chemical analysis is presented elsewhere (Davis, et al. 1998; Shackley 1998).

The geochemical sourcing was based on measurements in parts per million (ppm) for six elements: rubidium (Rb), strontium (Sr), yttrium (Y), zirconium (Zr), niobium (Nb), and barium (Ba) (see Appendix 2). Results were obtained for 14 of the 18 obsidian specimens. The geochemical signature for each sample was assigned to an obsidian source through comparison with source characterization values outlined in Jackson (1989) and others. The majority of the obsidian derived from the Annadel flow (n=9; 64%) near Santa Rosa, California, while the remainder (n=5; 36%) came from Glass Mountain in Napa Valley, California (see Appendix 2).

The obsidian hydration analysis was undertaken by Thomas M. Origer when he directed the Sonoma State University Obsidian Hydration Laboratory. For each specimen, a four-inch diameter circular saw blade mounted on a lapidary trimsaw was employed to cut two parallel lines along an appropriate edge. The cuts resulted in the isolation of small samples with a thickness of about one millimeter. The samples were removed from the specimens and mounted with Lakeside Cement on to etched glass micro-slides. The thickness of each sample was then reduced by manual grinding with a slurry of #500 silicon carbide abrasive on plate glass. When samples had been ground to an appropriate thickness, a coverslip was affixed over each sample. The obsidian hydration bands were measured with a strainfree 60 power objective and a Bausch and Lomb 12.5 power filar micrometer eyepiece on a Nikon petrographic microscope. Six separate measurements, taken along the edge of each thin section, were used to calculate a mean hydration rim measurement (Appendix 2). The hydration measurements have a range of +/– 0.2 microns.

Obsidian hydration is best used as a relative dating method based on the observation that newly created obsidian surfaces will absorb water over time. Thicker hydration rims tend to be older than thinner ones, but the hydration rates vary between sources and are also affected by temperature and other local environmental conditions. Research over the past three decades has refined a chronology for the southern Coast Ranges that provides some confidence in distinguishing obsidian artifacts that date to the historical era from those dating to earlier prehistoric times (Fredrickson 1989; Fredrickson and Origer 2002; Jackson 1989; Origer 1987, 1989; Tremaine 1989; Tremaine and Fredrickson 1988). Tremaine (1989) has devised a series of "comparison constants" based on induced obsidian experiments that allow investigators to compare directly the hydration rims of obsidian specimens from different sources in northern California. Her findings indicate that obsidian specimens from Napa Valley can be compared directly to those from the Annadel flow by multiplying the former readings by 0.77. In employing this calculation for the Napa Valley specimens (see Appendix 2), we standardize all our values to the hydration rate of the Annadel source.

Origer (1987:55–59) has constructed a chronology for Annadel hydration rims based on the association of obsidian artifacts in well-dated (radiocarbon) contexts from six sites in the southern North Coast Ranges. His chronology, based on a regression calculated for the dated materials, assigns obsidian artifacts into prehistoric and historical periods depending on their hydration rim values. They are as follows:

6.6–5.3 microns	Lower Archaic (6000 BC–3000 BC)
5.2–4.1 microns	Middle Archaic (3000 BC–1000 BC)
4.0–2.9 microns	Upper Archaic (1000 BC–AD 500)
2.8–1.7 microns	Lower Emergent (AD 500–AD 1500)
1.6–1.0 microns	Upper Emergent (AD 1500–AD 1812)
< 1.0 microns	Historical (post AD 1812)

As noted elsewhere (see Lightfoot et al. 1991:67; Lightfoot and Silliman 1997:338; Silliman 2005b:85–87), we recognize that obsidian hydration chronologies will continue to be refined as our understanding of hydration rates for different sources in northern California becomes more sophisticated, especially with respect to how differential temperature, moisture, and depositional contexts influence hydration rim readings over time. However, in analyzing the Metini obsidian, Origer's chronology provides an excellent means for assessing how many of the artifacts may have been knapped in pre-contact times or possibly worked later during the historical period. Previous studies of the artifact assemblages from the nearby Native Alaskan Village Site (NAVS) and the Fort Ross Beach Site (FRBS) suggest that much of the obsidian found in sealed contexts dating to the 1820s and 1830s had been worked many hundreds of years earlier. In our interpretation of this finding, we recognize that some of the older obsidian artifacts may have derived from the mixing of pre-contact and historical deposits. However, we believe this pattern may have been largely produced from people (especially local Native women) scavenging and recycling obsidian artifacts from nearby prehistoric sites for use in this historical village complex (see Lightfoot and Silliman 1997:350–353).

The results of the obsidian hydration analysis of the Metini artifacts suggest that many of the chipped stone materials were probably produced in the historical period. Of the 13 obsidian artifacts that yielded readable hydration values, four exhibit hydration rims measuring between 0.77 and 0.9 microns, and another two are 1.0 microns thick. Another four yielded readings of between 1.3 and 1.6 microns, while the remaining three values are 2.4, 3.2, and 4.2 microns, respectively (Table 3). The thinner hydration rims that appear to date to historical times include obsidians from both the Annadel and Napa Valley sources; a similar pattern is found for the presumably earlier pre-colonial artifacts with hydration rates of 2.4 microns or greater, as they include both Annadel and Napa Valley obsidians. The findings suggest that at least some of the obsidian artifacts were knapped or modified during historical times (post AD 1812), while a few specimens appear to be much earlier pre-colonial artifacts. The presence of pre-colonial artifacts mixed into the Metini assemblage may be due to several different factors: possible problems with the obsidian chronology, the potential use of the Metini place during pre-colonial times (an issue that will be discussed in more detail later), and/or the recycling of older obsidian artifacts from nearby prehistoric sites for use at the historical settlement of Metini (see Lightfoot and Silliman 1997 for a full discussion of these different factors).

In contrast to previous research on obsidian artifacts from nearby sites, the Metini assemblage stands out in two significant ways. First, our investigation of obsidian artifacts recovered from survey sites in the greater Fort Ross region suggests that while various sources from northern California were used in pre-colonial times (e.g., Borax Lake, Mt. Konocti, Annadel, and Napa Valley), the historical age sites are almost completely overshadowed by

Table 3. Mean Hydration Rim Widths (Temaine's Comparison Constant) for Obsidian Artifacts.

Catalogue Number	Obsidian Source	Mean Hydration Rim Width (Tremaine's Comparison Constant)	Estimated Age	n
ME-4/16/99-01-LI-02	Annadel	1 micron	AD 1500–1812	1
ME-4/16/99-05-LI-01	Annadel	1.6 micron	AD 1500–1812	1
ME-4/16/99-06-LI-01	Annadel	1.6 micron	AD 1500–1812	1
ME-4/30/99-05-LI-02	Annadel	1 micron	AD 1500–1812	1
ME-6/18/98-07-LI-01	Napa	4.2 micron	3000–1000 BC	1
ME-6/19/98-03-LI-01	Napa	0.77 micron	Post-AD 1812	1
ME-6/20/98-02-LI-01	Napa	3.2 micron	1000 BC–AD 500	1
ME-6/26/98-09-LI-02A	Annadel	0.9 micron	Post-AD 1812	1
ME-6/26/98-09-LI-2B	Napa	0.77 micron	Post-AD 1812	1
ME-4/30/99-01-LI-01	Annadel	2.4 micron	1000 BC–AD 500	1
ME-4/30/99-07-LI-01	Annadel	1.3 micron	AD 1500–AD 1812	1
ME-4/29/99-06-LI-02A	Annadel	1.6 micron	AD 1500–AD 1812	1
ME-4/29/99-06-LI-02B	Annadel	0.9 micron	Post-AD 1812	1

Napa Valley obsidians. Whereas Annadel obsidians remained the dominant source for most of the early and late prehistoric periods, they were almost completely replaced by obsidian from Napa Valley with Russian colonization (Lightfoot et al. 1991:116).

In interpreting this diachronic pattern for the survey sites, we cited Farris' (1989:492) study that indicated the flow of obsidian to the local Kashaya Pomo people had been disrupted at the time of the founding (AD 1823) of the Franciscan mission (Mission San Francisco Solano) in Sonoma, as well as with the construction of later Mexican period ranchos situated between Colony Ross and the obsidian sources. We suggested that these historical settlements had essentially cut off the Kashaya Pomo from the Annadel obsidian, but that exchange relationships or direct procurement continued to allow Napa Valley materials to reach Kashaya Pomo territory. However, the findings from Metini Village suggest that at least some obsidian derived from the Annadel source continued to be transported to the Sonoma County coast after the establishment of Russian, Spanish, and Mexican settlements.

Gonzalez's (2011:238) XRF study of obsidian artifacts from the North Wall Community supports the finding that a variety of obsidian sources, including Annadel, remained in use and circulation during Russian occupation of Fort Ross and during the operation of the Benitz Rancho. Of

308 samples submitted for XRF analysis, the majority are from the Annadel obsidian flow (n=146; 47%), with the remainder from Glass Mountain in Napa Valley (n=125; 41%), Franz Valley in Petaluma (n=14; 4%), Mt. Konocti (n=13; 4%) and Borax Lake (n=5; 2%) in Clear Lake, in addition to unknown sources (n=5; 2%). This distribution of obsidian sources is similar to that observed at early and late prehistoric period sites on the Fort Ross terrace, which were investigated during the 2004–2005 field seasons of the Kashaya Pomo Interpretive Trail Project. The XRF study of obsidian artifacts (n=63) recovered through the surface collection of terrace sites in 2004–2005 revealed a greater proportion of Napa Valley obsidian (n=28; 45%) to Annadel obsidian (n=20; 32%), with the remaining sources coming from Franz Valley (n=5; 8%), Mt. Konocti (n=3; 5%), Borax Lake (n=3; 5%), and unknown sources (n=4; 5%). Thus, at both Metini Village and the North Wall Community it appears that residents continued to access and make use of a wide variety of obsidian sources despite the potential barriers of access to Annadel obsidian that were noted by Farris (1989).

Second, although the sample size is admittedly small at Metini Village, there is a greater percentage of obsidian that appears to date to the historical period than that observed for either NAVS or FRBS. Only one of the 76 (1%) obsidian artifacts at FRBS and six of the 96 (6%) obsidian specimens recovered from NAVS that yielded interpretable hydration rims are identified as possibly historical in age (band measurement less than or equal to 1.0 microns) (Lightfoot and Silliman 1997:350). In contrast, six of the 13 (46%) readable hydration measurements from Metini exhibited rim widths of 1.0 micron or smaller. Annadel obsidian also comprises the majority (4 out of the 6) of the obsidian that appears to be of historical age at Metini, while at NAVS and FRBS there is slightly more Napa Valley obsidian (n=4) that appears younger in age (1.0 or less microns) than Annadel (n=3) (Lightfoot and Silliman 1997:352). Despite the small sample size, these findings indicate that at least during the time that Metini Village was occupied, Native people were able to access both Annadel and Napa Valley obsidians.

Ground Stone and Other Lithic Artifacts

We identified several categories of ground stone artifacts, intentionally shaped by grinding, pecking, and/or polishing, in the Metini Village lithic assemblage. These include: milling hand stones (MH) (or manos), defined as convex, hand-sized tools with one or more grinding surfaces; pestles (PE), which are cylinder-shaped tools with evidence of battering on the distal or proximal end; and mortars (MO) identified by their bowl or hopper shape that exhibit evidence of pecking and grinding. Additional ground stone artifacts are classified as ground stone "other" (GO). These include what appear to be broken fragments of ground stone tools, such as pestles or milling stones that exhibit evidence of fire-alteration. These ground stone artifacts may have been recycled as cooking stones. Fire-cracked rocks (FC) also exhibit evidence of fire-altered surfaces, but they do not appear to be recycled ground stone artifacts, but rather cobbles or angular pieces of rocks used primarily as cooking stones. We believe that both FC and GO probably functioned at Metini Village as cooking stones in underground ovens, hearths, and for heating liquids/foods in watertight baskets. Other artifacts (OT) include materials that do not fit any of the above categories. The basic raw materials employed in the production of the other lithic artifacts include sandstone (SA), basalt (BA), igneous rock (IG), granite (GR), slate (SL), quartz (QZ) and unidentified rock material (UN). Allyson Leigh Milner (2009) completed the analysis of the other lithic artifacts. Appendix 3 presents specific details on the other lithic artifacts.

Surface Collection Units

Twenty-eight "other" lithic artifacts were collected in the surface collection units (Table 4). The majority was classified as fire-cracked rocks (n=19; 68%) and ground stone other (n=6; 21%). One milling hand stone was identified, along with one worked piece of slate and a quartz crystal. The raw materials identified for these artifacts include sandstone (n=18; 64%), basalt (n=3; 11%), igneous rock (n=1; 3.5%), granite (n=1; 3.5%), slate (n=1; 3.5%),

Table 4. Counts of Other Lithic Artifact Classes.

Other Lithic Classes	Surface Collection	ON 10W Excavation	15S 4E Excavation	20S 21E Excavation	SUM
FC	19	0	2	3	24
GO	6	0	2	2	10
MH	1	0	1	0	2
MO	0	0	0	1	1
PE	0	0	1	0	1
OT	2	0	0	1	3
SUM	28	0	6	7	41

Table 5. Counts of Other Lithic Artifact Raw Material Types.

Other Lithic Raw Material	Surface Collection	ON 10W Excavation	15S 4E Excavation	20S 21E Excavation	SUM
SA	18	0	6	6	30
BA	3	0	0	0	3
SL	1	0	0	1	2
GR	1	0	0	0	1
IG	1	0	0	0	1
QZ	1	0	0	0	1
UN	3	0	0	0	3
SUM	28	0	6	7	41

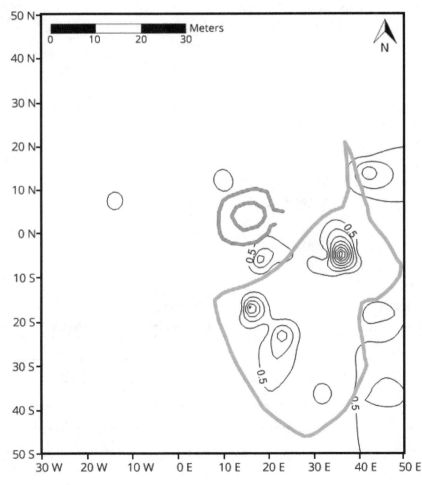

quartz (n=1; 3.5%), and unidentified rock material (n=3; 11%) (Table 5).

We plotted the expected spatial distribution of other lithic artifacts across Metini Village based on the counts from the 183 surface collection units. The output from the Surfer software program indicates that other lithic artifacts are concentrated in three to four discrete clusters along the terrace edge east of the pit feature (Figure 25). A sparse number of artifacts are also found along the terrace slope and on the west side of the pit feature. Since the majority of these artifacts are either fire-cracked rocks or ground stone other, this spatial configuration probably reflects the location of ovens and hearths and/or the discard of materials from these features along the terrace edge, with some materials sliding down the terrace slope.

Excavation Units

0N 10W. No "other" lithic artifacts were recovered.

Figure 25. Surface distribution of other lithic artifacts (0.5 artifact per m² contour interval). Pit depression outlined in red, midden in green.

15S 4E. The six specimens unearthed in this unit include two fire-cracked rocks, two groundstone others, one milling hand stone, and a pestle fragment. All were manufactured from local sandstone and all were found in the midden deposit, between 0 and 20 cm below unit datum.

20S 21E. Field crews excavated seven objects identified as other lithic artifacts: three fire-cracked rocks, two ground stone others, one large hopper mortar, and an etched piece of slate. The hopper mortar (ME-4/29/99-06-LI-09; Figure 13) was found 14 cm below unit datum in a cluster of artifacts. Nearby was discovered the etched slate piece (ME-4/29/99-06-LI-1, Figure 26) that had a cross with a circle at its intersection. With the exception of the etched piece of slate, all the artifacts were identified as sandstone. All of the artifacts were found in the midden deposit, 10–30 cm below unit datum.

Summary: Other Lithic Artifact Assemblage

The majority of the other lithic artifacts recovered from Metini are fire-cracked rocks (n=24; 58%) and ground stone others (n=10; 24%) probably from hearths or underground ovens, or from the hot rocks method of heating foods in watertight baskets (Table 4). The remaining objects are various kinds of processing tools—two milling hand stone fragments (Figure 27), one pestle fragment (Figure 28), and one hopper mortar (Figure 13)—along with several objects classified as "other" artifacts. The latter were identified as a quartz crystal and two slate pieces, one of which exhibited evidence of engraving (Figure 26). Most of the assemblage was manufactured from local sandstone (n=30; 73%) with the remaining 27% consisting of an assortment of raw materials: basalt (n=3), slate (n=2), igneous rock (n=1), granite (n=1), quartz crystal (n=1), and three unidentified (Table 5).

Figure 26. Etched slate artifact (20S 21E, Level 2, ME-4/29/99-06-LI-01).

Figure 27. Milling handstone fragment, lithic (17S 16E, Surface, ME-6/20/98-07-LI-02).

Figure 28. Pestle fragment, lithic (15S 4E, Level 2, ME-5/01/99-02-LI-04).

Ceramic Artifacts

We employed the same methodology for analyzing Metini ceramics as that developed for the Native Alaskan Village Site (NAVS) and the Fort Ross Beach Site (FRBS) assemblages (see Silliman 1997:136–138 for a full discussion). Ceramics were classified by (1) class (e.g., refined earthenware, stoneware, porcelain), (2) ware group (e.g., pearlware, creamware, ironstone, etc.), and (3) type (method and kind of decoration, such as hand-painted, transfer print, annular, undecorated). Identification of vessel forms (flat ware, hollow ware, etc.) was also undertaken when possible. David Palmer's analysis of the ceramics from Metini Village identified a relatively limited diversity of ceramic classes/groups within the assemblage. The basic categories include porcelains, classified as white (PO-WH) or non-white (PO-NW) porcelains, and four groups of refined earthenwares: whiteware (RE-WW), pearlware (RE-PW), ironstone (RE-IS), and a later hotel ware (RE-HW). A few white ball clay (kaolinite) pipe stems and bowls (KP) are also represented in the Metini Village assemblage. Detailed information on the ceramic artifacts is presented in Appendix 4.

Surface Collection

Field crews recovered a total of 27 ceramic sherds from surface collection units (Table 6). The surface ceramic assemblage is comprised of relatively small sherds (less than 20 mm diameter) from which the type (design elements) and vessel forms are often difficult to discern. The majority are identified as refined earthenware, ironstone vessels (n=11; 41%). Two of the ironstone ceramics (ME-6/20/98-07-HC-01B, Figure 29; ME-4/30/99-05-HC-01)

Table 6. Counts of Ceramic Artifacts.

Ceramic Classes	Surface Collection	ON 10W Excavation	15S 4E Excavation	20S 21E Excavation	SUM
PO-WH	1	0	0	2	3
PO-NW	6	0	0	0	6
RE-WW	3	0	2	0	5
RE-PW	1	0	0	0	1
RE-IS	11	0	0	3	14
RE-HW	0	0	0	1	1
KP	5	0	0	1	6
SUM	27	0	2	7	36

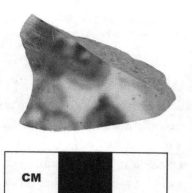

Figure 29. RE-IS ceramic with blue transfer print design (17S 16E, Surface, ME-6/20/98-07-HC-01B).

Figure 30. RE-IS ceramic with blue hand-painted underglaze (31S 33E, Surface, ME-4/17/99-03-HC-01).

Figure 31. PO-NW ceramic with hand-painted overglaze, earth-tone colored design (6S 43E, Surface, ME-4/29/99-01-HC-01).

exhibit blue transfer print designs, which may date between 1800 to 1860. Another (ME-4/17/99-03-HC-01, Figure 30) is distinctive for its underglaze, blue hand-painted, scalloped edge, which may date it to the period of 1800 to 1860. The rest of the ironstone vessels appear to have been produced later, probably between 1840 to 1900, and they include one with a blue molded shell edge } design, while the rest are undecorated. The vessel forms include three rims from plates, a shoulder from a bowl, a rim from a cup, a rim from an unknown vessel type, and the rims of one bowl and two hollow forms (probably bowls). Two of the undecorated ironstone vessels exhibit evidence of burning (see Appendix 4).

The next most common ceramics are non-white porcelains (n=6; 22%). One (ME-4/29/99-01-HC-01, Figure 31) is distinguished by overglaze hand-painting with an earth-tone floral sprigged design. Another (ME-4/16/99-02-HC-01, Figure 32) is an overglaze hand-painted vessel with red latticework designs. Both of these ceramics were produced sometime in the late 1700s to the late 1820s/1830. Two sherds are characterized by underglaze blue hand-painted decoration that was common in non-white porcelains up until about 1850, with one identified as the rim of a saucer (ME-6/20/98-01-HC-01). Another ceramic displays a hand-painted overglaze (color unknown) that may have been produced prior to 1850, while one other sherd is undecorated. The latter exhibited possible signs of being worked.

The three ceramics defined as refined earthenware whitewares include two (ME-6/20/98-04-HC-01; ME-4/16/99-05-HC-01B, Figure 33) distinguished by underglaze blue hand-painted decoration, while the third sherd is undecorated. The refined earthenware pearlware ceramic (ME-6/20/98-05-HC-01) displays transferprint blue designs (employing a double-sided transfer), although

Figure 32. PO-NW ceramic with hand-painted overglaze, red latticework design (21S 29E, Surface, ME-4/16/99-02-HC-01).

Figure 33. RE-WW ceramic with blue hand-painted underglaze (26S 28E, Surface, ME-4/16/99-05-HC-01B).

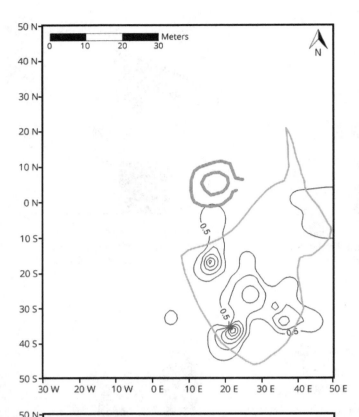

Figure 34. Surface distribution of ceramics (0.5 artifact per m² contour interval). Pit depression outlined in red, midden in green.

the sherd (less than 6 mm diameter) is so small that the designs cannot be identified. This sherd is from the base of a pearlware cup that was probably manufactured between 1785 and 1830. The one white porcelain in the surface assemblage is an undecorated piece from a hollow ware form. The five clay pipe artifacts include fragments of three bowls and two stems (for details see Appendix 4).

The spatial plotting of the ceramics using the SURFER software indicates that they are primarily found in the central and southern midden area, along the terrace edge and terrace slope (Figure 34). When the three ceramics, whose manufacture date predates 1830 are plotted, they are found in the central midden area, while the ceramics (primarily ironstones) that post-date 1840 are distributed in the southern midden area (Figures 35, 36, respectively).

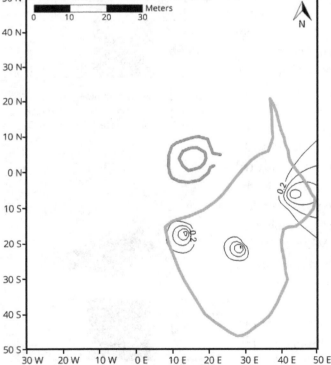

Figure 35. Surface distribution of ceramics produced before 1830 (0.2 artifact per m² contour interval). Pit depression outlined in red, midden in green.

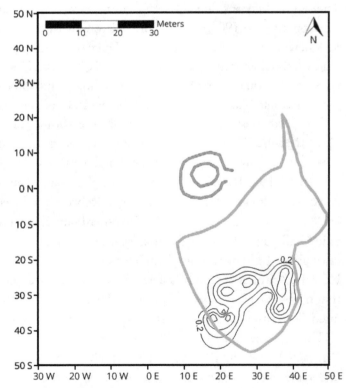

Figure 36. Surface distribution of ceramics produced after 1840 (0.2 artifact per m² contour interval). Pit depression outlined in red, midden in green.

Excavation Units

0N 10W. No ceramics were recovered in this 1-by-1 m unit.

15S 4E. Two ceramics were identified from the excavation. Both were identified as refined earthenware white wares. The rim of a plate (ME-5/01/99-02-HC-01, Figure 37) exhibited an underglaze, hand painted blue edge. The holloware ceramic (ME-5/01/99-11-HC-01, Figure 38) was decorated with an underglaze, transfer print flow blue design on both sides of the vessel. Both ceramics have production dates that span sometime between 1835 and 1870. Excavators recovered both artifacts in the midden deposit, 0–20 cm below unit datum.

Figure 37. RE-WW ceramic with dark blue underglaze (15S 4E, Level 1, ME-5/01/99-02-HC-01).

Figure 38. RE-WW ceramic with underglaze, transfer print flow blue design (15S 4E, Level 2, ME-5/01/99-11-HC-01).

20S 21E. Seven ceramic artifacts were uncovered during excavation including three undecorated, refined earthenware ironstone sherds that were probably used sometime between 1840 to1900. Another two white porcelain fragments were identified—one (ME-4/29/99-03-HC-01, Figure 39) is the rim of a lid with an overglaze, decal (ghost) design (possibly a tan flower), which may have a manufacture date post-dating 1880, and the other (ME-4/29/99-06-HC-01B) is the rim of a saucer with an overglaze, hand-painted decoration along the edge that was produced sometime after 1790. One piece of refined earthenware hotel ware, the rim of a bowl, was analyzed. It exhibited an overglaze hand-painted grayish-blue (ghost) design. This ceramic piece may also be associated with a late production date, post-dating 1880. The final artifact is that of an undecorated kaolinite pipe stem. One of these ceramics was recovered from the surface of the unit; the remaining pieces were excavated from the midden deposit, 0–20 cm below the unit datum.

Figure 39. PO-WH ceramic with overglaze decal (ghost) design (20S 21E, Surface, ME-4/29/99-03-HC-01).

Summary: Ceramic Assemblage

Of the 36 ceramic artifacts recovered from the Metini fieldwork, the majority (n=14; 39%) are identified as refined earthenware ironstone, followed by non-white porcelains (n=6; 16.5%), kaolinite pipe bowls and pipe stems (n=6; 16.5%), refined earthenware whitewares (n=5; 14%), white porcelains (n=3; 8%), a refined earthenware pearlware (3%), and a refined earthenware hotel ware (3%) (Table 6). A summary of the chronological information derived from the ceramic assemblage will be discussed later in the report.

Glass Artifacts

The glass remains from Metini were analyzed using the same methodology as that employed for the glass assemblages at NAVS and FRBS (see Silliman 1997:138–139). David Palmer completed the basic analysis of the glass materials, while the detailed investigation of the worked glass artifacts was undertaken by Emily Darko (2007) as part of her Senior Honors Thesis in the Anthropology Department at UC Berkeley. Her pioneering work was supplemented by further analyses by Roberta Jewett, Brandon Patterson, Allyson Leigh Milner, Elizabeth Campos, and Fanya Becks (see Darko 2007; Milner 2009).

Vessel, Flat, Lamp/Globe, and Mirror Glass

Glass sherds were separated into three basic groups: vessel (VS), flat glass (FG), lamp/globe (LA), and mirror (MI), while those that were uncertain were placed in the unidentifiable (UN) category. Color was then observed for each glass specimen; the major colors discerned in the Metini assemblage include light green (GR), dark green (DG), brown (BR), colorless (CO), blue-green (BG), yellow-green (YG), and aqua (AQ). Vessel glass was further differentiated by a manufacture method that involved free blown glass (BL), and various kinds of molding methods, such as dip molding (DP), machine molding (MM), and plate molding (PM). When we could not identify the particular method for molding the bottle, the specimens were simply designated as "molded" (MO) glass. In cases where we could not distinguish the manufacture method (e.g., free-blown or molded), we used the unidentifiable (UN) category. Whenever possible, we identified vessel form (bottle type), and vessel part [base (BA), neck (NE), shoulder (SH), and finish/collar (FC)]. However, similar to the NAVS, FRBS, and NWC assemblages, the vessel remains from Metini are highly fragmented, and identification of manufacture method, vessel form, and vessel element was not possible for many specimens.

The entire glass assemblage was carefully evaluated under a low power binocular microscope for evidence of knapping and/or use, and all glass edges were analyzed for signs of modification (e.g., nibbling, scratching, or the removal of small flakes from one or more edges). Glass artifacts exhibiting evidence of production and/or use were assigned to the category, worked glass (WG). These artifacts were classified in the same manner as the chipped stone artifacts discussed earlier. The categories include debitage [complete flake (CP), proximal flake (PX), flake shatter (FS), angular shatter (SH)] and core and core fragments (CO, CF), projectile point fragment (PF), uniface (UN), and biface (BI) (for examples, see Figures 40–43). The one exception to this classificatory system is the addition of the glass sherd (GS) category (Figure 44). It is defined as a glass fragment that exhibits indications of edge modification, usually nibbling, scratching, or the removal of small flakes from one or more edges, but in which no evidence of glass reduction by percussion or pressure flaking is visible. Glass sherds thus exhibit none of the criteria established for identifying formal tools or debitage (complete and proximal flakes or flake shatter with identifiable ventral or dorsal surfaces, striking platform, bulb of percussion, termination points), but potentially indicate usage in manners consistent with edge-modified lithic tools and debitage. We recognize that edge modification on glass artifacts may be produced by trampling by people and livestock, or by so-called "bag retouch" once they were collected by archaeologists. Given that edge modification on glass artifacts can be produced by a variety of actions, we recommend a conservative approach in considering the glass sherd category. Detailed observations about the glass artifacts (non-worked or non-modified) are provided in Appendix 5, while the worked glass assemblage is presented in Appendix 6.

Figure 40. Example of complete flake, worked glass (20S 25E, Surface, ME-4/29/99-04-WG-02B).

Figure 41. Example of proximal flake, worked glass (4S 40E, Surface, ME 4/30/99-04-WG-02).

Figure 42. Example of flake shatter, worked glass (6S 43E, Surface, ME-4/29/99-01-WG-03).

Figure 43. Example of core, worked glass (20S 21E, Surface, ME-4/29/99-06-WG-03).

Figure 44. Example of glass sherd, worked glass (35S 43E, Surface, ME-4/30/99-05-WG-03).

Surface Collection

A total of 269 glass artifacts were recovered during the surface collection of the 183 1-by-1 m units. The assemblage includes 250 (93%) vessel glass fragments, 17 (6%) flat glass pieces, and two (1%) lamp/globe sherds (Table 7). Glass color is dominated by 181 (67%) dark green pieces, then 54 (20%) colorless, 18 (7%) light green, 10 (4%) brown, five (1.5%) aqua, and one (0.5%) blue-green sherd (Table 8). Most of the flat glass appears to be the fragments of window panes. For the 250 vessel fragments, the most common manufacture technique was the dip molding method (n=147; 59%), followed by the generic molding category (n=67; 27%), plate molding (n=3; 1%), free-blown methods (n=3; 1%), and machine molding (n=2; 1%). Manufacture technique could not be identified for a total of 28 (11%) vessel sherds (Table 9). While the majority of the vessel fragments appear to be the remains of liquor/spirits bottles, others include fragments of three mineral bottles, three patent/perfume bottles, one pharmaceutical bottle, one beer bottle, and one ketchup bottle. The analysis identified 13 pieces of case bottles and six square, flat-sided panel bottles. The most common vessel sections identified in the surface assemblage were the bottle base (n=22), lip/finish (n=6), shoulder (n=3), neck (n=2), and tumbler rim (1).

Table 7. Counts of Glass Artifacts by Basic Groups.

Glass Groups	Surface Collection	ON 10W Excavation	15S 4E Excavation	20S 21E Excavation	SUM
VS	250	7	72	77	406
FG	17	0	0	15	32
LA	2	0	0	0	2
MI	0	0	1	0	1
SUM	269	7	73	92	441

Table 8. Counts of Glass Artifacts by Color.

Glass Color	Surface Collection	ON 10W Excavation	15S 4E Excavation	20S 21E Excavation	SUM
GR	18	4	5	1	28
DG	181	3	49	62	295
BR	10	0	3	4	17
CO	54	0	16	22	92
AQ	5	0	0	2	7
BG	1	0	0	0	1
YG	0	0	0	1	1
SUM	269	7	73	92	441

Table 9. Counts of Vessel Glass by Manufacture Techniques.

Vessel Manufacture Technique	Surface Collection	ON 10W Excavation	15S 4E Excavation	20S 21E Excavation	SUM
MO	67	2	32	21	122
DP	147	4	27	48	226
MM	2	0	0	0	2
PM	3	0	0	0	3
BL	3	0	0	0	3
UN	28	1	13	8	50
SUM	250	7	72	77	406

Table 10. Counts of Worked Glass Artifact Classes.

Worked Glass	Surface Collection	ON 10W Excavation	15S 4E Excavation	20S 21E Excavation	SUM
SH	20	2	6	12	40
FS	26	1	8	17	52
PX	6	0	3	1	10
CO	4	0	0	1	5
CP	13	0	7	6	26
CF	7	0	0	0	7
UN	0	0	0	0	0
BF	1	0	0	0	1
GS	66	1	11	13	91
SUM	143	4	35	50	232

We defined a total of 143 (53%) pieces from the entire surface collection assemblage as worked glass (Table 10). The majority are identified as glass sherds (n=66; 46%), followed by flake shatter (n=26; 18%), angular shatter (n=20; 14%), complete flakes (n=13; 9%), core or core fragments (n=11; 8%), proximal flakes (n=6; 4%), and bifaces (n=1: 1%). The biface is a fragment of an undiagnostic projectile point. Given the diversity of worked glass forms, it appears that a wide range of glass modification and tool manufacture and use took place at Metini Village.

In plotting the spatial distribution of glass artifacts across Metini Village (based on the counts from the surface collection units), the SURFER isopleths indicate glass remains cover the entire midden area along the terrace edge and terrace slope (Figure 45). A few pieces are found to the west of the pit feature.

Figure 45. Surface distribution of glass artifacts (0.5 artifact per m² contour interval). Pit depression outlined in red, midden in green.

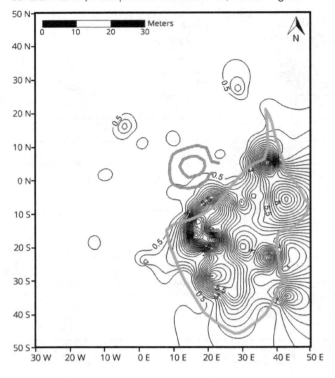

The worked glass fragments, when mapped out separately, follow a similar pattern as that of the entire glass assemblage (Figure 46). There are several clusters along the terrace edge with materials radiating down the slope of the terrace throughout the midden area. In plotting the worked glass categories involving tool production (shatter, flake shatter, complete flakes, proximal flakes, and cores), an analogous spatial distribution is evident—discrete clusters along the terrace edge and other materials distributed downslope throughout the midden area (Figure 47).

Figure 46. Surface distribution of worked glass artifacts (0.5 artifact per m² contour interval). Pit depression outlined in red, midden in green.

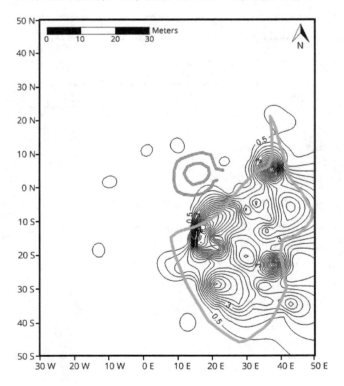

Figure 47. Surface distribution of worked glass categories involving tool production (shatter, flake shatter, complete flakes, proximal flakes, and cores). (0.5 artifact per m² contour interval). Pit depression outlined in red, midden in green.

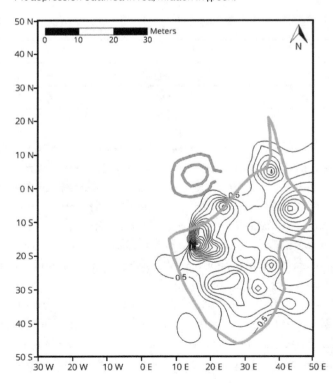

Excavation Units

0N 10W. Seven vessel glass pieces were unearthed in the 1-by-1 m excavation unit. Glass color ranged from light green (n=4) to dark green (n=3), with four of the bottle fragments exhibiting evidence of dip molding manufacture and two others some form of contact molding technique. The manufacture method of one sherd was unidentifiable. Given the small size of the glass pieces, no other information could be obtained about bottle type or bottle section. Four of the seven glass artifacts were classified as worked glass, including two pieces of angular shatter, one flake shatter, and one glass sherd (See Tables 7–10). All the glass fragments were recovered in the A horizon or the underlying dark brown sandy loam.

15S 4E. Of the 73 glass artifacts recovered from the unit, 72 were vessel fragments and one was a piece of mirror glass. Dark green glass (n=49) dominated the assemblage, followed by colorless glass (n=16), light green colored glass (n=5), and brown colored glass (n=3). The vessel glass, which could be identified as to manufacture technique, was either some form of contact molded glass (n=32, 44.4%) or dip-molded glass (n=27, 37.5%), with 13 sherds (18%) undiagnosed as to method of manufacture. Vessel forms that could be identified from the relatively small sherds include fragments of eight case bottles. The only section of a bottle identified in the assemblage was that of the base of a colorless molded bottle. Thirty-five of the 73 glass specimens (47.9%) were classified as worked glass artifacts. These included 11 glass sherds, eight flake shatter artifacts, seven complete flakes, six pieces of angular shatter, and three proximal flakes. No formal tools or cores were unearthed (See Tables 7–10). The majority of the glass objects were found in the midden deposit 0–20 cm below datum.

20S 21E. Field crews unearthed a total of 92 glass specimens, including 77 vessel glass fragments, 15 pieces of flat glass, and no lamp/globe sherds. Glass color varied from dark green (n=62), to colorless (n=22), light green (n=1), brown (n=4), aqua (n=2), and yellow-green (n=1). For the 77 vessel glass fragments that could be classified by manufacture technique, 48 are dip-molded glass and 21 are generic molded glass, while eight were unidentifiable. Vessel forms distinguished in the glass assemblage include one case bottle and one fragment of a flat-sided patent-proprietary bottle. Bottle sections recognized for the unit assemblage include two bottle bases and one square sided bottle neck. Worked glass artifacts accounted for 50 of the 92 glass artifacts (54.3%). The most common worked glass classes are flake shatter (n=17), glass sherds (n=13), and angular shatter (n=12), followed by six complete flakes, one proximal flake, and one core (See Tables 7–10). Almost all the glass objects were recovered in the midden deposit, 0–30 cm below unit datum. One small worked glass piece was found 30–40 cm below datum in the mottled loamy sand level.

Summary: Vessel, Flat, Lamp/Globe and Mirror Glass

The investigation of the Metini Village yielded a total of 441 glass artifacts. The majority are vessel fragments (n= 406; 92%), followed distantly by flat glass (n=32; 7%), lamp/globe glass (n=2; 0.5%), and a mirror fragment (n=1; 0.5%) (Table 7). Glass color is dominated by dark green (n=295; 67%), colorless (n=92; 21%), light green glass (n=28; 6%), and brown (n=17; 4%). Aqua colored glass (n=7; 2%) was also recognized, along with trace amounts of blue-green (n=1) and yellow-green (n=1) fragments (Table 8). For the 406 vessel glass fragments, the manufacture technique involved dip molding (n=226; 55.5%), generic molding (n=122; 30%), plate molding (n=3; 1%), free blown glass (n=3; 1%), and machine molding (n=2; 0.5%). We were unable to classify 50 (12%) vessel fragments by manufacture technique (Table 9). The majority of the bottle types appear to be liquor or spirits bottles, along with some patent/proprietary bottles, a few mineral bottles, and an occasional pharmaceutical bottle, ketchup bottle, or beer bottle. Vessel elements include a few examples of bottle parts from the finish/collar, neck, and shoulder, but the majority are bottle bases, including several well-formed kick-ups.

The most salient characteristic of the glass assemblage is the large number of worked glass pieces. Worked glass artifacts accounted for 232 (53%) of the 441 glass specimens recovered from surface and excavation units at Metini (Table 10). The most common artifact category in the worked glass assemblage is the "glass sherd" (n=91; 39%), followed by flake shatter (52; 23%), angular shatter (n=40; 17%), complete flakes (n=26; 11 %), core and core fragments (n=12; 5%), proximal flakes (n=10; 4%), and one biface fragment (1%). The Metini residents appear to have been highly selective about the kinds of glass they employed in tool manufacture and/or modification through use. All the worked glass fragments are derived from bottles and it appears that particular kinds of bottles were selected for glass working. The vast majority are dark green (n=188; 81%), followed distantly by light green (n=17; 7%), colorless (n=11; 5%), brown (n=10; 4%), and aqua (n=6; 3%). In regards to the kind of bottle glass employed for working, the majority are dipped molded (n=155; 67%) and generically molded (n=48; 21%), with only one free blown and another plated molded. We could not identify the manufacture method for 27 of the worked glass vessel fragments.

The most common vessel types employed for glass working were stocky dark green, dip-molded bottles (n=141; 61% of the entire worked glass assemblage), followed distantly by dark green, generically molded bottles (n=26; 11%). In contrast, while colorless glass makes up over 20% of the entire glass assemblage at Metini Village (92 out of 441 sherds), the total number of colorless glass sherds exhibiting evidence of use or manufacture is only 11 (only 5% of the entire worked glass assemblage). This pattern is not only the consequence of

Metini residents not using window glass for glass working, but also apparently their decision to limit the number of available colorless glass vessel fragments as raw materials for tool production and/or use. Thus, the preferred kind of raw material employed for glass working at Metini was the dark green glass from dip-molded (and generic molded) vessels—most likely from heavy, thick bottomed, dark glass alcohol bottles. There is also a strong tendency for people to use the base of these bottles for glass production. In identifying the parts of the dark green, dip-molded bottles represented in the worked glass assemblage, we counted 19 bottle bases, including thick kick-up components in some cases, along with two bottle shoulders, and two lips with champagne finishes. One bottle lip was identified for the dark green, generically molded bottles pieces. The majority of the dark green, dip-molded and molded glass appear to be derived from case bottles (n=12).

Our observations of the worked glass assemblage suggest Metini residents employed the glass artifacts as tools in two different ways. The first way was to select pieces of broken, dark green bottle glass with sharp edges as expedient tools. Whether these glass fragments were obtained from bottles used by Metini workers or scavenged from the Russian stockade or the Benitz residential dump is not clear at this time. As noted earlier, the artifacts classified as "glass sherds" exhibit evidence of some form of edge modification, typically nibbling or seriated edges that may signify their use as tools. There is little evidence that they were produced through traditional core reduction methods involving the creation of flake or core tools using percussion or pressure flaking methods as traditionally employed with lithic raw material. We surmise that these expedient tools were used to perform various activities that required a sharp edge, and after one or a few uses, they were often discarded.

We caution that not all of the glass sherds exhibiting some evidence of edge modification may have been intentionally used by Metini residents. We recognize that some of the "glass sherds" may have been modified by the trampling of people or cattle or by other actions not involving their use as tools. But at least some glass sherds exhibit clear indications for what appears to be tool use. In particular, we observed a pattern where the edges of some glass sherds (n=23) were intentionally sharpened by glass removal either by scraping or in a few cases by the removal of pressure flakes along the edge. We also noted that some glass sherds (n=6) exhibited evidence for their use in smoothing wood or some other raw material. Referred to as "spoke shaves" by some of our analysts, these glass sherds displayed a rounded, smooth edge that appeared to be produced by repeated rubbing or smoothing.

The other pathway for glass tool use at Metini involved glass modification through the reduction of thick chunks of glass into smaller flakes. In selecting the remains of heavy, dark green glass bottles, the Metini craftspeople preferred the heel or base of these thick vessels for glass modification. We identified the

Figure 48. Example of core fragment, worked glass (5N 38E, Surface, ME–4/21/99–02-WG–01A).

Figure 49. Biface fragment, worked glass (8S 22E, Surface, 6/26/98–03–WG–02).

remains of 23 bottle bases, including three kick-ups, in the entire worked glass assemblage. Significantly, all 12 of the core and core fragments were produced from bottle bases. Our observations suggest the glass knappers typically employed the bases of the dark green, dip-molded bottles as cores in the expedient production of choppers/cutting implements (Figure 48). The bottle bases and finishes/necks were repurposed as expedient tools using both percussion and pressure flaking techniques. We observed that some of the worked glass artifacts (particularly a number of small complete flakes and flake shatter; n=29) exhibit the diagnostic attributes for pressure flakes from bifacial reduction. Our observations suggest that this is consistent with retouch and use-wear. The interpretation of expedient manufacture is consistent with the lithic data—a preponderance of debitage, very few formal tools, and some flake tools, which indicates that repurposing and recycling of both the lithic and glass raw materials were being undertaken at Metini. There is minimal evidence for formal tool production for either the lithic or glass raw materials. For example, only six formal lithic tools and one glass biface fragment, exhibiting signs of pressure flaking along its edge (Figure 49), were recovered at Metini during our field investigation.

Glass Beads *by Elliot H. Blair*

Forty-six glass beads were recovered during excavations at Metini. Appendix 7 provides detailed attributes of the individual beads in the assemblage. Method of manufacture (e.g., drawn, wound, blown, molded), construction (e.g., simple, compound, complex, composite), finishing method (e.g., none, faceted, heat rounded), shape, diameter, length, color, and diaphaneity were recorded for each specimen—following standard bead analysis protocols and terminology (see Beck 1928; Blair et al. 2009; Karklins 2012[1982]; Kidd and Kidd 2012[1970]; Stone 1974; van der Sleen 1973). Additionally, Kidd and Kidd (2012 [1970]), and Ross (1997) type designations are included in Appendix 7 for comparative purposes.

Table 11 summarizes the method of manufacture, construction, and color data for the assemblage. Of the forty-six beads recovered, five specimens are of wound manufacture (10.9%). Four of these are white and of simple construction (Figures 50, 51). The final specimen is of compound construction and consists of two distinct layers of white glass (Figure 52). The remaining 41 beads (89.1%) are all of drawn manufacture (Figures 53–57). Sixteen of these are of simple construction, including 11 white, four blue, and one light green. These include two faceted hexagonal tubes (Bohemian cut beads)—one cobalt blue (Kidd and Kidd If5) and the other light green (Kidd and Kidd If3). The remaining 25 drawn beads are all of compound construction. These include 18 heat rounded white-over-white beads, three Bohemian cut clear-over-white beads (Kidd and Kidd IIIf1), three red-on-white (cornaline d'Aleppo) beads (Kidd and Kidd IVa2), and one red-on-green (Kidd and Kidd IVa6, green heart) bead.

Table 11: Glass Bead Manufacture, Construction, and Color Summary.

Manufacture	Construction	Color
Wound (n=5)	Simple (n=4)	White (n=4)
	Compound (n=1)	White over white (n=1)
Drawn (n=41)	Simple (n=16)	White (n=11)
		Blue (n=4)
		Light green (n=1)
	Compound (n=25)	White over white (n=17)
		Clear over white (n=3)
		Red over white (n=3)
		White over cream (n=1)
		Red over green (n=1)

Figure 50. Wound white oblates. Left to right: ME-6/20/98-02-BE-01; ME-6/26/98-05-BE-01A; ME-4/17/99-01-BE-01.

Figure 51. Wound white bead: ME-6/26/98-03-BE-01A.

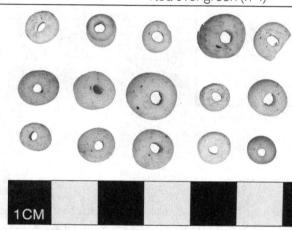

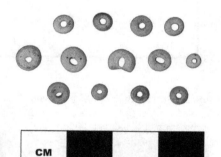

Figure 52. Wound compound white bead: ME-6/26/98-01-BE-01.

Figure 53. Simple and compound drawn white beads. Row 1, (left to right): ME-6/20/98-04-BE-01A; ME-6/23/98-04-BE-01A; ME-6/26/98-03-BE-01B; ME-6/26/98-05-BE-01B; ME-6/26/98-05-BE-01C. Row 2: ME-6/26/98-08-BE-01A; ME-6/26/98-09-BE-01; ME-4/29/99-02-BE-01A; ME-4/29/99-02-BE-01C; ME-4/29/99-04-BE-01A. Row 3: ME-4/29/99-04-BE-01B; ME-4/29/99-06-BE-01A; ME-4/29/99-06-BE-01B; ME-4/29/99-06-BE-01C; ME-5/01/99-11-BE-01A.

Figure 54. Simple and compound drawn white seed beads. Row 1, (left to right): ME-6/20/98-04-BE-01B; ME-6/23/98-04-BE-01B; ME-4/16/99-06-BE-01; ME-4/29/99-02-BE-01D. Row 2: ME-4/29/99-06-BE-01D; ME-4/29/99-06-BE-01E; ME-4/29/99-06-BE-01F; ME-4/29/99-06-BE-01G; ME-4/30/99-12-BE-01. Row 3: ME-5/01/99-02-BE-01C; ME-5/01/99-07-BE-01; ME-5/01/99-11-BE-01B; ME-5/01/99-11-BE-01C.

Figure 55. Blue seed bead: ME-5/01/99-02-BE-01D.

Figure 56. Bohemian cut beads. Row 1, (left to right): ME-6/25/98-08-BE-01; ME-6/26/98-08-BE-01B; ME-4/29/99-02-BE-01B; ME-5/01/99-02-BE-01A; ME-5/01/99-02-BE-01B.

Figure 57. Compound red-on-white and red-on-green beads. Left to right: ME-6/20/98-04-BE-01C; ME-6/26/98-03-BE-01C; ME-5/01/99-02-BE-01E; ME-5/01/99-11-BE-01D.

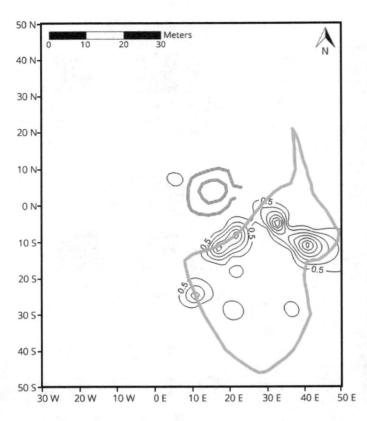

Figure 58. Surface distribution of glass beads (0.5 artifact per m² contour interval). Pit depression outlined in red, midden in green.

The Metini glass beads are distributed in three discrete clusters along the terrace edge east of the pit feature. Another cluster of beads cascades down the northern face of the terrace slope (Figure 58).

The bead assemblage from Metini is small and few major conclusions can be drawn from it. I will, however, make some brief observations regarding chronology, color composition, and possible sources of the beads, highlighting similarities and differences to other bead assemblages from Fort Ross, including the North Wall Community (Ballard 1995; Blair 2011; Smith 1974), the Tomato Patch and Ridge Village sites (Ross 1998), the Native Alaskan Village site and Fort Ross Beach site (Ross 1997), the Fort Ross Industrial Complex (Allan 2001), the Fort Ross Magazin (Farris 1981, 1990; Newland and Meyer 2003), the Fort Ross cemetery (Goldstein 2012; Goldstein and Brinkmann 2003[2008]; Osborn 1997), and several additional sites (e.g., CA-SON-670, CA-SON-174) summarized by Atchley (Atchley 1990; Meighan 1967, n.d.; Ross 1998) (see also Lightfoot, Wake, and Schiff 1991; Motz 1979).

Chronology

The Metini bead assemblage contains few beads that are temporally diagnostic. The few that are include red-on-white (cornaline d'Aleppo) beads and Bohemian cut beads, often erroneously referred to as "Russian" beads (Kidd and Kidd types If and IIIf). While red-on-green beads have circulated in North America since the early seventeenth century, many researchers have noted that red-on-white beads do not appear on California sites until after 1841 (Atchley 1990; Meighan 1967, n.d.; Motz 1979; Ross 1998). Recently, Billeck (2008) conducted an extensive study reviewing the dates when red-on-white beads first appear in historical documents, trade ledgers, ethnographic beaded objects, and archaeological sites in the North American Great Plains region. His synthesis of these multiple lines of evidence indicates that this bead type is *extremely* rare during the mid-1830s and only becomes common by the mid-1840s. This appears to be similarly true in California. Atchley (1990:47–48) suggested that California sites containing red-on-green beads but lacking cornaline d'Aleppo beads date prior to 1844. Crowell's (1997) seriation of Alaskan bead assemblages also supports a post-ca. 1840 date for the introduction of red-on-white beads in the west.

At Metini Village the ratio of red-on-green to red-on-white beads is 1:3. While the sample only includes four beads, when compared to other contexts at Fort

Ross (regardless of sample size) the contrast is stark. For example, at the North Wall Community this ratio is 9:2 (Ballard 1995; Blair 2011), at the Ritter excavations between Metini and the North Wall Community the ratio is 3:0 (Smith 1974), at NAVS the ratio is 101:2 (Ross 1997), and at the Fort Ross Industrial Complex the ratio is 4:0 (Allan 2001). Indeed, in almost all contexts across the Fort Ross landscape, which are directly associated with Russian occupation, red-on-green beads significantly outnumber red-on-white specimens. Other than Metini Village, the only contexts where the ratio differs are at CA-SON-174 (Atchley 1990) and in several burials within the Fort Ross Cemetery. At CA-SON-174 the ratio is 6:5; this is entirely consistent with the later date (1840s–1850s) that has been suggested for the site (Lightfoot, Wake, and Schiff 1991:75–76; Lightfoot 1993:169). A large quantity of red-on-white beads found with a few burials at the Fort Ross cemetery is the only anomaly for Russian-occupied colonial spaces and requires further study.

The other chronologically significant bead type at Metini Village is the Bohemian cut bead, of which there are five (10.9% of the assemblage). This type is conspicuously absent from most other contexts at Fort Ross (see also Motz 1979:14–15). For example, only two (3%) were recovered during the numerous excavations at the North Wall Community and only three were recovered from NAVS (0.5%). The only contexts in which this type appears to be numerous are at Tomato Patch (n =15, 9.5%) (Ross 1998) and possibly in the Fort Ross cemetery (Goldstein and Brinkmann 2003[2008]:14, Fig. 7). Meighan (n.d., cited in Motz 1979) has suggested that these bead types date to the 1847–1867 period, while Ross (1997) states that they are certainly post-1820s types and are primarily associated with the Hudson's Bay Company trade. Francis (1994:296) suggests 1819 as the earliest manufacturing date for this type, but notes a major time lag before they become common in the North American trade. The absence of this bead in clear Russian contexts at Fort Ross supports the late, post ca. 1840 date for this type.

A late date for this type at Metini Village is also supported by the chemical composition of bead P1190-017-A (ME-5/01/99-02-BE-1), type If3. This bead has a distinctive green color, sometimes known as Annagrün or Anna green, caused by the addition of uranium oxide. Uranium glass was invented ca. 1830 and did not become common as a glass additive until the 1840s (Brill 1964:54; Langhamer 2003:71).

Together, the presence of eight (17.4%) relatively "late" beads at Metini Village—the three red-on-white beads and the five Bohemian cut beads (including one manufactured from uranium glass)—strongly supports a post-Russian occupation at the site, especially when compared to other sites from across the Fort Ross landscape, where these bead types are largely absent. Whether the occupation is entirely post-Russian, however, is impossible to determine from the bead assemblage. Despite the relative absence of red-on-green beads, nothing about the assemblage precludes the possibility of a Russian period occupation of Metini Village.

Color Composition

The Metini Village bead assemblage consists of 34 white beads (73.9%), four red beads (8.7%), four blue beads (8.7%), three clear beads (6.5%), and one green bead (2.2%). In order to compare the bead color preferences at Metini—an important research question in terms of Native bead consumption across California (e.g., Meighan 1985; Panich 2014; Ross 1997)—with other sites around Fort Ross, the bead color diversity from Metini and other Fort Ross sites was reduced to the following categories: white/clear, blue/green/purple, red, black, and amber/yellow. The percentage of beads in each of these color categories from a number of sites at Fort Ross is presented in Figure 59. Metini's bead color profile—dominated by white/clear beads, with smaller numbers of red and blue/green/purple beads—is most similar to the Ridge Village site (Ross 1998) and the Fort Ross Industrial Complex (Allan 2001). The color profile of the Metini site is also distinctly different than the unique pattern found at NAVS, which included an unusually large number of black and red beads (Ross 1997). Also clearly evident

Figure 59. Glass bead color profiles.

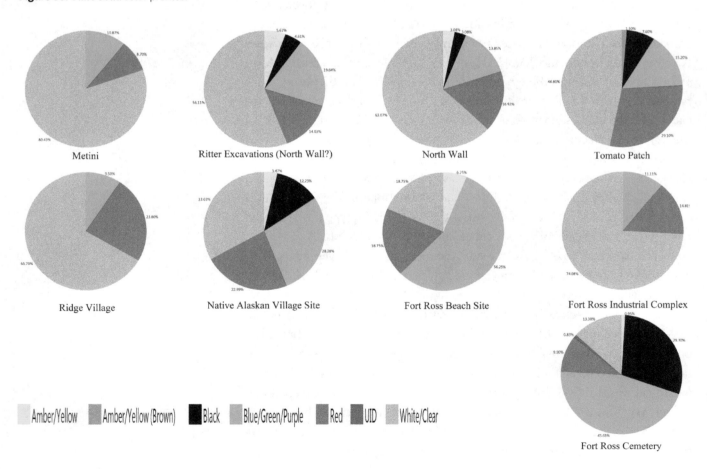

in this figure is a distinct similarity between the North Wall Community beads and those recovered during the 1972 Ritter excavations (Smith 1974), both of which are readily distinguishable from the Metini Village assemblage.

The North Wall Community and the 1972 Ritter excavations are also linked by the presence of an unusual bead type in common—a complex black (dark purple) barrel shaped bead with white stripes. These specimens, Kidd and Kidd Type IIb13's, are exact matches of two beads recovered at Fort Vancouver (1829–1860)—Variety IIb-op/tpl-1 (Blair 2011, Ross 1990, Smith 1974). The specimens from Fort Vancouver and the one from the 1972 Ritter excavations each had 26 stripes, but the North Wall bead is fragmented and it is unclear how many stripes the intact specimen possessed. While the presence of this bead in both contexts is hardly conclusive, combined with the other similarities between the North Wall Community and the Ritter excavation materials, it highlights the distinctions between these Native Californian bead assemblages and Metini Village.

Bead Sources

With the exception of the previously discussed Bohemian cut beads (from Bohemia), the majority of the Metini Village beads appear to be of Venetian manufacture, most likely distributed by the Hudson's Bay company (Ross 1990, 1997). No beads from Metini suggest Russian or Chinese manufacture. Indeed, despite Bychkov's provocative hypothesis that glass and glass beads for the Russian-American trade were manufactured in Siberia (Bychkov 1997; Farris 1992), no evidence has yet to emerge that any glass beads found in Russian-American colonies were manufactured in Russia (see also Brackett, Kleyman, and McMahan 2008; Dovgalyuk and Tataurova 2010). Similarly, Ross (1997) has commented on the unusual absence of Chinese beads from Fort Ross, and indeed, with the exception of wound blue beads pictured from the Fort Ross cemetery (Goldstein 2012:239, Fig. 4; Goldstein and Brinkmann 2003[2008]:14, Fig. 7) that appear to be examples of Canton beads, no Chinese beads have been identified at Fort Ross.

Discussion

The Metini Village bead assemblage, while small in number, hints at important temporal and social distinctions across the Fort Ross Landscape. While the bead assemblage is equivocal as to whether the site was occupied during the Russian period, the relatively high number of red-on-white and Bohemian cut beads, types that likely post-date the Russian period in California, strongly suggests that the site was occupied after the Russian abandonment of Fort Ross. The general absence of these types from almost all other contexts at Fort Ross strengthens this interpretation. The color profile of the Metini bead assemblage (see Figure 59)—dominated by white/clear beads—is also strikingly different from the Native Alaskan Village site and is easily distinguished from the North Wall Community. In the case of NAVS the difference is partly temporal, but also likely indicates differences in bead color preferences between Native Alaskans and Native Californians. The differences between Metini Village and the North Wall Community (including the 1972 Ritter excavations), which include different color profiles and starkly different red-on-green to red-on-white bead ratios, also suggest that the two sites were likely not part of a single, larger and contemporaneous zone of occupation—at least during the post-Russian period.

Buttons

Most of the artifacts classified as buttons were manufactured from glass, but there were also some specimens made from brass, iron, and bone. David Palmer completed the analysis of the button assemblage. The button assemblage is presented in Appendix 8.

Surface Collection

Field crews collected a total of eight buttons from surface units at Metini, including five made from glass, one from iron, one from brass, and one from bone (Table 12). The five glass objects are molded, opaque white colored, four-hole buttons with a diameter of between 10 and 20 mm (Figure 60). The iron artifact is a cast/molded, snap fastener with a diameter of 16 mm. It may have once had a decorated face, but the artifact is highly corroded (Figure 61). The brass specimen (ME-4/16/99-04-ME-02) is a United States army issue, cast/molded, button cover with a diameter of 3.4 cm (Figure 62). The button cover exhibits the eagle with shield and olive branches and arrows. It was manufactured sometime between 1850–1900 (Luscoms 1992:11). The final button recovered from the surface collections was carved from bone (Figure 63). It exhibits a five-hole pattern (with a central hole surrounded by the other four) and is 16 mm in diameter.

Table 12. Counts of Glass and Other Buttons.

Button Classes	Surface Collection	ON 10W Excavation	15S 4E Excavation	20S 21E Excavation	SUM
Glass	5	0	1	3	9
Iron	1	0	0	0	1
Brass	1	0	0	1	1
Bone	1	0	0	0	1
SUM	8	0	1	4	13

The eight buttons collected from the surface are distributed only in the midden area. The isopleth densities plotted using SURFER show button artifacts along the terrace edge and down the terrace slope (Figure 64).

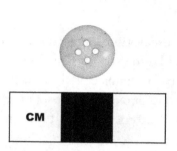

Figure 60. White molded prosser 4-hole pattern button (12S 17E, Surface, ME-6/20/98-04-BU-01).

Figure 61. Iron snap fastener (5N 38E, Surface, ME-4/21/99-02-BU-01).

Figure 62. Brass button cover (23S 38E, Surface, ME-4/16/99-04-ME-02).

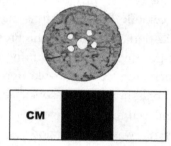

Figure 63. Bone 5-hole pattern button (5.1N 35E, Surface, ME-6/05/98-01-BU-01).

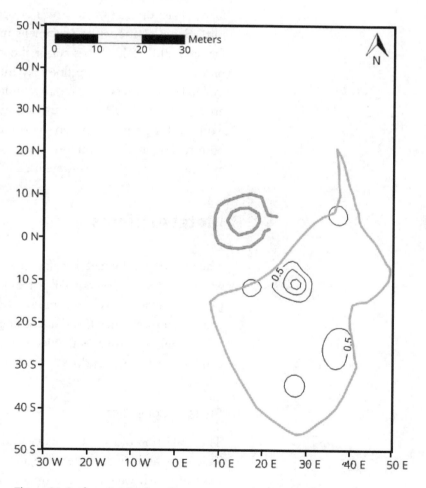

Figure 64. Surface distribution of buttons (0.5 artifact per m² contour interval). Pit depression outlined in red, midden in green.

Excavation Units

0N 10W. No buttons were recovered.

15S 4E. One opaque white, four-hole glass button with a diameter of 11 mm was found in the lower midden deposit.

20S 21E. We unearthed four buttons in the excavation of this 1-by-1 m unit. They include one opaque white, four-holed button; two opaque blue, four-holed buttons; and one brass single-holed (post manufactured) artifact that may be a work clothing fastener for denim pants or overalls. The four buttons were recovered in the upper midden deposit, 0–10 cm below unit datum.

Summary: Button Assemblage

The majority of the 13 buttons recovered from Metini appear to be glass artifacts, either opaque white (n=7) or opaque blue (n=2), with a four-hole pattern. Some of the white specimens may be ceramic Prosser buttons manufactured after 1840 (Farris personal communication, 2/22/2016). The Prosser process involved pressing fine clay into cast-iron molds and then firing the molded clay objects at high temperatures, which produced a glass-like appearance (Sprague 2002). Other artifacts include a brass army button cover, a brass work clothing button, an iron snap fastener, and a custom made five-hole bone button. The small button assemblage suggests that western style clothing—or at least their accessories—were used by Metini Village residents.

Metal Artifacts

The majority of the metal artifacts recovered from Metini Village are classified as wrought iron objects (nails or staples), cut iron nails, and various metal pieces of scrap, as well as some household or construction objects such as a thimble, a shovel head, and a clothing fastener. David Palmer completed the initial analysis of the metal objects. Specific information on the metal artifacts can be found in Appendix 9.

Surface Collection

The collection of surface units yielded a total of 19 metal objects (Table 13). The materials include three wrought nails, one wrought staple, and five cut nails, most of which were highly corroded. Two of the wrought nails exhibited rose heads, while the cut nails appear to be square cut and two exhibited square heads.

Table 13. Counts of Metal Artifacts.

Metal Class	Surface Collection	ON 10W Excavation	15S 4E Excavation	20S 21 Excavation	SUM
Wrought Nail	3	0	0	0	3
Wrought Staple	1	0	0	0	1
Cut Nail	5	0	5	2	12
Spike	0	1	0	0	1
Metal Scraps	4	1	11	3	19
Can Fragment	1	0	0	0	1
Wire Fencing	0	1	0	1	2
Shovel Handle	0	0	1	0	1
Shovel Head	0	0	1	0	1
Thimble	1	0	0	0	1
Round Capsule	1	0	0	0	1
Disk Object	1	0	0	0	1
Clothing Fastener	1	0	0	0	1
Plow Blade	0	0	0	1	1
Spring	1	0	0	0	1
SUM	19	3	18	7	47

One of the wrought nails (ME-6/24/98-06-ME-01) had either been bent into a hook-like object or was a clinched nail (Figure 65). A similar looking specimen from the nearby Native Alaskan Village Site was identified as a possible sturgeon hook (Glenn Farris, personal communication 2/22/2016). Four of the relatively complete nails indicate that they may have been originally used in construction with the lengths of two wrought nails ranging from 9.1 to 11.2 cm, and the lengths of two cut nails measuring between 8.0 and 10.0 cm. The four metal scrap pieces appear to have been from sheet trimming—one is from a fragment of corrugated sheet metal. One other metal specimen was a can fragment with part of the seam still visible. Other artifacts include a copper spring (possibly from a bed), a brass clothing fastener (ME-4/29/99-02-ME-01, Figure 66), a brass thimble (possibly dented in use) (ME-4/16/99-04-ME-01, Figure 67), and two unknown objects—one made from copper and the other possibly lead. The unidentified copper item resembles a round capsule and it may have functioned as a bell or even as a button, while the lead object is a disk with four pierced holes that could have been used as fishing weight or weaving/spinning weight (ME-6/26/98-09-ME-01, Figure 68).

Figure 65. Wrought iron nail, bent (36S 18E, Surface, ME-6/24/98-06-ME-01).

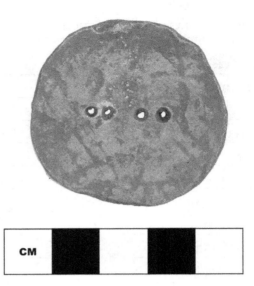

Figure 66. Brass clothing fastener (11S 41E, Surface, ME-4/29/99-02-ME-01).

Figure 67. Brass thimble (23S 38E, Surface, ME-4/16/99-04-ME-01).

Figure 68. Lead disk with four pierced holes (18S 22E, Surface, ME-6/26/98-09-ME-01).

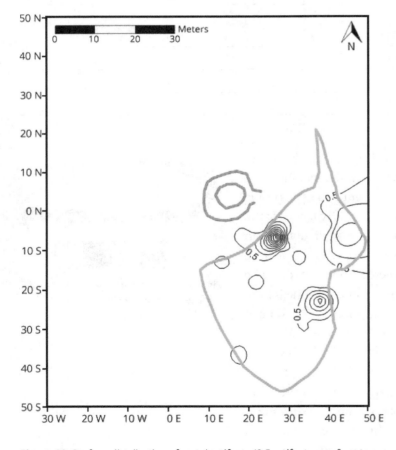

The spatial plotting of the metal objects using the SURFER software program suggests that they are concentrated in a cluster along the terrace edge directly south of the pit feature, while other metal artifacts are found directly south of this cluster along the terrace slope (Figure 69).

Figure 69. Surface distribution of metal artifacts (0.5 artifact per m² contour interval). Pit depression outlined in red, midden in green.

Excavation Units

0N 10W. Three metal artifacts were unearthed from the unit: a square-headed iron spike measuring 15.3 cm in length (ME-5/01/99-03-ME-01; Figure 70), a fragment of a fence (possibly barbed wire), and one iron scrap (Table 13). The artifacts were found 0–26 cm below unit datum.

Figure 70. Square-headed iron spike (0N 10W, Level 3, ME-5/01/99-03-ME-01).

15S 4E. Field excavators recovered 18 metal artifacts, including five cut nails, 11 pieces of scrap metal, and a shovel head (ME-5/2/99-05-ME-01) and shovel handle (ME-5/1/99-18-ME-01) (Table 13). The latter were found in the 40-cm-wide pit feature (Figure 16) described earlier for unit 15S 4E. The shovel parts were found between 11–16 cm below unit datum. The majority of the other artifacts were also detected in the midden deposit about 10–20 cm below unit datum.

20S 21E. The excavation of this unit yielded seven metal remains. One unusual item was the iron "ripper" blade of a plow (ME-5/01/99-10-ME-01, Figure 71), found in the east wall of the unit. Other materials include two cut nails, a fragment of fencing or wire material, and three iron sheet fragments (Table 13). The materials were detected in the midden deposit, between 10 and 30 cm below unit datum.

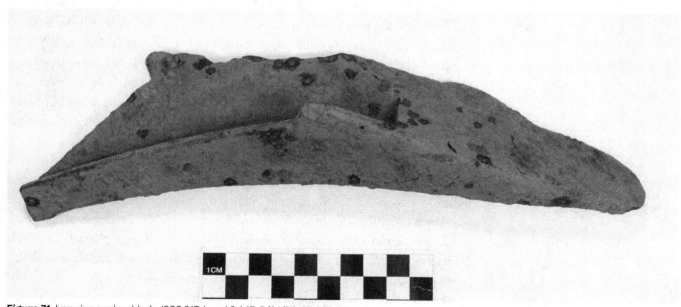

Figure 71. Iron ripper plow blade (20S 21E, Level 2, ME-5/01/99-10-ME-01).

Summary: Metal Assemblage

The 47 metal artifacts recovered from Metini Village represent a varied range of construction, agrarian, and household materials (Table 13). Both wrought (n=3) and cut (n=12) nails are well represented, along with one large iron spike. A couple of fragments of possible fencing material, a wrought iron staple, and an impressive plow blade were also found. An almost intact shovel head and handle were unearthed during excavation. Other materials include a used thimble, a clothing fastener, a spring (possibly from a bed), a can fragment, and two unidentified artifacts (a round capsule and disk object). Nineteen small pieces of metal scrap were also identified.

Faunal Remains

Shellfish

The majority of the shellfish species recovered from Metini thrive in the nearby rocky intertidal, benthic environments that comprise much of the Kashaya coastline. The primary taxa identified in the Metini assemblage are abalone (AB) (*Haliotis* sp., mostly Red Abalone, *H. Rufescens*); barnacle (BA) (*Balanus* sp.); clam (CL) (*Saxidomus* sp., *Protothaca* sp.); chiton (CH) (probably the Black Chiton, *Katharina tunicata*, but could be Mopalia sp. and other smaller species of chitons); Gumboot Chiton (GC) (*Cryptochiton stelleri*; identifiable by its large plate size); limpets (LI) (e.g., *Acmaea* sp., *Notoacema* sp. *Collisella* sp.); horned slipper shell (HS) (*Crepidula* sp., mostly *C. adunca*); California Mussel (MU) (*Mytilus californicus*); turban snails (TU) (*Tegula funebralis, T. Brunnea*); dog whelk or dog winkle (DW) (*Nucella* sp., primarily *N. Emarginata* and *N. Lamellosa*); terrestrial snails (TS); and *Olivella* shells (OL) (*Olivella biplicata*, renamed *Callianax biplicata*). Our analysis involved classifying the shellfish assemblage into the above classes, then identifying and counting diagnostic elements for specific classes of shellfish. The diagnostic elements are employed in defining Minimum Number of Individuals (MNI), which provides the baseline for quantifying the mollusk assemblage.

The diagnostic elements for gastropods are caps (CA) for limpets and horned slipper, and shell apertures (openings) (AP) or columellae (CO)(interior central axis) for dog whelks, *Olivella* shells, marine snails and terrestrial snails. Diagnostic elements identified for bivalves include the umbo (UM) of the mussel and clam. Diagnostic elements of chitons are based on the number of plates (PL). Since diagnostic elements are tough to distinguish for both barnacle and abalone shells, we counted them as present or absent within specific archaeological units. Minimum number of individuals (MNI) is based on one diagnostic element per individual for gastropods (i.e., limpets, horned slipper shell, dog whelks, *Olivella* shells, marine snails, and terrestrial snails), two diagnostic elements (umbos; two umbos per individual) for bivalves (i.e., mussels, clams), and eight diagnostic elements (plates; eight plates per individual) for Gumboot Chitons and other species of chitons. Information on the shellfish assemblage is presented in Appendix 10.

Surface Collection

The surface assemblage of the Metini shellfish is composed of 1390 diagnostic elements of various classes, as well as 44 collection units where abalones were collected and 38 units where barnacles were identified (Table 14). This table also includes the MNI estimates for the different classes of shellfish based on calculations for the entire surface assemblage (MNI=575).

Table 14. Counts of Shellfish Remains (P= present, DI = diagnostic element, MNI=minimum number of individuals).

Shellfish Class	Surface Collection	ON 10W Excavation	15S 4E Excavation	20S 21E Excavation	SUM
AB	P =44 units	0	P	P	P=46 units
BA	P=39 units	0	0	P	P=40 units
CH	DI=546 MNI= 68	0	0	DI=22 MNI=3	DI=568 MNI=71
GC	DI=49 MNI=6	0	0	DI=2 MNI=1	DI=51 MNI=7
CL	DI=7 MNI=4	0	0	0	DI=7 MNI=4
DW	DI=5 MNI=5	0	0	0	DI=5 MNI=5
HS	DI=2 MNI=2	0	0	0	DI=2 MNI=2
LI	DI=36 MNI=36	0	0	DI=1 MNI=1	DI=37 MNI=37
MU	DI=583 MNI=292	0	0	DI=5 MNI=3	DI=588 MNI=295
TU	DI=122 MNI=122	0	0	DI=9 MNI=9	DI=131 MNI=131
TS	DI=24 MNI=24	0	0	DI=5 MNI=5	DI=29 MNI=29
OL	DI=16 MNI=16	0	0	DI=1 MNI=1	DI=17 MNI=17
SUM	P=83 DI=1390 MNI=575	0	P=1	P=2 DI=45 MNI=23	P=86 DI=1435 MNI=598

The most common shellfish classes in order of abundance based on MNI calculations are: California Mussels (MNI=292; 51%); turban snails (MNI=122; 21%); chiton (MNI=68; 12%); limpets (MNI=36; 6%); terrestrial snail (MNI=24; 4%); *Olivella* Shell (MNI=16; 3%); Gumboot Chiton (MNI= 6; 1%); dog winkle (MNI= 5; 1%); clam (MNI=4; 0.5 %); and horned slipper shell (MNI=2; 0.5%). Abalone and barnacle were present in 44 and 39 of the 183 surface collection units, respectively.

The spatial distribution of surface mollusk remains based on SURFER plots covers the entire midden area, stretching across the most of the terrace edge and down the terrace slope in a series of discrete clusters (Figure 72). The mapping of individual shellfish classes suggests that there is no distinctive patterning of specific kinds of shellfish within this area. Abalone, barnacle, mussels, marine snails, chitons, limpets, and *Olivella* shells, for example, are dispersed across the midden area on both the terrace edge and down the slope.

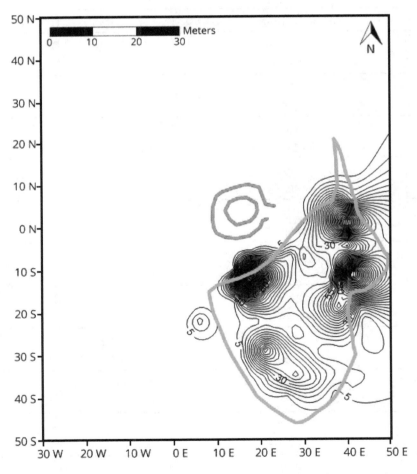

Figure 72. Surface distribution of shellfish remains (5 mollusk specimens per m² contour interval). Pit depression outlined in red, midden in green.

Excavation Units

0N 10W. No shellfish remains were unearthed in this unit.

15S 4E. Our field team recovered only a few fragments of shellfish remains. Abalone is present, but barnacle is not present and no diagnostic elements for any other shellfish remains were recorded.

20S 21E. A diverse range of shellfish remains were unearthed in the midden deposit of this unit. Abalone and barnacle are both present here. The most common shellfish classes based on MNI calculations for the entire unit include turban snails (MNI=9), terrestrial snails (MNI=5), California Mussels (MNI=3), chitons (MNI=3), Gumboot Chiton (MNI=1), limpet (MNI=1), and *Olivella* snail (MNI=1) (Table 14). The *Olivella* snail specimen appears to be worked with the removal of the spiral (see the next section).

Summary: Shellfish Assemblage

The shellfish remains are found almost exclusively in the midden deposit of Metini village. Excavations at 0N 10W outside the midden area yielded no shellfish remains, while 15S 4E situated on the western edge of the midden produced only a few fragments. The one excavation unit, 20S 21E, that was located in the thick of the midden contained a diverse assemblage of shellfish remains. Abalone and barnacle shells are found in 46 and 40 units that were surface collected, respectively (including the excavation units). California Mussel comprises almost half of the shellfish found at Metini, based on MNI calculations (MNI=295; 49%). The next most common class is turban snail (MNI=131; 22%), followed by chiton (MNI=71; 12%), limpet (MNI=37; 6%), terrestrial snail (MNI=29; 5%), Olive Snails (MNI=17; 3%), Gumboot Chiton (MNI=7; 1%), dog winkle (MNI=5; 1%), clam (MNI=4; 0.5%), and horned slipper snail (MNI=2; 0.5%) (Table 14).

There is some evidence for worked shell at Metini Village. A worked abalone specimen was found on the surface at 12S 40E that was not included in the formal surface collection. An animal burrow had disturbed this area and the worked abalone and pieces of daub were found on the surface by Bill Walton and Kent Lightfoot. The presence of burned daub possibly indicated the presence of a formal floor or hearth/underground oven. The worked abalone specimen (ME-10/27/01-WS-01) had been carefully worked and smoothed into an oval shape with a hole drilled in the upper section of the artifact. It would be classified as a Perforated Haliotis Disk or Oval, Type K1a by Gifford (1947:15). In addition, twelve of the 17 *Olivella* specimens exhibit evidence of manufacture and/or use. A detailed analysis of these materials by Fanya Becks is presented in the next section.

Shell Bead Production *by Fanya Becks*

In accordance with the Bennyhoff and Hughes (1987) typology, the twelve worked *Olivella* materials from Metini were analyzed and measurements were recorded for the length, width, thickness, and diameter of each piece of worked shell (see Appendix 11). Modifications made to individual artifacts were recorded, such as perforation diameters. While this latter measurement is not used to determine bead type under the Bennyhoff and Hughes typology, it provides a more detailed understanding of the use and modification of these artifacts. All of the *Olivella biplicata/ Callianax biplicata* shell artifacts have been heat treated and are a chalky white color instead of the natural brown, purple, or white-grey (Gibson 1992:8). Out of the 12 worked shell artifacts, eight are categorized as beads, two artifacts as large whole heat treated *Olivella* shells, and one artifact as a piece of broken shell with the shelf and spire still attached, and the final shell object can be considered a bead fragment, with the spire neatly broken off or ground down and a fragmentary shell body.

The eight *Olivella* beads are categorized as type A1c, which are large (with a maximum diameter between 9.51 mm and 14 mm) whole shell, shell spire removed beads (Figure 73). These beads occur across all time periods in California. The average lengths of these beads is 21.07 mm (SD= 1.71) and the average maximum diameter is 12.58 mm (SD= 0.9164). The perforation diameters varied depending on the type of modification present: the range for the ground spires was 2.01 mm to 2.46 mm, the range for broken spires was 4.15 mm to 6.3 mm, and the range for water worn spires was 2.33 mm to 5.36 mm. Five (62.5%) of the beads had broken or ground outer lip, which is often done to increase the ease of stringing whole shell beads (Bennyhoff and Hughes 1987:117). While Bennyhoff and Hughes (1987:116) write that "the spire may be broken or ground down, or naturally water worn," this description does not take into consideration whether these shells have broken naturally and collected with their spires already removed, or if they were made into beads. Looking at the bead materials conservatively, two out of eight beads are clearly ground and are the most reliably modified beads. Of the other six beads, one is either ground or water worn, one is water worn and the other four beads had the spires broken off. While all of the beads have been heat treated, which is consistent with bead making, two of the A1c beads with the spires roughly broken off are relatively ambiguous.

Figure 73. *Olivella* shell bead (6S 43E, Surface, ME-4/29/99-01-MO-01A).

Vertebrate Faunal Remains *by Thomas A. Wake and Kent G. Lightfoot*

The vertebrate faunal assemblage was analyzed at the UCLA Cotsen Institute of Archaeology Zooarchaeology Laboratory. All specimens were sorted by vertebrate class and identified to the most discrete taxonomic level possible (see Appendix 12). All identifications were confirmed using the comparative osteological collection housed in the laboratory facility. More detailed taxonomic assignment is limited to elements with sufficient distinguishing features allowing identification to the given family, genus, or species. Bones lacking discrete morphological features were sorted into broad size categories by class. Size categories are as follows: for mammals, large represents deer size or greater, medium represents smaller than deer but larger than jackrabbit, and small represents jackrabbit or smaller sized animals.

For each discretely identified animal bone a series of data were recorded including catalog number, provenience, screen size information, skeletal element, part of element, side, age, and modification (Appendix 12). Information on modification of specimens includes evidence of burning, cut marks or gnaw marks, and indications of tool or other artifact manufacture (worked bone). The bone elements were counted and weighed to the nearest 0.01 g using electronic scales. Complete information for the vertebrate faunal assemblage is presented in the Appendix 12.

The Metini vertebrate remains are highly fragmented. No complete bones were encountered. The classes of vertebrate mammals found at Metini include Domestic Cow (*Bos taurus*) (BT), goat/sheep (*Capra/Ovis* sp.) (C/O), Black-Tailed Deer (*Odocoileus hemionus*)(OH), Bobcat (*Lynx rufus*) (LR), California Vole (*Microtus californicus*) (MC), eared seal (*Otariidae*) (OT), Cabezon (*Scorpaenichthys marmoratus*) (SC), and rockfish (*Sebastes* sp.) (SE). Some mammal remains could only be identified by size, such as large (Mlrg) and medium (Mmed) mammals, while still others could only be classified as mammal (MA) or in the artiodactyl order (AR). Given the relatively small sample size and fragmented nature of the assemblage, we present only the number of individual specimens (NISP). No attempt is made to determine minimum number of individuals (MNI) beyond the presence of specific species or genus on the site.

Surface Collection Units

Field crews recovered 245 bone elements from the 183 surface collection units (Table 15). The most common elements were large mammals (n=165;67%), Domestic Cow (n=29; 12%), Black-Tailed Deer (n=16; 6%), and mammals not distinguished by size (n=16; 6%). Other vertebrate faunal classes represented in the surface assemblage include goat/sheep (n=4; 2%), California Vole (n=2; 1%), Bobcat (n=1; 1%), medium mammal (n=1; 1%), eared seal (n=1; 1%), Cabezon (n=1; 1%), rockfish (n=1; 1%), and unidentifiable (n=1; 1%) (Table 15).

Table 15. Counts of Vertebrate Faunal Elements.

Vertebrate Faunal Remains	Surface Collection	ON 10W Excavation	15S 4E Excavation	20S 21E Excavation	SUM
AR	7	0	0	2	9
BT	29	0	1	7	37
C/O	4	0	0	0	4
LR	1	0	0	0	1
MA	16	0	16	5	37
Mlrg	165	0	15	53	233
Mmed	1	0	0	0	1
MC	2	0	0	2	4
OH	16	0	1	1	18
OT	1	0	0	0	1
SC	1	0	0	0	1
SE	1	0	0	0	1
UN	1	0	0	0	1
SUM	245	0	33	70	348

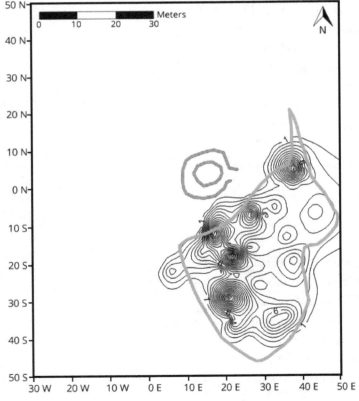

We generated a number of SURFER maps based on the density of vertebrate faunal elements recovered in the 183 surface collection units. The faunal remains are distributed in a series of clusters along the terrace edge of the midden area. Faunal remains are also distributed down the terrace slope (Figure 74). The spatial plotting of the domesticated species (cattle, goat/sheep) suggest they are found in the central and southern areas of the midden (Figure 75), while those identified as wild species (both mammal and fish) are mostly mapped in the central and northern area of the midden (Figure 76).

Figure 74. Surface distribution of vertebrate faunal remains (1 faunal element per m² contour interval). Pit depression outlined in red, midden in green.

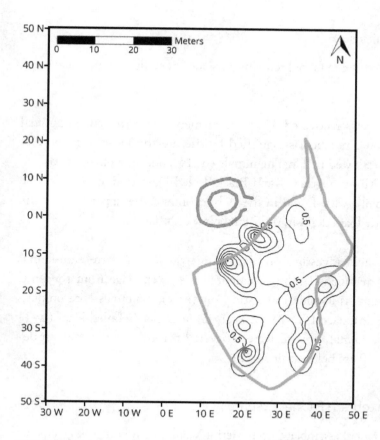

Figure 75. Surface distribution of domesticated mammals (cattle, goat/sheep) (0.5 faunal element per m² contour interval). Pit depression outlined in red, midden in green.

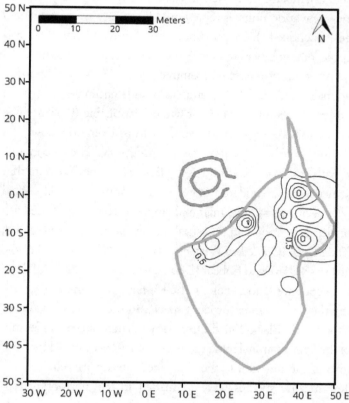

Figure 76. Surface distribution of wild vertebrate faunal species (both mammal and fish) (.05 faunal element per m² contour interval). Pit depression outlined in red, midden in green.

Excavation Units

0N 10W. No vertebrate faunal remains were identified during the excavation of this unit.

15S 4E. Field crews recovered 33 faunal elements from the unit. Mammal remains that could not be distinguished by size are the most common elements (n=16), followed by large mammals (n=15), and one element each of Domestic Cow (limb fragment) and Black-Tailed Deer (radius) (Table 15). The faunal remains were found in the A horizon and the upper level of the dark brown sandy loam deposit, 0–27 cm below unit datum.

20S 21E. The field investigation of this unit yielded 70 vertebrate faunal remains. Large mammals (n=53) dominated the assemblage from the unit. Other faunal remains include Domestic Cow (n=7), mammals (size unidentifiable) (n=5), artiodactyl (n=2), voles (n=2), and Black-Tailed Deer (n=1) (Table 15). The faunal remains were recovered throughout the midden deposit, from 0 to 30 cm below unit datum.

Summary: Vertebrate Faunal Assemblage

The vertebrate faunal assemblage from Metini Village, comprising 348 elements from the surface and excavation units, is represented by seven vertebrate genera and five species (see Appendix 12). Only mammal and fish remains were identified and no bird, reptile, or amphibian remains were recovered. The vast majority of the assemblage is made up of terrestrial mammal species. A large proportion are either large mammals (n=233; 67%), mammals of indeterminate size (n=37; 11%), or artiodactyls (n=9; 2%). One element was unidentifiable (0.33%). The mammal assemblage includes domesticated species such as Domestic Cow (*Bos taurus*) (n=37; 11%) and goat/sheep (*Capra/Ovis* sp.) (n=4; 1%). These economic animals were raised both at Colony Ross and at the Benitz Rancho. We note that number of cattle elements may be underestimated given that two bones identified as artiodactyl and 20 specimens as large mammal are reported as "cow" sized animals. A number of elements from wild terrestrial mammals are also represented, including Black-Tailed Deer (*Odocoileus hemionus*) (n=18; 5%), California Vole (*Microtus californicus*) (n=4; 1%), and Bobcat (*Lynx rufus*) (n=1; 0.33%). All three of these mammals are commonly found along the Kashaya coastline today, with the voles comprising the most common rodent species in the grassy meadows at Fort Ross State Historic Park. Black-Tailed Deer elements may also be under represented since six of the large mammal remains are defined as "deer size." However, sheep and goat elements may also fit into the "deer size" category as well.

Interestingly, few marine species were identified in the vertebrate faunal assemblage. Only one marine mammal remain was identified—a single element of carpal bone from the eared seal (Otariidae) (0.33%). Fish are represented by two bone elements (0.33% each), one identified as Cabezon (*Scorpaenichthys marmoratus*) and the other as rockfish (*Sebastes* sp.). Both fish genera are common to the rocky subtidal zone along the Sonoma County coast (Eschmeyer et al. 1983).

Cut marks were noted for six specimens (3 cattle, 3 large mammals), with one of the Domestic Cow elements exhibiting evidence of being butchered with a saw. About 10% of the faunal assemblage (n=36) showed signs of burning. The burned specimens included 1 Black-Tail Deer (2.8%), 1 Domestic Cow (2.8%), 1 sheep/goat (2.8%), and 33 mammal remains (91.6%).

Ethnobotanical Remains

Field crews systematically collected sediment samples from excavation units for the primary purpose of extracting ethnobotanical remains. A total of 46.75 liters of sediments was collected, including column samples from 0N 10W (n=3), 15S 4E (n=3), and 20S 21E (n=4), along with two samples from in and around Feature 1 in 15S 4E. The 12 sediment samples, ranging in volume from 2.4 to 8.0 liters in size (Table 16), were floated in the California Archaeological Laboratory at UC Berkeley. The processed light fractions were then sent to the Paleoethnobotany Laboratory, Cotsen Institute of Archaeology at UCLA, where they were analyzed under the direction of Dr. Virginia S. Popper (2006).

Table 16. Provenience Information and Sample Size for Sediment Samples from the Metini Village.

Cat Number	Unit	Level	Sample Size (liters)
ME-5/1/99-4-S	0N 10W	0–10 cm	4.0
ME-5/1/99-5-S	0N 10W	10–25 cm	4.0
ME-5/1/99-6-S	0N 10W	25–40 cm	3.7
ME-5/2/99-8-S	15S 4E	0–15 cm	3.2
ME-5/2/99-9-S	15S 4E	15–30 cm	3.4
ME-5/2/99-2-S	15S 4E	Feature 1 (20–25 cm)	3.0
ME-5/1/99-17-S	15S 4E	East of Feature 1	2.75
ME-5/2/99-11-S	15S 4E	40–60 cm	3.5
ME-5/1/99-13-S	20S 21E	0–10 cm	3.8
ME-5/1/99-14-S	20S 21E	10–20 cm	5.0
ME-5/1/99-15-S	20S 21E	20–30 cm	8.0
ME-5/1/99-16-S	20S 21E	30–40 cm	2.4

At the Paleoethnobotany Laboratory, the light fractions were sifted through a series of nested sieves (2.00, 1.00, and 0.50 mm), yielding four size fractions to be sorted (>2.00 mm, 2.00–1.00 mm, 1.00–0.50 cm, and <0.50 cm). Popper divided the light fraction samples into those four size groups to facilitate the sorting of material using an incident light binocular microscope (10–40x). It also allowed her to identify and recover distinct materials from each fraction size. She applied the following method for recovering material that would be further analyzed. Carbonized wood, pine cone fragments, and amorphous material were removed only from the >2.00 mm fraction. Pulse and nutshell/seedcoat fragments were recovered only from the >1.00 mm fractions. All other plant material was removed from the 2.00–1.00 mm and 1.00–0.50 mm fractions. Only whole or identifiable carbonized seeds were removed from the <0.50 mm fraction.

Most of the seeds and plant parts were counted, but wood charcoal, California Bay (*Umbellularia californica*) seedcoat fragments, nutshell/seedcoat fragments, and amorphous material were weighed because variations in fragmentation can make weight a more representative measure of abundance. Since all the samples contained uncarbonized seeds of modern weedy annuals (e.g., *Calandrinia* sp., *Silene* sp.), common contaminants in macrobotanical samples from open-air, coastal California archaeological sites, only carbonized or partly carbonized plant remains were included in the study. Wood charcoal specimens were fractured to provide a clean transverse section and then examined under an incident light binocular microscope at 60x. If available, a random selection of 20 pieces of wood charcoal from the >2.00 mm fraction from each flotation sample was taken. Previous research indicates that this subsample size usually provides a representative selection of the diversity of taxa in the larger sample (Smart and Hoffman 1988:186). But for some of the soil samples, the charcoal proved too small or too friable for the identification of 20 fragments. The recovered plant remains were identified through the use of various manuals and comparative plant and seed collections housed at the Paleoethnobotanical Laboratory in the Cotsen Institute of Archaeology at UCLA.

The results of the macrobotanical analysis are presented in Appendices 13–15. Appendix 13 lists the absolute counts and weights (grams) of the recovered carbonized remains. Appendix 14 provides density values (counts/liter or grams/liter) for the recovered carbonized remains, which facilitates comparisons between samples since the volume of soil per sample varied somewhat. Appendix 15 presents the identified and amorphous wood charcoal absolute counts and weights for fragments >2mm. Almost no charred seeds or charcoal fragments were recovered from 0N 10W. The majority of the ethnobotanical remains derived from the midden deposits originate from the excavation units of 15S 4E and 20S 21E. The density of seeds was relatively low, ranging from 0.0 to 2.8 seeds/liter per sample, possibly due to poor preservation conditions. The wood charcoal densities varied from 0.0 to 0.72 grams/liter.

Seeds: Cultigens

Agrarian crop plants found at Metini Village include wheat (*Triticum* spp.), barley (*Hordeum vulgare* cf.), and possibly bean or pea fragments, classified as pulse fragments. The wheat and barley were detected only in the soil samples from 15S 4E. All of these specimens were fragmented, eroded, or distorted, making their identification difficult. Popper (2006:3) observed that one wheat grain has the rounded shape of bread (*T. Aestivum*) and club (*T. Compactum*) wheats, while the other specimens were narrower in shape. Significantly, wheat (*Triticum* spp.) is the highest density of any type of domesticated or wild seed varieties in the Metini collection. Popper suggested that the concentration of burned wheat and barley in and around Feature 1 could indicate that the shovel head protected the remains, thereby creating better preservation conditions. She also noted that the concentration of cultivated plants may also reflect the disposal of cooking debris (e.g., from a hearth or oven) in the 15S 4E area.

Seeds: Non-Domesticated Plants

Charred seeds recovered from other plants include California Poppy (*Eschscholzia* sp. cf.), bluegrass (*Poa* sp.cf.), knotweed/dock (*Polygonum/Rumex* sp.), and California Bay (*Umbellularia californica*). However, seeds were rarely identified to species because specimens within the same genus are often morphologically similar and carbonization often distorts seeds, which obscures their diagnostic characteristics. Some seeds that Popper could not identify to the genus level were assigned to the family level based on morphology. These include pink (Caryophyllaceae cf.), legume (Fabaceae), grass (Poaceae), rose (Rosaceae cf.) and nightshade (Solanaceae cf.) families. For seeds that were too fragmented or distorted to assign to the family level, Popper assigned these to the Unidentifiable Seeds category. She also noted any uncertain identification with "cf."

Popper's study revealed that all of the identified non-domesticated plants could be found in the nearby environs of Metini Village. Her review of the extant literature on local ethnographic uses of the plant remains suggests the following uses:

> California poppy (*Eschscholzia* sp.) roots and leaves were used as
> medicines, and the leaves may have been eaten. Many types of
> wild legumes (Fabaceae) have edible leaves and seeds. Leaves
> were usually picked in the spring and seeds were harvested in the
> summer. Similarly, Native Californian groups gathered several types
> of grass seeds, including bluegrass (*Poa* sp.) in late spring/summer,
> parching and grinding them to prepare *pinole*. Grasses could also be
> used as kindling, matting, or roofing material. Knotweed and dock

(*Polygonum/Rumex* sp.) seeds and leaves were edible. The seeds ripen in late spring and summer, and were cooked as *pinole*. Given the low density of these seeds, they could be accidental inclusions in the deposits. But it is also possible that these useful plants were encouraged or protected around the village to provide easily available resources when needed.

The most common seed in the samples is California bay (*Umbellurlaria californica*), with seedcoat fragments recovered in three samples from two units. In addition, California bay charcoal was found in one of these samples. Native Californian groups ate California bay fruit flesh raw or boiled when ripe in the fall. In addition, the seed kernels were roasted and eaten or stored for later consumption. After shelling, the hard seed coats were probably disposed of in hearths. The leaves had medicinal and other uses. California bay grows along streams and most likely came from the Fort Ross Creek drainage. Historic accounts report that laurel wood was exported from the Fort, so it must have been abundant (Popper 2006:5–6).

Charcoal Wood and Other Floral Remains

Other ethnobotanical materials recovered from the flotation samples are wood charcoal, unknown nutshell/seedcoat fragments, amorphous material, and conifer cone fragments.

The nutshell/seedcoat pieces were about 0.8 mm thick, with a spongy cross section and a smooth outer surface. Botanical remains that lacked any diagnostic characteristics and could not be positively identified to a known taxon were placed in the "amorphous" category. Amorphous materials typically possess minimal vessel structure and lack distinctive shapes. The wood taxa recovered from the flotation samples are sunflower (Asteraceae cf.), pine (*Pinus* sp.), willow (*Salix* sp. cf.), Coast Redwood (*Sequoia sempervirens*), and California Bay (*Umbellularia californica*). Conifer fragments were too small or distorted to identify more specifically, but they could be pine, coast redwood, or some other type of conifer. Other unidentified pieces came from a diffuse porous wood with multiseriate rays. Type A (listed in Appendix 15) is a diffuse porous wood that may be willow (*Salix* sp).

Pine and Coast Redwood charcoal are the most ubiquitous remains in the flotation samples, with the former identified in seven samples and the latter in six. Cone fragments were recovered from four samples. Some of the conifer fragments could also come from pine taxa or the Coast Redwood. However, we would not be surprised if some of the conifer specimens may have derived from Douglas Fir (*Pseudotsuga menziesii*) trees, which along with the Coast Redwood along the Fort

Ross Creek drainage are quite abundant along the coastal facing slope of the ridge system adjacent to Fort Ross and Metini Village. The pine specimens may have originated from the nearby closed-cone pine forest along the Fort Ross coastline (up to an elevation of about 365 m) where Bishop Pine (*Pinus muricata*) thrives today in large numbers, along with some Beach Pine (*Pinus contorta*). A few Sugar Pine (*Pinus lambertiana*) trees are also found in the nearby Douglas Fir forests, which produce edible pine nuts. The possible willow (*Salix* sp.) specimen may have been collected along the Fort Ross Creek drainage.

We believe the majority of the charcoal wood probably represents the remains of fuel used in hearths and underground ovens by Metini residents. All of the taxa are located within close walking range to Metini Village where they flourished along the Fort Ross Creek drainage and on the adjacent coastal ridge system. They could have been gathered as firewood throughout the year. Popper (2006: 6) also emphasized that the pine species may have provided basketry material and medicine, the Coast Redwood bark could have been used as cover for dwellings and its leaves and sap as medicine, while the willow may have provided construction material, baskets, and tools, among other items.

Summary: Ethnobotanical Remains

Fifteen taxa of plants (identified to family or more specifically) were recovered from the 46.75 liters of soil collected from the three excavation units. The ethnobotanical remains, similar to the artifacts and faunal remains, are distributed primarily in the midden deposit at Metini Village. The wood charcoal pieces from pine, Coast Redwood, and unidentifiable conifer specimens—all available from the nearby environs of the Fort Ross Creek drainage and coastal ridge system today—probably represent fuel used in hearths and underground ovens. The Metini residents appear to have used crops known to have been cultivated at both Colony Ross and the Benitz Rancho, such as wheat, barley, and possibly beans or peas. They also gathered locally available plants, such as California Bay, California Poppy and various kinds of seed-bearing plants. Popper (2006:7) makes the following summary observation about the Metini plants, particularly the seeds.

> Some of the small seeds recovered from the samples may have been
> gathered for food or may be accidental inclusions in the site deposit.
> Small edible seeds would have burned while being parched in
> preparation for grinding and cooking. Only seeds burned on purpose
> or by accident had the potential of being preserved and recovered
> for this study, so many food plants that were not processed or eaten
> near fires would leave no archaeological trace. The discussion
> above shows that Native Californian groups used some of the

recovered taxa for medicinal and utilitarian purposes. Although we have no archaeobotanical evidence of these uses at this site, we know the plants were available. The recovered taxa could have provided resources from early spring through the fall. In the spring the inhabitants could have collected a variety of greens and in late spring and summer the seeds of grasses and knotweed/dock. Wheat, barley and beans were harvested in the late summer/fall along with California Bay and possibly pine nuts. These and the small seeds could have been stored to provide food during the winter. These samples provide only a partial picture of plant use at Metini village because we will not find evidence of plants such as vegetables, ornamentals, and medicines that were never burned or burned completely to ash.

Chapter 7

Evaluating Four Research Issues

Issue 1: Chronology

There has been some debate about the chronology of Metini Village in recent years. When the senior author began working on this project in the late 1990s he believed CA-SON-175 was probably occupied in the early-to-mid 1800s during the colonial regime of the Russian-American Company. He went so far as to argue that it was one of the principal settlements inhabited by the Kashaya Pomo "in the heart of the multi-ethnic colonial community of Fort Ross" (Lightfoot et al. 2001:1). Glenn Farris proposed an alternative interpretation, suggesting that the occupation of Metini Village was considerably later—that it was not founded until about 1855–1859 (personal communication, June 2001). He suggested that the Kashaya Pomo working for the Benitz family may have initially lived at CA-SON-174, a site situated a short distance west of the Ross Settlement stockade complex. In undertaking field work at CA-SON-174 in 1983, Farris and his field crew uncovered an extensive Native occupation that appears to date to the 1840s and 1850s. Archaeological materials included glass projectile points, glass trade beads, obsidian and chert debitage, various types of buttons, and an 1854 dime with a hole drilled through it (Farris 1983; Newquist 2002). Based on these findings, he proposed that Metini Village may have been used by the Kashaya Pomo in the years immediately following their occupation of CA-SON-174, and that its use probably ceased about 1870 when the Benitz Rancho was sold and most of the Native workers moved up the coast to Haupt's Ranch. Thus, Farris suggested the occupation dates for Metini Village probably extended from the 1850s and 1860s to about 1870. In addition to these alternative views about the historical chronology of Metini Village, Kashaya elders believe that the location served as a major village center for Kashaya from ancient history through to their removal from Ross to Haupt's Ranch.

Subsequent analysis of archival materials and the archaeological remains from Metini Village largely supports Farris' interpretation that CA-SON-175 was in use during the 1850s and 1860s. As noted by Farris (1986:16) some years ago, the site is marked as an Indian Rancheria on the 1859 Plate map of the Muñiz Rancho (Matthewson 1859). Many of the temporally diagnostic artifacts (e.g., ceramics, glass, metal artifacts) support the idea that the primary occupation of the village took place in the 1850s and 1860s. However, the possibility also exists that the site was used a little before and after this period of primary use and probably overlapped with the occupation of nearby CA-SON-174.

The analysis of the ceramics suggests most of the diagnostic artifacts were probably manufactured and available for consumption sometime between the mid-to-late 1800s. While some of the porcelains, refined earthenwares, and kaolinite pipe fragments could not be dated precisely, or had long production spans that extended across discrete colonial regimes, others were more temporally discrete. The most common ceramics on the site, the refined earthenware ironstones making up almost 40% of the ceramic assemblage, have manufacture dates that typically occur after the Russian-American Company occupation, sometime between 1840 and 1900. A few of the ceramics, such as the porcelain white ware with an overglaze, decal (ghost) design (ME-4/29/99-03-HC-01) and the refined earthenware hotel ware (ME-5/01/99-09-HC-01), may have been produced after 1880. Still other ceramics suggest they were available for consumption at an earlier date, possibly during the latter end of the Russian-American Company occupation. These ceramics include the refined earthenware pearlware (ME-6/20/98-05-HC-01) with blue transfer print designs (circa 1785–1830), and the two non-white porcelains (ME-4/16/99-02-HC-01, ME-4/29/99-01-HC-01) with hand-painted overglaze (circa late 1700s to the late 1820s). Finally, two non-white porcelains (ME-6/20/98-06-HC-01, ME-6/20/98-01-HC-01) with underglaze decorations and one with an overglaze decoration (ME-6/24/98-03-HC-01) may have been produced prior to 1850.

Most of the vessel, flat, and lamp globe glass that could be dated is not very useful for evaluating the alternative interpretations proposed for the occupation of Metini Village. The primary glass vessels found at Metini, the dark green, dip-molded alcohol bottles, were probably available for consumption sometime between 1730 and 1870. However, some of the vessel glass fragments are temporally diagnostic. The glass assemblage boasts several that have relatively late manufacture dates. These include the colorless, plate-molded paneled bottle fragment (ME-4/17/99-05-GL-01) (circa 1867–1920); the colorless, machine molded, mineral bottle piece (ME-4/30/99-04-GL-01) with the prescription lip (circa 1889+); and the worked piece of molded, embossed paneled bottle glass (ME-6/24/98-02-WG-01) (circa 1876–1920+).

The most temporally diagnostic artifacts analyzed for Metini Village are the glass beads. Elliot Blair's analysis indicates that a large percentage of the beads—the diagnostic late beads include the red-on-white and Bohemian cut beads, as well as the green colored bead composed of uranium glass—were probably manufactured after 1840. This indicates a later, post-Russian Kashaya occupation at the village. While the other varieties of glass beads (white-over-white, red-on-green, etc.) do not preclude an earlier, Russian period occupation of Metini Village, their period of manufacture and use is more extensive and less precise for dating purposes.

A few of the metal objects are useful for distinguishing pre-1850 from post-1850 dates for individual artifacts. The United States army button cover (ME-4/16/99-04-ME-02) was probably issued between 1850 and 1900. The hand wrought nails with rose heads (e.g., ME-6/26/98-04-ME-01, ME-6/26/98-04-ME-02, ME-6/24/98-06-ME-01) may indicate an earlier date. Diamond (2009:166–167), for example, suggests that these kinds of nails were used in frontier settings in the Intermountain West until about 1830 or 1840.

The obsidian hydration chronology for Metini Village suggests that some of the obsidian artifacts with hydration readings of between 0.77 and 1.0 microns were probably knapped sometime in the 1800s. It is difficult to be more precise than this in evaluating the historical use of obsidian at Metini. However, several obsidian artifacts exhibit thicker hydration rims, ranging from 2.4–4.2 microns, suggesting they were probably worked in pre-contact times, possibly many centuries ago. This raises the question of whether the later historical occupation at Metini may have been built upon an earlier, prehistoric deposit.

Given our limited subsurface explorations of the site, it is possible that earlier, ancient occupations of the site were not fully represented in our investigations. However, based on the available data from our archaeological investigation of Metini at this time, there is little concrete evidence for a significant pre-colonial component underlying the historical occupation. We base this interpretation on four observations. First, the archaeological deposits at Metini Village are shallow. Excavations in the midden area indicate it is only about 40–45 cm deep with historical materials dispersed throughout the deposits. Of course, active bioturbation taking place in the soils of open-air sites along the coast of California tend to mix together materials of different ages. But we have yet to observe a discrete component at Metini underlying the historical midden deposits. Second, the spatial distribution of artifacts and faunal remains are clustered almost exclusively along the terrace edge and terrace slope, which follows the boundaries of the historical midden area. We would not expect that an earlier pre-colonial component would necessarily fit within the exact footprint of the historic deposits.

Third, outside of a rather sparse lithic assemblage recovered at Metini Village, the other artifacts (e.g, ceramics, metal, glass) date to the colonial era. If a significant prehistoric site component underlaid Metini, then we would expect to find a larger number of lithic artifacts and greater variation in the classes of lithic artifacts employed at the site. We identified only 123 chipped stone artifacts and 41 ground stone and other lithic artifacts, which is considerably fewer than the 232 worked glass artifacts recovered during the field work. To put this disparity in perspective, if instead of examining worked glass as a distinct material technology. we group it as a material type within the chipped stone assemblage, worked glass is 67% (n=232) of the assemblage, chert 28% (n=99) and obsidian only 5% (n=18). In our previous discussion of the obsidian assemblage from Metini Village we noted that residents of the village continued to use and circulate obsidian from both the Napa Valley and Annadel sources. This finding, on the surface, suggests little change in Metini residents' access to obsidian. However, the predominance of worked glass recovered from the site suggests that the issue of access to raw resources for chipped tools may have been a factor in the daily lives of Kashaya.

Comparing the chipped tool assemblage from Metini Village to that observed at the North Wall Community (Gonzalez 2011) underscores this issue of disparate access to raw materials during the historic period. In the case of the North Wall Community, which was occupied throughout the Russian-period and into the Benitz Rancho period, the chipped tool assemblage is as follows: obsidian tools and debitage comprise 69% of the assemblage followed by chert, 24%, and worked glass, 7%. While our hydration study of obsidian artifacts from Metini Village indicates that the majority of lithic artifacts date to the historical period, suggesting some degree of continued access to traditional sources, the disparity between raw materials for flaked tools suggests that access to obsidian decreased significantly in the late nineteenth century when Metini Village appears to be most heavily occupied. The fact that worked glass becomes the predominant raw material used to produce flaked tools demonstrates how, despite potential issues of access or disruption to local and regional exchange networks, Kashaya residents turned to a different, but functionally equivalent raw material: dark green, heavy duty bottle glass.

Finally, our previous survey work in the region indicates that the coastal terraces are covered by low-density lithic manifestations that were probably produced by foraging and hunting activities by local Native people over many hundreds and even thousands of years (Lightfoot et al. 1991:110–112). Our work suggests that some of the historical sites along the coastal terrace, including the North Wall Community (CA-SON-190), the Native Alaskan Village Site (CA-SON-1897/H), and even CA-SON-174, were built on top of these non-residential lithic manifestations. Consequently, there is a tendency to find older lithic artifacts mixed into the historical deposits. These stone tools may have resulted from the mixing of earlier prehistoric materials deposited along the coastal terrace into the later historical occupations. Alternatively, these earlier lithic materials may have been scavenged from nearby non-residential lithic manifestations by later Native residents living in historical villages along the coastal terrace. Examining the chipped tool assemblage from Metini Village suggests that while recycling of lithics continued into the late nineteenth century, increased reliance upon glass suggests that this raw material was easier to obtain than obsidian, either through payments received for work (Kennedy 1955) or from reuse of the material from historical midden deposits associated with Fort Ross and the Benitz Rancho.

In sum, our analysis of the extant archaeological and archival materials suggests that the primary occupation at Metini Village took place in the 1850s and 1860s, and would have been contemporaneous with the Benitz Rancho. There is some limited evidence that suggests the site may have been used in the late 1830s and 1840s in the latter phase of the Russian-American Company's tenure at Colony Ross and the early years of the Benitz Rancho based on a handful of ceramics, wrought iron nails, and some glass beads whose dates span this period. However, these could also be materials that were later reused by the residents of Metini Village or they may have been heirlooms of the earlier colonial days that were curated by Metini residents at the site.

There is also some evidence that Metini may have been used after 1870, when the Kashaya Pomo are known to have moved to Haupt's Ranch after William Benitz sold his ranching operation in 1867 to James Dixon and his partner Lord Charles Fairfax (Tomlin 1993:10). A few of the ceramic and glass artifacts recovered from Metini Village were manufactured in the post-1870 period. It is possible that these materials originated from people working for the commercial timber operation that Dixon and Fairfax established at Fort Ross from 1867 to 1873, or from workers associated with the ranching empire established by George Washington Call in 1873. However, all of these post-1870 artifacts are found in the discrete historical midden area, which suggests they are associated directly with the Metini Village archaeological deposits.

We suggest that Kashaya Pomo people probably revisited the Metini location after 1870, using it as a sacred place for contemplation or spiritual guidance by individuals or small groups, or possibly for larger communal gatherings for ceremonies, dances, feasts, and other such activities. Some Kashaya people may have even reused the site occasionally during the time when the Call family administered their extensive ranch operation in the post-1873 years. For example, John McKenzie (1963:1–2), the early park ranger at Fort Ross who interviewed members of the Call family, noted that a family of Kashaya Pomo (Lucaria and Mary) were known to have lived and worked on the Call ranch in the early 1900s. It is thus possible that some of the Kashaya working for the Call family may have reused the Metini site periodically and/or that Kashaya people from Haupt's Ranch, and later the nearby Rancheria, came down to visit the site. In recognizing Metini as a sacred place that once contained an ancestral dance house, the site remains particularly significant to the Kashaya Pomo community today.

Our field work at Metini Village detected minimal archaeological remains that would support the idea of a substantial, earlier pre-colonial component at the site. The few pre-contact obsidian artifacts probably originated from the extensive low-density lithic manifestations that blanket much of the coastal terrace or from the recycling of older artifacts from nearby sites by the historic residents at Metini. There is no question that the broader region of *Metini* is characterized by occupations and use going back at least 8000 years, but the specific site of CA-SON-175, known as Metini Village, does not appear, based on our current archaeological investigations, to contain major pre-contact archaeological deposits suggestive of an earlier, prehistoric settlement. However, it is important to stress that this interpretation is based on minimal subsurface sampling of the site. More extensive subsurface sampling might be necessary to detect earlier, pre-colonial deposits.

Issue 2: Spatial Structure of Metini Village

An important facet of our study is understanding how Metini Village was laid out, where domestic and religious structures may have been situated, where food processing and consumption took place, and where different kinds of activities occurred. The archaeological investigation identified three primary spatial components of the settlement: the large pit feature, the midden area, and the so-called "clean zone." The following discussion examines how Metini residents may have employed the pit feature, midden area, and clean zone in the organization and use of their village space.

The Large Pit Feature

At the core of the village—the most visible signature of the archaeological site today—is the circular pit feature and surrounding berm. Pomo people constructed several kinds of architectural buildings at important villages, including semi-subterranean lodges, sweat houses, and dance houses, which involved digging out extensive areas to create semi-subterranean dirt floors. Any of these kinds of buildings could have produced large surface depressions in archaeological sites, such as the one mapped at Metini Village (CA-SON-175). We begin by presenting background information for each type of structure, and the purposes they served in historical Pomo communities. We then evaluate the possible function that the large pit feature may have served at Metini Village, employing diverse lines of evidence drawn from contemporary Kashaya Pomo perspectives, ethnohistorical observations, and our archaeological findings.

Semi-Subterranean Lodges

Samuel Barrett, the well-known anthropologist who worked with Pomo communities in the early-to-mid 1900s, noted that wealthy families occasionally built semi-subterranean structures in villages, especially for use during the winter months. These structures would have left characteristic pit depressions on the surface of archaeological sites.

Men of means, such as chiefs, good hunters, lucky gamblers, medicine-men, and others, often had semi-subterranean, earth-covered lodges similar in every respect to the sweat and dance houses shortly to be described, except that the pit was only about a foot and a half deep and the tunnel only about four feet long. These lodges were called *ga'hmarkak* (E) and *ma'cane* (C). Frequently, a small room was built out on either side of the tunnel as a storage place for wood. The roof was constructed with much care. Its frame of poles was covered with brush, grass, and matting, and finally with a layer of three or four inches of earth. Over this was plastered a layer of clay, any kind except white or blue being used. It was mixed in baskets and poured on from the top downward, being spread and patted into place by means of flat, wooden paddles, finally being smoothed very carefully with water. At last a thin layer of sand was applied to prevent cracking. A man wealthy enough to afford one of these houses engaged others to build it, and custom prescribed that he pay liberally for the services (Barrett 1975:42).

Employees of the Russian-American Company and other foreign visitors who visited the Ross Colony described earth-covered lodges in local Indian villages that were used as winter houses. Peter Kostromitinov, who served as the manager of the Colony Ross from 1830 to 1838, made the following observation.

Their residences can be classified into summer or winter quarters. During the summer they find shelter in bushes, which are thinned below, and tied together above; in winter, however, they construct barabaras. A pit is dug, some vertical fixed poles are driven into the ground with their pointed ends first, and covered with wood bark, twigs, and grass; an opening is left on top and on the side, the former to let the smoke escape, the latter to serve as entrance into the barabara. Grass and a few goat hides serve as clothing and as bedding. A bow, arrows, a large pot, and sometimes fishing nets constitute the only household goods (Kostromitinov 1974:8).

Peter Corney, the chief officer on the merchant vessel *Columbia*, stumbled onto a nearby Indian village while visiting Port Rumiantsev (Bodega Harbor). His observation, made in December 1814, provides additional information about such semi-subterranean structures.

We landed, and found ourselves *above* an Indian village, for here they live underground, and we could hear their voices beneath us. Several old women and children made their appearance; we gave them some beads and by signs inquired where the Russians were.... We then left them, and, on passing the village, some of our party had the curiosity to venture into their subterraneous abodes, but were obliged to make a hasty retreat, pursued by swarms of fleas, and an intolerable stench from a mess of filth (Corney 1896:33–34).

Fedor Lütke, a Russian officer aboard the *Kamchatka*, provides an additional glimpse of the summer houses in September 1818 when his ship anchored at Port Rumiantsev. He probably toured the same village or Indian community that Corney had visited four years earlier during the winter season of the year.

Their living quarters are more like beehives or anthills than human habitations. They are made of sticks stuck in the ground in a semicircle about one and one-half arshins high; these are fastened together and then covered with dry grass or tree branches. These dwellings do not give them shelter from rain or foul weather, which, fortunately for them, is quite rare in the area where they live (Lütke 1989:275).

Ferdinand Wrangell, Chief Manager for the Russian-American Company, presents yet another account of the summer houses when he toured the Russian River region in September 1833.

We found the Indian village on sandy soil, entrenched behind shrubbery and dry ditches. It was inhabited by five or six inter-related families. The women had furnished these temporary dwellings, made of flexible shafts of sand-willow and other willows, which can be pushed into the ground quite easily, in such an extraordinarily tasteful manner, that I was most pleasantly surprised by the sight. The colorful shading and the variety of sizes of the willow-leaves (a tree which grows there in great abundance) lent a quite special rustic aspect to the open huts; the side opening, which serves as a door, is decorated with foliage with special care; several of the huts also communicate with each other by means of internal openings (Wrangell 1974:3–4).

Finally, as already quoted earlier, Captain Cyrille Théodore Laplace, the French naval officer who visited the Ross Settlement in August 1839 described the "miserable huts formed of branches through which the rain and wind passed without difficulty" (see Farris 2012b:250).

Sweat Houses

The sweat house or "sudatorium" was a semi-subterranean, earth-covered structure built with a smoke hole, center pole, and tunnel entrance (Barrett 1975:44–45; Kniffen 1939:362). These structures tended to be used by men and older boys for taking sweats, which they did on a daily basis, by building hot fires in the fire pit. Traditional sweats involved men running outside and plunging themselves into a cold source of water. The sweat house also served as a male clubhouse where many of the men and older boys spent their nights and days, especially during the colder winter months. It is reported that women were allowed into the sweat houses for short periods of time during the day. While some ceremonies and dances may have originated in sweat houses, especially in the winter (Halpern 1988:3), most of the communal ritual activities of the village took place in the dance houses. It is important to note that some scholars tend to employ the term sweat house interchangeably with that of ceremonial structures (Kniffen 1939:385).

Sweat houses appear to have considerable antiquity among Pomo people. There are at least three accounts of sweat houses by Russian era observers in the vicinity of Colony Ross.

The earliest known account is a brief account by Fedor Lütke in his visit to a Bodega Harbor village in September 1818 who noted "These Indians use a special kind of bathhouse which is really just an underground iurt. An opening is made on one side, through which one must crawl. There is smoke hole in the top" (Lütke 1989:278).

Peter Kostromitinov, the manager of the Colony Ross in the 1830s, made the following observation.

> The bathhouses are constructed almost the same as the barabaras (houses). A pit is dug, a few poles are placed around it and the whole is covered first with bark, then with earth; on the side a small air vent is made to allow the smoke to escape, and at the bottom of the wall an opening is made to allow entrance but it is so small that it can be entered only by crawling (Kostromitinov 1974:8).

A third observation was made by the French officer Cyrille Laplace in his visit to Colony Ross in August 1839.

> In order to survive they have recourse to their ordinary remedy, which with the use of several simple things gathered in the woods, composes all their means of curing. This remedy is the sweat bath of which the Red Skins in this part of America have made habitual use since time immemorial. Down in a circular hole, dug into the soil, and being about five meters in diameter and a quarter of this measure in depth, is placed a roof of a flattened, conical form, constructed of branches covered with sod, such that the air could not pass through. In this type of sweating room, into the interior of which one can only enter by a very narrow opening, of which the entry is severely forbidden to women, are assembled, sitting on rocks ranged around an enormous hearth, the bathers, among whom the

last arriving is careful to close with a flat rock or a plank, the single entrance so that in a moment the air rises to a very high temperature. The consequence of this excessive heat is, of course, an abundant perspiration among the patients, who after having been submitted to this ordeal during a fairly long space of time, according to their taste, return to the fresh air, scrape the body streaming with sweat with little wooden sticks, then go about their ordinary occupations as if nothing happened (Farris 2012b:255).

Dance Houses

The dance house or assembly house is where important village assemblies took place, especially those involving ceremonial practices. Barrett (1975:44–51) emphasized that this structure served as the center of village life. Gifford (1967:40) also noted, based on his interview with Herman James, that some dance houses were employed as winter residences for one or more families. Barrett's analysis of the semi-subterranean dance house suggests they consisted of a 0.9 to 1.8 m (three to six feet) deep pit that measured about 12.2–18 m (forty to sixty feet) in diameter. A wooden superstructure was then built over the pit, including the ritually significant center-pole and eight primary support poles, along with their stringers, upon which roof poles, thatching, and a thick layer of mud were carefully laid down. The dance house typically had a tunnel entrance, as well as a smoke hole for the fire pit. The tunnel entrance might have been oriented to the east or west (Gifford 1967:40) or to the southeast (Barrett 1975:49). The fire pit was placed near the entrance of the dance house; opposite the tunnel entrance the builders dug a trench in which they placed a large log drum. Pomo dance houses sometimes had benches built along the perimeter of their interior, while the center of the structure was reserved as a dance area. Barrett noted that the dance houses he observed often had a thick coat of rich black earth and adobe, along with a coat of sand, laid down in the center of the structure.

Dance or assembly houses are well documented in the ethnographic literature among the Pomo people of northern California (Barrett 1975; Gifford 1967:27–28, 40; Halpern 1988; Kennedy 1955; Kniffen 1939:362; Stewart 1943:50). There is some evidence that dance houses, as an architectural form, have undergone considerable innovations over time. Omer Stewart (1943:50) suggested that dance houses or assembly houses were an important component of the late prehistoric settlements system of the Kashaya Pomo. On the basis of discussions with tribal consultants, he suggested that important villages with chiefs tended to be associated with assembly houses, while less politically important settlements lacked these buildings. These tribal consultants reported that in some of the important old villages you could still see large pit depressions where assembly houses once stood. However, it is not clear whether these large pit depressions may have once served as dance houses, sweat houses, or even large residential structures. Fred Kniffen (1939:384–385) in his ethnographic work with the Kashaya Pomo also indicated that large pit features tended to be associated with important villages, in contrast to lesser villages and camp sites.

> One important criterion of a village's importance is found in the presence or absence of a ceremonial structure or "sweat house," since only the most important villages had them. Unfortunately, information on just what villages contained sweat houses is lacking.

However, it is not clear in this case whether the large depressions associated with important village sites were dance houses or possibly sweat houses.

Edwin Loeb also argued for considerable antiquity for the semi-subterranean dance houses, suggesting they were used by Pomo people to perform the Old Ghost ceremony in ancient times. He believed that more recent innovations in dance house designs, such as the inclusion of an interior gallery, painted interior poles, and a tunnel entrance, were additions to an ancient architectural form (Loeb 1926:338, 395–396). Barrett (1975:45) noted that the large, earth covered, semi-subterranean dance house he observed at Sulphur Bank in 1902 was "the last of the truly aboriginal type of dance house built in the Pomo region." The emergence of the dreamer or "Bole-Maru" religious practices that derived from the 1870 Ghost Dance movement and ancient forms of Kashaya belief, eventually led to the transformation of this architectural form to that of above ground, redwood-planked dance houses by the early 1900s that could hold about 150 people (Kennedy 1955:125–135).

Interestingly, while European visitors to Indian villages during Russian colonial times described in some detail semi-subterranean lodges and sweat houses, no such observations are known for the large dance houses (see Kennedy 1955:11). It is possible that these sacred structures were off-limits to the Russians and their visitors, thus perhaps explaining why there are no historical reports of dance houses for the north coast. It should be noted, however that these structures would have been the largest and most centrally located structures in Indian settlements, and thus highly visible to visitors.

Evaluating the Metini Village Pit Feature

In considering the purpose and meaning of the large pit feature at CA-SON-175, we consider three lines of evidence: contemporary Kashaya Pomo perspectives, ethnohistorical observations, and our archaeological findings.

Contemporary Native Perspectives

Kashaya elders and tribal scholars who collaborated on our joint project interpreted the pit structure as the remains of a ceremonial "round house" (*aka* dance house) based on their oral traditions. They believe it was employed as a communal structure for dances, spiritual prayers, and healing ceremonies, and would have served as a central foundation in the Kashaya Pomo community at that time. They noted that the spiritually invested center pole was probably removed from the Metini Village structure and carefully transported to Haupt's Ranch when the first of the dance houses was constructed there.

Ethnohistorical Accounts

There are no known observations of large, semi-subterranean, earth covered, dance houses being used during Russian colonial times, while there are numerous observations of semi-subterranean lodges and sweat houses. It is possible that dance houses were not built in Native villages situated near the Ross Settlement or Port Rumiantsev during the early 1800s. An eyewitness account appears to corroborate this observation. Marie James (the mother of Herman James, a key Kashaya consultant to both Edward Gifford and Robert Oswalt) remembered that the first dance house was built in the Fort Ross area when she was about eight years old (circa 1857). Prior to that, Marie James recalled that brush shelters were constructed for major dances and ceremonies (see Kennedy 1955:11). We know of other dance houses being built by Pomo people in the mid-1800s, such as the large dance house among the Clear Lake Pomo dating to the late 1850s or early 1860s (Barrett 1952:414).

Archaeological Findings

While semi-subterranean structures employed as lodges, sweat houses, or dance houses may produce similar kinds of archaeological signatures, such as large pit depressions, as well as fire-cracked rock, charcoal and other debris from associated fire pits, we believe they can be distinguished using basic archaeological data. A significant criterion is size. According to Barrett (1975:44), dance houses tend to be larger (12.2–18 meters or 40–60 feet in diameter) than sweat houses (4.5–9 meters or 15–30 feet in diameter) or residential structures. Observations from Russian colonial times suggest that semi-subterranean lodges were about the same size as sweat houses, or somewhat smaller. The pit feature recorded at Metini Village measures about 13 meters (43 feet) total in diameter, including the berm; the pit alone appears to be between 10 and 11 meters (32.8 to 36 feet) in diameter. Its dimensions fall within the size range of a small Pomo dance house.

Other findings from the archaeological investigation support the idea that the pit feature may have served as a dance house. The gradiometer survey revealed a significant magnetic anomaly in the southeast corner of the feature. Tribal elders working with us believe that this magnetic anomaly probably marked the location of a hearth with fire-cracked rocks. According to their oral traditions, as well as Barrett's ethnographic account, it is a characteristic pattern for dance or round houses to have hearths, typically situated near the entrance of the structure. The gradiometer survey also indicated a possible anomaly within the eastern berm of the pit structure that looks like it may be the remains of a former entrance to the structure.

The pit feature at Metini Village may very well be the dance house built by the Kashaya Pomo as remembered by Marie James from when she was eight years old. The 1857 construction date as recalled by Marie James fits nicely with the chronological analysis of Metini Village that suggests its primary occupation took place in the 1850s and 1860s. Significantly, other possible sites where the 1857 dance house may have been erected do not exhibit the footprints for a dance house. The most likely other village site is CA-SON-174, which appears to have also been used during the Benitz Rancho period in the 1840s and 1850s. While pit depressions have been mapped on this site (see below), the largest are somewhat smaller than the one at Metini Village, measuring only eight meters in diameter (Lightfoot et al. 1991:69–70).

Large earth-covered, semi-subterranean dance houses or assembly houses may have considerable antiquity among the Kashaya Pomo (and other nearby Pomo groups) as suggested by Barrett, Stewart, and Loeb. However, few details are known about these ancient forms of dance houses. The paucity of early colonial observations of these structures may be a reflection of the Kashaya Pomo deciding not to build these large structures in villages that were regularly visited by the Russian-American Company and European visitors. They may have chosen to make dance houses relatively invisible to the colonial invaders during the early years of culture contact at Colony Ross. It is also possible that large semi-subterranean earthen structures were not commonly employed as dance houses on the Kashaya coast until the 1850s. Prior to this time other kinds of structures, such as brush houses or even sweat houses, may have incorporated many of the duties and ceremonial performances that ethnographers have attributed to later dance houses. In any event, the dance house at Metini Village represents the emergence of an architectural form that had not been observed by the Russian merchants and visitors in the early years of Colony Ross.

Midden Deposit

The midden deposit located to the east of the pit feature along the terrace edge and slope contains a diverse range of archaeological materials that resulted from the daily activities of Metini households, along with the production of possible feasts and large gatherings that would be associated with periodic ceremonies at the dance house. The archaeological findings indicate that people processed, cooked, and consumed a diverse range of domesticated and wild foods. They utilized cuts of beef and mutton, as well as wheat, barley, and possibly peas, which were probably provided as rations by William Benitz (see below). Metini dwellers also obtained wild game, particularly Black-Tail Deer (*Odocoileus hemionus*), gathered various shellfish varieties (e.g., mussel, turban snails, chitons, limpets, abalone, barnacles) from the nearby rocky coastline, and collected a diverse range of seeds [e.g., and from California Poppy (*Eschscholzia* sp. cf.), blue grass (*Poa* sp.cf.), knotweed/dock (*Polygonum/Rumex* sp.), California Bay (*Umbellularia californica*), as well as from various families of pink (Caryophyllaceae), legume (Fabaceae), grass (Poaceae), rose (Rosaceae cf.), and nightshade (Solanaceae cf.) plants]. Some coastal fishing took place, probably by hook and line from the rocky shoreline, as indicated by the presence of Cabazon (*Scorpaenichthys marmoratus*) and rockfish (*Sebastes* sp.). While no fishhooks made of shell were recovered during the archaeological investigation, it is possible that some of the iron nails were reworked into hooks. However, only one specimen of a marine mammal [eared seal (Otariidae)] was detected.

Native residents employed both lithics and glass as raw materials in the production and use of sharp-edged tools. The large percentage of shatter and flake shatter, primarily from local chert and imported obsidian, indicates that core reduction and flake production took place on the site. The substantial number of worked glass objects indicates that glass, particularly from heavy duty, dark green alcohol bottles, was a significant raw material for creating expedient tools. The significant number of worked glass sherds, flake shatter and shatter artifacts indicates that some glass working took place on site. There is also some indication that shell bead production may have also taken place at Metini given the number of *Olivella* shells (12 out of 17) that exhibited evidence of modification.

Other archaeological remains recovered at Metini Village may have served as household furnishings. These include various ground stone tools, such as milling hand stones, pestles, and a hopper mortar, which may have been employed in the processing of various kinds of foods.

The original use of ceramic and glass objects at Metini is not entirely clear. The ceramic-refined earthenware ironstone pottery plates, bowls, and cups may have been utilized as serving vessels, while the glass bottles may have held medicinal remedies, ketchup, condiments, and various kinds of liquid, particularly alcohol. However, another interpretation is that these pieces of plates, bowls, cups, and bottles may have been obtained in fragmentary forms for use as raw materials for making tools, gaming pieces, and decorative items, an observation made for similar assemblages in the Native Alaskan Village Site (see Farris 1997:130–131). Other objects that may have been associated with household furnishings are the thimble and the spring (possibly from a bed). The manufactured brass and glass buttons, along with the metal clothing fastener, provide a glimpse of some of the clothing probably utilized by Metini residents.

The above findings indicate that much of the archaeological assemblage appears to be related to the accoutrements of residential living. However, it is not clear at this time where specific house structures may have been located. Gifford (1967:9) observed in 1950 possibly 12 to 15 "house pits," in addition to the "dance-house pit." However, no known map of these house pits currently exists. We attempted to re-locate the house pits by visiting the site during different seasons of the year. But we were unable to detect their location. As Gifford and other early investigators noted, the small pit features were probably obliterated by plowing and other historical landscape uses in the area. It is possible that some of the house pits observed by Gifford may have been located to the south towards the former intersection of Highway 1 and Seaview Road near the North Wall Community. Future analysis of the Ritter collections might resolve this issue.

We believe that if house structures once existed at Metini Village then they were probably situated either in or near the midden area along the terrace edge. To the east of the small dance house feature we mapped a 10 to 15 m wide midden deposit which extends about 60 m along the terrace edge. The midden deposit then continues down the terrace slope about 20 m or so to the east towards Fort Ross Creek (see Figure 4). The terrace edge and slope of the midden deposit contain the great majority of archaeological materials associated with Metini Village. Intermixed with the artifacts, faunal and floral remains, as described earlier, are the fire-cracked rocks and wood charcoal that were probably deposited from hearths and underground ovens. Our investigation of the midden deposit did yield some fired daub samples that may be the product of underground ovens or even house structures.

Our interpretation is that at least some of the house structures at Metini Village were situated along the 60 m strip of terrace edge (either within the midden deposit and/or adjacent to it). Some of these house structures may have been built as semi-subterranean lodges, as suggested by Gifford's observation of house pits, particularly for use in the winter months. Other structures used by laborers primarily during the warmer harvest season may have been much more ephemeral pole and thatched houses, as described by Corney, Wrangell, and Laplace. Some structures may have even been built from slabs of redwood bark and wood, which leaned together on a center pole, as observed by later ethnographers (e.g., Barrett 1975:37). However, it is interesting that none of the early colonial period Russian observations mention these conical slab structures (Lightfoot et al. 1991:142). It is possible that the conical redwood slab structures may have become more common with the commencement of the redwood timber operations in the region in late 1800s, such as that initiated by the Benitz Rancho at Timber Cove, which is located a couple miles north of Fort Ross cove.

The finding of both wrought and wire nails, along with the window glass fragments, also indicates that some innovations may have been employed in the residential architecture at Metini. Powers (1976:189) describes one such frame house used by the Kashaya Pomo at Haupt's Ranch in the early 1870s. Barrett (1975:53) photographed "modern" log houses, adjacent to more "traditional" conical slab houses, among the Pomo during his field work in 1901 and 1902.

In sum, we suggest that people probably would have performed many of their mundane domestic tasks (food processing, cooking, tool production) near structures along the terrace edge facing Fort Ross Creek. Food residue, hearth and oven contents, and spent materials were then discarded down the adjacent terrace slope. However, at this time we have found only circumstantial evidence (e.g., presumed house pits recorded by Gifford, nails, window glass) for the possible existence of residential structures along the terrace edge. If structures were built, we suspect that a diverse range of winter and summer architectural styles were probably employed.

Clean Zone

One of the most striking findings during our archaeological investigation was that the site area beyond the midden deposit and pit feature was almost totally devoid of artifacts and faunal remains. It appears as if Metini dwellers intentionally kept the area west of the pit feature clean of debris and household residue by either limiting activities to the terrace strip or deliberately cleaning the area. The tribal elders working on the project believed that this might have been a sacred area associated with the round house for outdoor dances and large gatherings of people. The archaeological findings certainly support this interpretation. Other alternative interpretations for the "clean zone" is that it was an area possibly used by Benitz for crop production or livestock grazing that may have been of limited access to the Metini dwellers.

Relationship to North Wall Community

In examining the spatial layout of Metini Village, a significant question we pondered prior to the fieldwork was whether it was part of a larger, contiguous archaeological manifestation connected to the North Wall Community before the realignment of Highway 1 took place. We noted earlier that the results of our survey work at Metini Village suggested that they were probably two separate and discrete archaeological deposits. The density of artifacts declined noticeably along the southern edge of the site, while Gonzalez's (2011:160–162) work at the North Wall Community area showed that the density of artifacts declined substantially 20 m north of the stockade wall. The dating of the two areas supports this interpretation. Metini Village appears to be somewhat later (primarily post-Russian in age) than the Russian-period North Wall Community. This finding is exemplified by the glass bead assemblages in the two areas. As Elliot Blair noted (see earlier), not only is Metini Village associated with late bead types, but the color profile and red-on-green to red-on-white bead ratios are quite distinctive between these two areas, perhaps pointing to the fact that each represents a discrete residential area. Other lines of evidence discussed later in this chapter highlight the differences between these two places, including the lower ratio of obsidian to chert tools and debitage and the higher percentage of worked glass artifacts at Metini Village compared to the North Wall Community. Thus, while Metini Village and the North Wall Community may be located a short distance from each other, they appear to be discrete residential areas used by the Kashaya Pomo, probably along with other peoples, at different times in the colonial history of the region.

Issue 3: Colonial Laborers

Our original intention was to compare the processes and outcomes of the Russian-American Company and the Benitz Rancho on the Indian people residing at Metini Village who were employed as colonial laborers. However, in discovering that the primary occupation of the site (CA-SON-175) dates to the 1850s and 1860s, this investigation will focus primarily on laboring practices during the Benitz Rancho period. While some of the archaeological remains may date to the terminal phase of the Russian-American Company, this interpretation is difficult to substantiate through archaeology at this time.

The archaeological investigation provides additional sources of information for evaluating, modifying, and expanding upon historical accounts of the Indian workers at Benitz Rancho. Documentary sources indicate that William Benitz provided his workers with room and board, as well as $8.00 per month, and that the Native workers may have been fed at a communal kitchen and provided alcohol rations (Tomlin 1993:8; Kalani and Sweedler 2004:36:44; Kennedy 1955:76–79). The archaeological investigation suggests that while Indian laborers may have been fed breakfast and dinner at an off-site commissariat, there is excellent evidence that considerable food processing and consumption took place at Metini Village. Our findings suggest that Native workers may have been paid rations that were subsequently cooked by Kashaya people at the site. These rations probably included wheat, barley, peas, beef, and mutton, among other goods. It is also possible that some of these foods may have been raised by the Indian workers primarily for their consumption.

The 37 Domestic Cow (*Bos Taurus*) elements identified at Metini suggest that a diverse range of meat cuts were probably provided to the Native laborers. The cattle elements included pieces of the mandible and cranium, ribs, carpal, femur, and vertebrate sections. It is very possible that live cattle were given to the Kashaya Pomo workers who then slaughtered, processed, cooked, and consumed the meat at the village site. In a letter dated October 7, 1863, William Benitz wrote that he "killed four head a week, which usually gave 500 lbs. at 4 cents a lb." (Benitz 1863). Some of these cows may have been periodically allocated to Indian workers. Three of the *Bos tauras* elements exhibited cut marks; one was identified as being sawed. The charred wheat and barley grains also suggest that these non-Indian foods were also cooked and consumed at Metini.

The diverse range of wild foods recovered at the site—shellfish, fish, wild game, wild seeds, and nuts—strongly suggests that the Kashaya Pomo were supplementing rationed food stores with resources obtained through hunting, fishing, and gathering. Historical records document that William Benitz was supplying deer hides and live ducks and pigeons to the outside world. While it appears that Benitz was paying some non-Indians as hunters, it is not clear what duties these workers performed. Possibly they were hunting wild game, such as Black-Tailed Deer (*Odocoileus hemionus*), for hides. While this task may have also been undertaken by some of the Kashaya Pomo hunters, it is notable that there is relatively little evidence in the chipped stone or worked glass assemblage of hunting-related tools, such as projectile points. Most of the worked pieces appear to be expedient tools probably used for camp related domestic tasks. In any event, the 18 elements of *Odocoileus hemionus* represent a diverse range of parts (e.g., tarsal, fibula, mandible, metacarpal, carpal, radius) that suggests whole animals were probably being butchered and consumed at the village.

The recovery of the glass buttons and brass buttons from work clothes suggests that the Native workers were either purchasing clothes, exchanging goods for them, or obtaining such articles as payment for their laboring efforts. It is not clear how the ceramic vessels were obtained. Previous studies of the ceramic assemblages from other nearby colonial sites (e.g., the Native Alaskan Village Site, North Wall Community, see p. 117) documented high levels of ceramic fragmentation, modest numbers of ceramic artifacts, and evidence that some sherds had been intentionally worked (Farris 1997:131; Gonzalez 2011:233; Silliman 1997:174). We believe that local Natives may have been recycling colorful or distinctive ceramic fragments from Russian dumps for use in domestic contexts as gaming pieces, pendants, or charms. The Metini Village ceramic assemblage is also highly fragmented and relatively few sherds were recovered (n=36). It is possible that a similar cultural practice was taking place at this later colonial village. However, few of the Metini ceramics exhibit evidence of being worked, and the largest percentage are white ironstones, most of which are undecorated. Some of these ceramics may have been provided (or bought) as whole vessels by Benitz and used by the Native residents for serving or consuming food and liquids. The ironstone fragments include three bowls, one cup, one unidentified hollow form, and three plates.

The large number of glass fragments at Metini Village, many of which exhibit evidence of use, also raises the question of whether the glass materials were recycled from garbage dumps, or purchased by or provided to the residents as whole vessels. Again, prior research at the Native Alaskan Village Site and the North Wall Community suggests that many of the glass fragments were scavenged from Russian dumps and reused by Native people as raw materials for making glass tools (Farris 1997:131; Gonzalez 2011:243; Silliman 1997:174). The high level of fragmentation of the Metini glass assemblage combined with the increased use of glass as raw material for the expedient production of chipped tools would certainly support this interpretation. The large number of fragments from dip-molded, thick-bottomed, dark glass alcohol bottles is also significant. We believe many of the glass sherds were probably recycled from the Benitz Rancho. The observation that William Benitz allocated alcohol rations to his laborers to fend off the cold and damp may have produced a number of heavy duty, utilitarian bottles. These bottles may have been reutilized by the Indian workers as an expedient supply of raw materials for making glass tools.

A few of the archaeological finds may be indicative of the tools used by the Indian workers on the Benitz Rancho. These include the wrought and cut nails, fencing material, the iron ripper plow blade, and the shovel. However, these tools may have also been employed in the construction of structures in the village, or they may be the product of later ranching (or even artifact looting) activities on the site area. But their concentration in the village's midden deposit suggests they may have been associated with the Native workers.

Issue 4: Maintaining an Indian Community After Many Years of Sustained Colonialism

An important question in the archaeology of colonialism is how colonized populations maintain a sense of community and core values while living and working for coercive colonial societies over the course of many decades. The primary occupation at Metini Village in the 1850s and 1860s took place after the Kashaya Pomo had already been exposed to nearly a half century of close entanglements with members of an international mercantile company and then later ranchers and business entrepreneurs. The issue we address here is, to what degree did the Kashaya Pomo continue to maintain their Indian community during these later years of settler colonialism while serving as laborers for the Benitz family? We evaluate this issue through a comparison of the archaeological materials from Metini Village with those from earlier colonial age assemblages unearthed at the North Wall Community, the Native Alaskan Village Site (NAVS), Tomato Patch, and CA-SON-670, as well as the later occupation of CA-SON-174 during the Benitz Rancho period.

As outlined earlier, the North Wall Community may have been a colonial space in the Russian-American Company's enterprise (i.e., 1810s–1830s) where barracks of Native laborers, single Native Californian women, and/or multiethnic households comprised of Creole/Russian men and Native Californian women once stood. The materials unearthed at NAVS, produced by multiethnic households composed of Native Alaskan men and Native Californian women, date primarily to the 1820s and 1830s. Tomato Patch contains both late prehistoric materials and early colonial materials (pre-1841) that may have been discarded by people who occasionally labored for the Russian-American Company. CA-SON-670 is a Kashaya Pomo village with an extensive occupation spanning late prehistoric and historical times. Native workers probably resided here while laboring for the Russian-American Company and possibly for Benitz Rancho. Dixon and Charles Fairfax used the site as part of their logging operation in the late 1860s and 1870s. CA-SON-174 is interpreted as one of the villages where Native laborers resided while working at the Benitz Rancho in the 1840s and 1850s. It later became the site of the foreman's residence for the Call Ranch in the early 1870s and Carlos Call's residence beginning in 1902.

In undertaking this analysis, it is important to recognize that recovery methods and sample size may influence the comparison of archaeological assemblages from the six sites, particularly the recovery rates of small-sized artifacts and faunal remains in different mesh sizes (6 mm [1/4 in.], 3 mm [1/8 in.], 1.5 mm [1/16 in.]) used to screen archaeological deposits (Ames 2005; Grayson 1978; Lyman 1991). The study of the Native Alaskan Village Site involved geophysical survey, intensive surface collection, and trench excavations, as well as areal excavations that unearthed features detected in the hand-dug trenches. The strategy for screening sediments involved taking a 25% sample for wet screening through 1.5 mm mesh, and dry screening the rest through 3 mm mesh. The results of the field investigation summarized by Ballard for the North Wall Community focus on the excavation of two trenches directed by Donald Wood in 1970. It is not clear what mesh size was employed in screening sediments, but probably it was 6 mm mesh, the standard of the time. Gonzalez's (2011) recent investigations of the North Wall Community, however, followed the recovery methodology employed at NAVS and work at the site involved a combination of geophysical survey, intensive surface collection, and areal excavations. All sediments were screened through 3 mm mesh, and 5–10 L soil samples were obtained from each excavated level and subsequently floated using 1 mm mesh.

Martinez's field work at Tomato Patch included geophysical survey, intensive surface collection across the entire site area, and excavation units placed in several surface pit depressions and the midden deposit (Martinez 1997, 1998). Her investigation revealed a discretely structured site with pit features and a well-demarcated midden deposit. All sediments were screened through 3 mm mesh. David Fredrickson's 1971 excavation at CA-SON-670 involved the screening of 7.8 m³ of soil distributed across ten 2-by-2 m units through 6 mm mesh and then wet screening in the creek through 3 mm mesh. Some 1.5 mm mesh may have also been used (Fenner 2002:14). The 1983 field investigation of CA-SON-174 directed by Glenn Farris employed 3 mm mesh for screening the 42 units excavated from across several areas of the site.

Technology

The residents of the six sites (e.g., Metini Village, the North Wall Community, NAVS, Tomato Patch, CA-SON-670, and CA-SON-174) employed lithic and glass as significant sources of raw materials in the production of sharp edged tools. There is evidence at all six sites for the reduction of cores into core tools (bifaces) and flakes via percussion methods, as well as finer pressure flaking along the edges of flake and core tools. The primary artifact categories reported for the chipped stone and worked glass assemblages for all six sites consist of debitage, including shatter and various types of flakes, along with edge-modified glass sherds. For example, in considering the chipped stone assemblages, the ratio of flakes/cores/shatter to formal tools (e.g., bifaces, unifaces, etc.) is high for all six sites, ranging from 90.1 at Tomato Patch (n=6270 to 69) and 56.1 at NAVS (n=1348 to 24) to 48.45 at CA-SON-670 (n=1502 to 31), 31.88 at CA-SON-174 (n=1052 to 33), and 16.5 at Metini Village (n=116 to 7) (Fenner 2002:18; Lightfoot, Schiff and Wake 1997:227; Martinez 1998:144–146; Newquist 2002:35). This ratio ranges from 129 (n=2709 to 21) (Ballard 1995:213) to 25.5 (n=1254 to 49) (Gonzalez 2011:235–236) at the North Wall Community, a disparity that is the likely result of collection strategies employed in Wood's excavations versus those employed by Gonzalez.

We observed several significant differences in the craft production practices implemented at Metini Village in comparison to the other sites:

1. The proportion of obsidian worked by Metini Village craftspeople, in

comparison to other lithic raw materials, is lower. The ratio of obsidian to chert at Metini Village is only 0.18 (n=18 to 99). The next lowest ratio is found at CA-SON-670 with 0.31 (n= 368 to 1157) (Fenner 2002:18–22). The North Wall Community, CA-SON-174, and NAVS exhibit higher obsidian to chert ratios specifically 1.7 (n=950 to 547), 1.83 (n=694 to 380), and 1.94 (n=903 to 465), respectively (Ballard 1995:215,217; Lightfoot, Schiff, and Wake 1997:226; Newquist 2002:35). Gonzalez's (2011:234) more recent investigations at the North Wall Community place the ratio of obsidian to chert at 2.92 (n=2025 to 693). Tomato Patch residents employed higher proportions of chert than the craftspeople at the North Wall Community, NAVS, and CA-SON-174, but not as high as at Metini Village. Excavations of the pit features at Tomato Patch revealed that chert made up 46 to 70% of the chipped stone assemblage, while obsidian comprised between 13 to 20% (Martinez 1998:119–123).

The low ratio of obsidian to chert artifacts at Metini Village may indicate that access to obsidian became tougher for Native Californians living in the north coast in the mid-to-late 1800s. The establishment of Mexican ranchos and later American period ranches, farms, and towns must have dramatically increased the difficulties of coastal Native people obtaining obsidian from interior sources through exchange or direct procurement (Farris 1989:492; Lightfoot et al. 1991). Furthermore, while Napa Valley may have been the primary source of obsidian during Russian colonial times, it appears that obsidian from the Annadel source may have been increasingly used by the Kashaya Pomo after the founding of the Benitz Rancho, at least by the residents of Metini Village. Yet the findings from CA-SON-174, which exhibits a relatively high obsidian to chert ratio, do not support the idea that obsidian became limited for all Native people laboring at the Benitz Rancho. Furthermore, the obsidian to chert ratio at a nearby prehistoric coastal site (CA-SON-1455) occupied sometime between AD 800 and 1500 yielded a low obsidian to chert ratio (0.12) on the magnitude of Metini Village (n=63 obsidian; 519 chert) (Farris 1986:31). Why such marked differences in the obsidian to chert ratio exist for these sites is not clear at this time, but they may reflect the fact that other factors than ease of access to obsidian sources may be involved.

2. The craftspeople at Metini Village tended to employ glass over stone as a medium for producing sharp-edged tools. The ratio of worked glass artifacts (n=232) to chipped stone artifacts (n=123) at Metini Village is almost two to one (1.9), which is considerably greater than that of four of the other sites. The ratio of worked glass to chipped

stone artifacts ranges from only 0.001 at Tomato Patch (n=10 to 6339) and 0.001 at CA-SON-670 (n=2 to 1533) to 0.05 at NAVS (n=73 to 1486), and from 0.06 (n=80 to 1303) to 0.07 (n=191 to 2736) at the North Wall Community according to Ballard's and Gonzalez's analyses, respectively (Ballard 1995:213, 224, 225; Fenner 2002: 46; Gonzalez 2011:234, 240; Lightfoot, Schiff, and Wake 1997:359–361; Martinez 1998:144–146). The ratio at CA-SON-174, although lower than at Metini Village, is significantly higher than at the other sites. The ratio for worked glass and melted glass to chipped stone at CA-SON-174 is 0.82 (n=886 to 1085) and for only worked glass to chipped stone is 0.60 (n=647 to 1085).

The much higher ratios of worked glass artifacts at Metini Village and CA-SON-174 probably reflect several factors. One is the earlier use of the other sites by indigenous people in Russian colonial times when glass may not have been as accessible as it became in the mid-to-late 1800s. Of course, the late pre-colonial component at Tomato Patch and CA-SON-670 and their associated chipped stone industry also would have lowered the worked glass to chipped stone artifact ratio significantly.

Another important factor in the higher ratio of worked glass at Metini Village and CA-SON-174 may be related to the increasing skills that Native people developed in using recycled glass for making various kinds of expedient tools previously made from obsidian. Glass sources, and specifically glass from dark green, heavy duty alcohol bottles, appear to have been readily obtainable from the Benitz Rancho. At Metini Village, glass appears to have been increasingly used for making expedient tools for camp life. The vast majority of the worked glass assemblage at the site is comprised of debitage and edge modified flakes. As only one formal tool (a glass biface) was identified, the flakes/core/shatter to formal tool ratio is an incredible 231 (n=231 to 1). The analysis of CA-SON-174 yielded similar findings. The worked glass assemblage consists of 649 artifacts (not including the melted sherds). Of these, 641 were recorded as edge-modified flakes and debitage, four as bifaces, and four as projectile points yielding a flakes/core/shatter to formal tool ratio of 80.5 (n=641 to 8) (Newquist 2002:44, Appendix D)

The third factor possibly influencing the growing use of glass for expedient tool production may be related to the increasing difficulties in later colonial times of obtaining high quality, non-local lithic material, such as obsidian, from sources distributed across the broader region. But as discussed earlier, this factor may be only relevant for Metini Village since obsidian is relatively more plentiful at CA-SON-174.

3.   Shell bead production appears to have varied significantly among the Kashaya Pomo residing in different colonial contexts. At Metini Village we found spire-removed perpendicular beads (type A1c) produced from *Olivella* shells, but little evidence for the working of abalone or clams. It is not clear whether the residents were manufacturing *Olivella* shell beads at Metini Village, but the finding of heat-treated bead pieces and fragments is suggestive. There does not appear to be much direct evidence of shell working at Tomato Patch, CA-SON-670, and NAVS. Newquist's (2002:38, 57–59, Appendix K) analysis of the CA-SON-174 assemblage produced some evidence for the production of shell artifacts, including two lithic drills and one drilled abalone artifact. Donald Wood's archaeological investigations at the North Wall Community revealed possible shell ornament production involving four drilled abalone fragments and 19 cut abalone pieces, along with 13 chert drills (of which 10 are bipointed), which may have been used for cutting and drilling shell pendants (Ballard 1995:145–146, 148–149). Although Gonzalez's (2011) recent study similarly revealed evidence of shell ornament production, including an obsidian drill and spire-removed perpendicular beads, no drilled or cut abalone or other shell fragments were uncovered.

As Ballard points out, the differences between the North Wall Community and other colonial contexts (e.g., NAVS) in regards to shell working may be a consequence of such considerations as engendered work spaces, since Native Californian men were probably not present at NAVS, but may have been residing in the barracks at the North Wall Community where shell bead production may have taken place. The paucity of evidence for shell working at Metini Village, beyond the production process of removing the spiral elements of *Olivella* shells, also raises the question of how much time laborers could invest in labor intensive tasks such as shell bead production. However, the discovery of the worked abalone object does suggest that time was taken by someone at Metini or in the local region to work other shell materials. Of course, the paucity of evidence for shell working at Metini Village may also be a reflection of sample size issues.

Menu

There are both strong commonalities and significant differences in foodways practices at Metini Village in comparison to the other five sites. Shellfish remains are a common constituent for all the sites, with mussel, chiton, limpet, and turban snails comprising the majority of the MNI counts, along with abalone, barnacles, and various species of gastropods. The shellfish analyses of CA-SON-670 and CA-SON-174, which were based on shell weight, identified abalone as the most common species (Fenner 2002:26–28; Newquist 2002:57–58). Interestingly, at the nearby pre-colonial coastal site of CA-SON-1455, limpets, mussels, and turban snails (*Tegula funebralis*) made up the majority of the identified shellfish assemblage (Swiden 1986:57). It appears that Native people residing in various colonial settings associated with the Russian colony and Benitz Rancho regularly collected shellfish from nearby rocky intertidal habitats. The greatest diversity in shellfish species is found at NAVS, as it contains a number of small snails and sea urchin spines and parts (Schiff 1997). This may be a product of Native Alaskan participation in shellfish harvesting or their taste preferences, which may have influenced the kinds of mollusks collected by them and the Native Californian women who lived with them. However, the recovery of small-sized urchin spines and minute gastropods may also be related to recovery methods involving finer mesh (1.5 mm) employed in water screening sediments from NAVS.

While the identified species of terrestrial mammals represented at Metini Village are dominated by cattle, followed by Black-Tail Deer, as well as some goat/sheep, voles, and bobcats, most of the other sites tend to have greater numbers of skeletal elements from wild animals than domesticated species. The residents of Tomato Patch dined almost exclusively on deer-sized game (Cervidae) and Black-Tailed Deer (*Odocoileus hemionus*), along with some rabbit/cottontail (*Sylvilagus* sp.), squirrels (Sciuridae), and pocket gophers (*Thomomys* sp.) (Martinez 1998:149–151). No domesticated mammals were recovered from the site. The identified terrestrial mammals from the North Wall Community included (in order of abundance) Black-Tailed Deer (*Odocoileus hemionus*), Domestic Cow (*Bos taurus*), Botta's Pocket Gopher (*Thomomys bottae*), Pig (*Sus scrofa*), Mountain Lion (*Felis concolor*), Sheep (*Ovis aries*), Striped Skunk (*Mephitis mephitis*), Broad-Handed Moles (*Scapanus latmanus*), and Bushy Tail Woodrat (*Neotoma fuscipes*) (Ballard 1995:210). The identified terrestrial species from NAVS (in order of abundance) are Black-Tailed Deer (*Odocoileus hemionus*), Botta's Pocket Gopher (*Thomomys bottae*), Domestic Cow (*Bos taurus*), Sheep (*Ovis aries*), Elk (*Cervus elaphus*), Pig (*Sus scrofa*), California Vole (*Microtus californicus*), dog (*Canis* sp.), Mountain Lion (*Felis concolor*), Grizzly Bear (*Ursus arctos*), Coyote (*Canis latrans*), Black-Tailed Jackrabbit (*Lepus californicus*), and Broad-Handed Moles (*Scapanus latmanus*) (Wake 1997b:282). The analysis of the small quantity of vertebrate faunal remains recovered from CA-SON-670 identified only large, medium, and small artiodactyl specimens and rodents (Fenner 2002:25–26). The specific species have not yet been identified.

The terrestrial vertebrate faunal assemblage unearthed at CA-SON-174 follows a similar pattern as that found at Metini Village. The identified taxa are dominated by Domestic Cow (*Bos taurus*) followed distantly by Black-Tailed Deer (*Odocoileus hemionus*), leporidae, sheep/goat (*Capra/Ovis*), squirrel, rodent, and possible fox (Newquist 2002: 54–56). Newquist (2002:54) observes that the ratio of domesticated to wild species is 10 to 1. Her analysis suggests that the cows were probably butchered on site or close by given the diversity of faunal elements and evidence of butcher marks, including saw marks, cut marks, and chop marks. The beef cuts identified in the faunal assemblage represent relatively low value meat cuts for the period. Only the deer bones exhibited evidence of butchering using a knife or similar sharp edged tool. Most of the bones were highly fragmented and exhibited signs of burning.

Marine mammals were virtually absent in the vertebrate faunal assemblage from Metini Village, as we recovered only one element of an eared seal (Otariidae). CA-SON-670 and CA-SON-174 exhibit a similar pattern—no marine mammals were identified from these sites (Fenner 2002:25; Newquist 2002:56). Sea mammal remains are also rare at Tomato Patch, where only two elements of California Sea Lion (*Zalophus californianus*) and three elements of Sea Otter (*Enhydra lutris*) were identified (Martinez 1998:149–151). Likewise, the North Wall Community is characterized by a paucity of marine mammals, where only one element of a Harbor Seal (*Phoca vitulina*) was found in the Wood excavations (Ballard 1995:210) and an additional spinal vertebrae from an unidentified sea mammal was recovered during Gonzalez's (2011) investigations. In contrast, marine mammals at NAVS make up a sizeable component of the faunal remains from the site, including Harbor Seal (*P. vitulina*), California Sea Lion (*Zalophus californianus*), Steller Sea Lion (*Eumatopias jubatus*), Northern Fur Seal (*Callorhinus ursinus*), whale, porpoise, and Sea Otter (*Enhydra lutris*), which are strong signatures of the marine hunting prowess of the Native Alaskan residents at the site (see Wake 1995, 1997a, b).

A similar pattern exists for marine fish, which are found in abundance and considerable diversity at NAVS, but are sparse at the other sites. At least 22 species of fish were identified from NAVS; the most common taxa included Cabezon (*Scorpaenichthys marmoratus*), rockfish (*Sebastes* sp.), and Lingcod (*Ophiodon elongatus*), which make up over 90% of the identified skeletal elements (Gobalet 1997). The North Wall Community yielded elements of bony fish (Osteichthyes), rockfish (*Sebastes* sp.), kelp greenling (Hexagrammadae), and Cabezon (*S. marmoratus*) (Ballard 1995:210). CA-SON-670 yielded one element of unidentified fish (Fenner 2002:25–26). No marine fish are reported from Tomato Patch (Martinez 1998:149–153). Metini Village had trace amounts of Cabezon (*S. marmoratus*) and rockfish (*Sebastes* sp.), while CA-SON-174 yielded 48 elements of unidentified fish (Newquist 2002:55). Fish vertebrate were abundant from the prehistoric component of CA-SON-1455, but were not diagnostic enough to identify specific taxa (Farris 1986:44). Again, the differences in the variety and quantity of marine fish elements found at NAVS are probably related to two factors: one is the sophisticated marine harvesting technology (boats, fishing gear) of the Native Alaskans that enhanced the exploitation of fish species, while the other is the overall larger sample size for the excavation units and the fine mesh (1.5 mm, 3 mm) employed in screening archaeological deposits.

The greatest abundance and diversity of bird remains were also found at NAVS with 16 taxa. These include (in order of abundance) the Common Murre (*Uria aalge*), gull (*Larus* sp.), pelican (*Pelecanus* sp.), duck (*Anas/Aythya/Melanitta/Bucephala/Mergus/Oxyura* sp.), Chicken (*Gallus gallus*), cormorant (*Phalacrocorax* sp.), goose (*Anser/Chen/Branta* sp.), and loon (*Gavia* sp.) (see Simons 1997). The large number of seabirds found at NAVS point to the Native Alaskan presence at the site, but again the larger sample size and finer mesh size employed in the excavation must also be factors in the recovery of the diverse bird bone assemblage. While we detected no bird bones at Metini Village, some elements were recovered at Tomato Patch, including swans/geese/ducks (Anatidae), Common Murre (*Uria aalge*), cormorant (*Phalacrocorax* sp.), and owls (Strigidae), and at the North Wall Community, where elements of gull (*Larus* sp.), Chicken (*G. galus*), and generic birds were identified (Ballard 1995:210; Martinez 1998:149–150). Only a few elements of unidentified bird elements were recovered from CA-SON-670 and CA-SON-174 (Fenner 2002:26; Newquist 55). No bird remains are reported for CA-SON-1455 (Farris 1986:44).

The flotation analysis from Metini Village indicates that people processed wheat (*Triticum* spp.), barley (*Hordeum vulgare* cf.), California Poppy (*Eschscholzia* sp. cf.), bluegrass (*Poa* sp.cf.), knotweed/dock (*Polygonum/Rumex* sp.), and California Bay (*Umbellularia californica*), along with specimens from the pink (Caryophyllaceae cf.), legume (Fabaceae), grass (Poaceae), rose (Rosaceae cf.) and nightshade (Solanaceae cf.) families. Pea remains are also probably found at Metini Village. Unfortunately, charred ethnobotanical remains have yet to be fully identified from the other five sites. Initial analysis of the sediment samples from NAVS indicated poor recovery rates for burned plant remains (Lightfoot, Schiff, Martinez, et al. 1997). Some charred acorn nut fragments were recovered during the excavation of Tomato Patch, and on-going ethnobotanical analyses will provide further information on plant remains in the near future. Earlier field investigation at the North Wall Community summarized by Hannah Ballard did not include the flotation of sediment samples. Sara Gonzalez's ongoing analysis of sediment samples recovered from this area during her recent excavations will remedy the situation in the near future.

Food Processing

Metini Village residents appear to have maintained strong cultural continuities in how they processed meat and vegetable foods. Pomo chefs commonly employed underground earth ovens to cook meat dishes, such as shellfish and terrestrial game, along with acorn bread, buckeyes, and "Indian potatoes." As described in the ethnographic literature (Barrett 1952:61; Gifford 1967:20; Holmes 1975:22), these ovens consisted of small, bowl-shaped pits about 30 cm deep. The ovens were built outside houses for use in good weather and inside structures for use in inclement weather. The chefs built a fire in the pit to heat rocks, as well as to radiate the sides of the oven. After the fire burned down, the cooks laid down a layer of vegetable matter (such as seaweed, kelp, oak, or wild grape leaves, tule, etc.) on the hot rocks. Upon this vegetable mat, they then placed meat dishes, acorn bread, Indian potatoes, and other foods. Additional layers of hot rocks, seaweed/kelp or leaves, and meat/vegetable dishes were then stacked into the oven, the contents of which were covered with dirt. A fire might be built on top of the earth oven. The food cooked for at least five to six hours or overnight.

Archaeological investigations at Tomato Patch and NAVS indicate that underground earth ovens were a mainstay for cooking meat dishes (shellfish, terrestrial game, and sea mammal). Martinez (1998:159) excavated an earth oven in one of the pit features at Tomato Patch that consisted of a basin shaped concentration of fire-cracked rocks at 30–40 cm below surface. A concentration of charcoal, shellfish remains, and bone were found directly on top of the fire-cracked rocks. The use of underground ovens at NAVS was inferred from several lines of evidence associated with bone bed deposits. These deposits contained dense accumulations of relatively large fire-cracked rocks (5–15 cm in diameter), concentrations of terrestrial and sea mammal bones that exhibited little evidence of direct burning (only 1.7 to 1.9% of the faunal assemblage), the association of wood charcoal, and the correlation of shellfish, especially small species of mollusks that might be stranded on kelp and seaweed used for vegetable layers in earth ovens (Lightfoot, Schiff, Martinez, et al. 1997:404–406).

The evidence for earth ovens is more ambiguous at the North Wall Community, as few fire-cracked rocks were collected during archaeological excavations conducted by Donald Wood. Ballard (1995:149–150) believes the paucity of fire-cracked rock is a reflection of past recovery strategies that did not include the collection of this artifact type, a finding that is confirmed in Gonzalez's (2011:193–205) investigations at the site, which recovered dense accumulations of fire-cracked rocks, charcoal, and an assortment of fire-affected shellfish and other faunal remains in addition to a cooking feature that consisted of a platform of groundstone slabs surrounded by accumulations of charcoal. The evidence for earth ovens is ambiguous at CA-SON-670 and CA-SON-174 given the paucity of fire-cracked rock that was collected.

The archaeological findings at Metini Village strongly hint that local chefs probably continued to cook some meat dishes in underground earth ovens. The relatively large number of fire-cracked rocks (n=24) and ground stone other artifacts (n=10), which appear to be ground stone tools that have been recycled for use as "hot rocks," is suggestive of underground ovens. The combination of fire-cracked rocks and ground stone other artifacts comprise 83% (34 of 41) of the entire assemblage of other (non-chipped stone) lithic artifacts. The percentage of burned faunal bones is also low (about 10%), suggesting that meats were either filleted from the bone and then roasted or slow baked in earth ovens. There is also ample evidence of wood charcoal from local pine, Coast Redwood, and California Bay that could have been employed in earth ovens.

We also observed in the midden deposit evidence of burned daub that could have been the remains of an earth oven or some other architectural feature that had been thermally altered. However, the presence of fire-cracked rock, ground stone other artifacts, and wood charcoal may be indicative of other cooking methods. Small fire-cracked rocks and cobbles (fist size or smaller) may be indicative of the stone boiling method used for cooking gruels or soups in watertight baskets. Fire-cracked rock and wood charcoal may also be produced from hearths where terrestrial game and shellfish meats were cooked over embers or in the hot ashes of cooking fires (see Gifford 1967:16–21). Laplace's (Farris 2012b:251) description of the Kashaya Pomo village near the Ross settlement in August 1839 suggests that some meats were cooked directly over embers (see also Kostromitinov 1974:8).

> The majority were busy with the housekeeping, preparing meals for their husbands and children. Some were spreading out on the embers some pieces of beef given as rations, or shell-fish, or even fish which these unhappy creatures came to catch either at the nearby river [Fort Ross Creek?] or from the sea....

While the percentage of burned bone is relatively low at Metini Village (10%) it is still considerably higher than that for NAVS (1.7–1.9%). This may indicate a more common tendency for placing meat cuts directly over the fire or embers at Metini, or the deposition of bones directly into fires once the meat has been removed.

Although there is a tendency to find wild animal remains (primarily deer) in the north and central sections of the Metini Village midden (Figure 76), and domesticated faunal elements (e.g., cattle, sheep/goat) in the central and south areas of the midden (Figure 75), there is no indication that these meat cuts were processed differently based on the number of cut marks, evidence for burning, or associated materials found in the north or south areas of the midden. Fire-cracked rock, ground stone other artifacts, and wood charcoal appear to be dispersed throughout the midden deposit. It appears that terrestrial game and domesticated animals were probably cooked in underground ovens and on cooking fires, as described by Laplace and Kostromitinov.

The finding of charred seed remains, along with milling stones and a hopper mortar, are also consistent with observations of Kashaya culinary arts as observed during Russian colonial times and by later ethnographers. Small grass seeds were commonly parched in tightly woven winnowing baskets with glowing coals, then ground to a fine meal in hopper mortars with wooden or stone pestles (Barrett 1952:85–87; Gifford 1967:10–15). The resulting dry meal, known as pinole, could be made into cakes or balls, or added to other meats and dishes. Laplace (Farris 2012b:251) described the production of seed meal in his 1839 observations:

> ...while the others heated the [wheat] grain in a willow basket before grinding it between two stones. In the middle of this basket they shook constantly some live coals on which each grain passed rapidly by an ever more accelerated rotating movement until they were soon parched, without letting the inner side of the basket be burned by the fire.

It appears that a very similar process was probably employed at Metini Village in processing a variety of cultivated seeds (e.g., wheat, barley, peas) and wild plant seeds (California Poppy, bluegrass, knotweed/dock, legumes, grass, rose, and nightshade). California Bay seeds were probably roasted in hot ashes, hulled, and then the meat ground to a fine meal in a hopper mortar (Gifford 1967:13).

Dress

Archaeological evidence of dress and body ornamentation is limited to a relatively few classes of artifacts. Nonetheless, some interesting patterns are evident. All the sites exhibited assemblages of glass beads, primarily inexpensive, monochrome, undecorated embroidery beads, mostly drawn as hollow canes and then cut to length, with some exhibiting hot tumbled finishes.

A few wound bead types were also identified, but they are a small minority at any of the sites. White beads dominated in all the assemblages, while red, black, purple, and blue colors were also found in different proportions (Ballard 1995:150–152; Fenner 2002:34; Newquist 2002:45–54; Ross 1996, 1997). Ross (1996:223,1997:192–198) emphasized that the bead types found in Kashaya Pomo colonial contexts tend to be relatively inexpensive, undecorated embroidery beads that are associated with daily, secular contexts. He also notes that the combination of white, red, and black glass beads, in particular, may indicate the color preferences of Kashaya and Coast Miwok people, particularly women involved in inter-ethnic households.

As discussed by Elliot Blair, the glass beads recovered at Metini Village not only include some bead types that were later in age (red-on-white, Bohemian cut beads, at least one green colored uranium bead), but the color profile varied distinctly from the bead assemblages analyzed by Ross. At Metini Village the glass beads are dominated by white/clear beads, with smaller numbers of red and blue/green/purple beads, which is in contrast to the red and black bead colors identified by Ross as characteristic of Kashaya Pomo and Coast Miwok sites. The sample size at the Metini site is admittedly small, so this difference may not be significant, but it suggests the bead color scheme for Kashaya sites may be more complex than originally thought, and that color preferences may have changed over time or in different residential places. This observation is supported by the bead assemblage recovered from CA-SON-174, which is dominated by white beads, but also contains (in order of abundance) red-white, red-green, red-red, blue, black, opaque, red, and clear beads (Newquist 2002:53).

It is interesting that the varieties of shell beads and shell ornaments vary somewhat across the six sites. Abalone ornaments dominated early field work at the North Wall Community, where field crews also recovered three clam shell disk beads and six spire-lopped *Olivella* shell beads (Ballard 1995:196). Later excavations at this site by Gonzalez (2011) revealed 10 spire-lopped *Olivella* shell beads and 12 clam shell disc beads in addition to one piece of possibly ground abalone shell. While we found little evidence for abalone ornaments at NAVS (one abalone button), we did unearth 29 clam shell disk beads, three spire-removed *Olivella* shell beads, and one ground mussel umbo (Schiff 1997:332; Silliman 1997:161). The analysis of the shellfish assemblage from Tomato Patch identified 11 clam shell disk beads and *Olivella* shell beads in the midden deposit (Martinez 1998:146, 231). No shell beads were identified for the CA-SON-670 assemblage. Newquist (2002:38, 57–59, Appendix K) recorded eight shell disc beads (6 clam, 2 unidentified), one abalone pendant, and some possible spire lopped *Olivella* shell from CA-SON-174. At Metini Village we did not find any clam shell disk beads, but we did recover a small assemblage of spire-removed *Olivella* shell beads in addition to a worked, perforated abalone disc. The paucity of the worked shell objects at Metini Village may be a reflection of the small sample size of sediments that were excavated and fine screened.

Buttons are another artifact type that exhibited an intriguing distribution across the different colonial contexts. The investigation at Tomato Patch revealed one porcelain button (Martinez 1998:122). Two buttons were recovered from CA-SON-670: one appears to be a ceramic Prosser button and the other manufactured from metal (Fenner 2002:36). The buttons at NAVS consisted of five worked bone buttons (flat round disks with a single hole in the center), as well as eight brass/copper buttons and one brass button hook (Silliman 1997:163–164; Wake 1997a:256–259). Early investigations of the North Wall Community also exhibited six bone buttons, but these consisted of round disks, each of which has a four-hole pattern (Ballard 1995:191). Four brass buttons were also found, but two appear to be from modern jeans, as the artifacts are inscribed with "Can't Bust Em" and "Boss of the Road" (Ballard 1995:114, 121). Gonzalez's (2011) later investigation of this area recovered five glass buttons and one four-hole pattern bone button similar to those recovered from NAVS. The button assemblage from CA-SON-174 included five bone buttons, one abalone button, 62 Prosser buttons, 46 other ceramic buttons, 23 metal buttons (four embossed with military associated designs of stars, wreaths, and eagles), and some glass buttons (Newquist 2002:44, 57, 59, 71) We also unearthed ceramic Prosser and glass buttons at Metini Village (four-hole patterns, n=9), along with a worked bone button (five-hole pattern), a brass button (single-hole pattern), a US Army button cover, and an iron snap fastener.

NAVS also contained a series of beautifully incised bone tubes, made primarily from bird bones. These may have been used as ear spools. While some of the styles and designs may be associated with the Native Alaskan men and women, the worked bone artifacts with intricate cross hatching appear to be diagnostic of central California artistic imagery (Wake 1997a:258–261). None of these incised tubes are reported for Tomato Patch, the North Wall Community, CA-SON-670, CA-SON-174, or Metini Village.

Spatial Layout of Settlements

Previous investigations of late prehistoric sites along the Kashaya Pomo coast indicated a strong tendency for indigenous people to segregate their sites into spatially discrete residential areas that are separate from midden or trash areas. In designing village layouts with houses in upslope locations, occupants kept these places clean of debris, probably by sweeping houses regularly and removing the contents of hearths and earth ovens periodically. The detritus from daily living was then dumped into downslope middens that contained dense concentrations of shellfish and mammal remains, fire-cracked rock, ash, wood charcoal, and other materials (Lightfoot et al. 1991:116–119). While similar cultural prescriptions were followed in the construction and use of historical-era Indian villages, how these cultural practices manifested themselves varied in specific colonial contexts. The investigation of the North Wall Community, as reported by Ballard, did not involve areal surface collection, areal mapping, or geophysical survey. Gonzalez's (2011) subsequent geophysical survey, intensive surface collection of the site, and areal excavations at the North Wall area revealed the rock cobble foundations of timber-framed households dating to the Russian-period. These structures were associated with a dense concentration of shell midden and a variety of Native and European-manufactured artifacts, indicating that Native Californians lived in this locale and perhaps in the historically documented, multi-ethnic households with Russian and Creole employees of the colony. Unfortunately, the degree of preservation at the site does not allow for a detailed spatial analysis of trash disposal practices.

The spatial patterning of CA-SON-670 is not well understood. Fenner's (2002) plotting of archaeological materials using SURFER software indicates that shellfish remains are concentrated in the northeast edge of the site, while faunal remains are found here and in the southwest section of the site. Newquist's (2002) spatial plotting of archaeological remains from CA-SON-174 suggests that most of the shellfish remains, faunal elements, glass beads, buttons, and ground stone artifacts are concentrated in a midden deposit in the southern section of the site. However, chipped stone artifacts are distributed across the site area.

The areal investigation of Tomato Patch revealed a classic Kashaya pattern where upslope houses were kept clean of most trash, which was dumped in an extensive downslope midden deposit. Some lithic artifacts and ceramic sherds were found in and around the house structures, but most of the contents of hearths, ovens, and food preparation involving shellfish and faunal remains were dumped into the midden (Martinez 1998:132–133). A discrete lithic scatter is also situated to the east of the pit structures, but upslope from the midden deposit.

NAVS is characterized by a synergistic colonial spatial organization that integrates various components of Native Californian sensibilities with those of Native Alaskan sea mammal hunters. A series of shallow pit features were mapped in a north/south direction along the edge of the marine terrace. Based on the testing of these pit features, they appear to be the remains of small semi-subterranean house structures and associated middens. Our interpretation of the spatial pattern of NAVS is that it was a J-shaped village, with one to two tiers of houses built along the eastern edge of the marine terrace overlooking the Pacific Ocean. In the south area of the site, it appears that multiple tiers or rows of houses may have once existed. The central area of the site, based on geophysical survey, intensive surface collection, and selected excavation, is characterized by a paucity of midden deposits and artifacts in general. It appears to be an area that may have been kept intentionally clean, possibly for use as a plaza or open communal area (Lightfoot, Schiff, Martinez, et al. 1997:412–416).

We believe that the house structures and adjacent activity areas at NAVS were periodically swept clean following Kashaya Pomo principles of cleanliness and order. For example, house floors and associated extramural spaces tended to be clean of refuse. Even adjacent spaces containing fence lines, which tend to catch debris, were relatively sterile of material remains (Lightfoot et al. 1998:211–212). Domestic refuse was then discarded in nearby abandoned houses or dumped over the eastern slope of the marine terrace, into the nearby Fort Ross Beach Site (CA-SON-1898/H). However, we noted significant transformations in conventional Kashaya trash disposal patterns at NAVS. In using abandoned houses as dumps, people would eventually cap these places with clean fill and create new leveled surfaces. These new surfaces were then reused as external living space. This may reflect an accommodation to the packing of multiple households into a limited amount of space at NAVS, but is more likely a product of Native Alaskan principles of land use, where old trash surfaces were commonly capped with clean fill to create new spaces. This practice is well documented in the ethnographic record and archaeological investigations of indigenous people from Kodiak Island, Alaska, where many of the North Pacific workers in the Russian-American Company originated (Lightfoot et al. 1998:211–212; Lightfoot et al. 1997:410–416).

The residents of Metini Village incorporated various principles of space management and settlement design that are well documented for the Kashaya Pomo in late prehistoric and early colonial villages. Similar to Tomato Patch and NAVS, there is an unambiguous demarcation of space at Metini into areas kept clean of debris and areas where trash is placed. The clearly defined midden deposit, with an obvious boundary separating it from the rest of the clean zone, is a classic Kashaya Pomo pattern. However, it is not clear if residential spaces at Metini were kept clean, as the location of house structures remains unknown. But our current interpretation is that people may have built house structures near or along the eastern terrace edge where a variety of residential activities may have taken place. The 10–15 meter-wide strip along the eastern terrace edge that contains midden remains may have been a place where various food processing and production activities took place and/or an area designated for dumping refuse, including what may be the contents of earth ovens, hearths, and workshop debris.

Public Architecture

Since the large pit feature dominates the spatial layout of Metini Village, it is important to evaluate whether the other five sites contain similar kinds of architectural features, specifically those associated with public buildings, such as dance houses or sweat houses. The 1971 field investigation at CA-SON-670 did not appear to have recorded any known architectural features (Fenner 2002). Archaeological investigations at the North Wall Commmuity, as reported by Ballard, did not identify any large pit features or structural remains. Russian-era paintings depicting the area by Auguste Duhaut-Cilly (1828) and Ilya Gavrilovich Voznesenskii (1841) indicate that buildings were constructed along the north stockade wall, but they appear to be Russian-style wood buildings with gables and fenced areas for gardens. While these structures may be associated with individual households (possibly interethnic couples comprised of colonial men and Native Californian women), some may be larger structures employed as barracks or dormitories for workers, such as Native Californian laborers.

Gonzalez's (2011) investigation of this area revealed the remains of two Russian-period timber-framed house foundations in association with a rich shell-midden deposit consisting of a dense concentration of Russian-period ceramic and glass table wares; shellfish and other faunal remains; chipped stone and worked glass artifacts; glass beads; shell beads and deer astragali; fire-cracked rock; milling stones, pestles, and net weights; porcelain buttons; and ground ceramic pendants and tokens. While the nature of these deposits is such that Gonzalez could not determine who the residents of the households were (e.g., single Native Californian women documented in the 1836/1838 census records, Native Californian men employed as laborers, Native Californian women living with colonial men), there is sufficient evidence that Native Californians were living in and making use of this residential zone throughout the Russian and into the subsequent Mexican and American periods. There is no indication from either Gonzalez's recent work or from the Duhaut-Cilly and Voznesenskii paintings that a dance house or sweat house built in the traditional style of the Kashaya Pomo was located in this residential space.

Our archaeological investigation at NAVS did not reveal any surface pit features of the size or depth of the one mapped at Metini Village. None of the 13 mapped surface features measured much over five meters in diameter. Our excavations of what we interpreted as semi-subterranean structures also indicated relatively modest floor spaces, certainly not on the order of the Metini pit feature (Lightfoot, Schiff, Martinez, et al. 1997:410–412). We did not identify any archaeological feature at NAVS that may have functioned as public architecture. It is possible that the central area's clean zone may have served as communal space or plaza for village gatherings and ceremonies. We speculated in the NAVS volume that some geophysical features found near this space may mark the location of a structure that may have served some form of public or ceremonial purpose, but this area has not yet been ground-truthed (Lightfoot, Schiff, Martinez, et al. 1997:416).

The mapping, geophysical survey, and excavation at Tomato Patch revealed four surface depressions. One (D2) of the small depressions is the earth oven described earlier. Two other features (D3 and D4) appear to be residential structures. The fourth depression (D4) is larger than the others, measuring about ten meters in diameter. However, Martinez's analysis of architectural elements and contents of the structure suggests that it is secular in use, and probably not employed as public architecture (neither as a dance house or a sweat house)

(Martinez 1998:131–132). It appears to have been one of the large semi-subterranean lodges as described by Barrett and various Russian-American Company accounts.

Glenn Farris' 1983 field investigation of CA-SON-174 revealed architectural evidence of the foreman's/Carlos Call's residence that consisted of sandstone slabs, milled redwood timber remains, and brick fragments (Newquist
2002:23). No other features are identified except the midden deposit unearthed in the southern section of the grid system. Three pit depressions have
been mapped southwest of the excavation area on the other side of old Highway 1. Two of the features measure about eight m in diameter, while the other
is about six m across (Lightfoot et al. 1991:69–70). The size of these features
suggest they may be semi-subterranean lodges or sweat houses (Barrett 1975).
Interestingly, systematic surface collections undertaken in this place detected
a "clean" area that contains only of a sparse amount of lithic artifacts and
shellfish remains.

Summary

The comparison of Metini Village with four nearby sites (Tomato Patch,
North Wall Community, NAVS, and CA-SON-670) where indigenous people experienced the earlier Russian mercantile program in distinctive colonial
contexts indicates cultural processes of both cultural continuity and transformation. A fifth site, CA-SON-174, provided a comparison with a similarly
aged village associated with the Benitz Rancho. Clearly, significant changes in
material practices took place among the Kashaya Pomo people from their initial cultural contact with the Russian-American Company in the early 1800s
to their integration into the Benitz Rancho complex in the 1840s–1860s. Major transformations took place in the types of raw materials employed in the
manufacture of tools and cultural objects, the kinds of plant foods and meat
dishes consumed, items of dress, and even possibly the re-creation of new kinds
of public architecture that had not been seen in the region in earlier colonial
times. However, despite these changes manifested in the archaeological record, it is clear that the Kashaya Pomo maintained their core cultural values
and principles in negotiating their daily lives after decades of living and working within settler colonial contexts.

In the analysis of Metini Village, change and continuity cannot be viewed
as mutually exclusive concepts, but rather as two sides of the same process that
enabled the Kashaya Pomo to survive and persist as successive waves of colonists
invaded their homeland (e.g., Panich 2013; Silliman 2009; Stahl 2012; Vizenor
2008). As Native residents at Ross and the Benitz Rancho incorporated new
raw materials, foods, and cultural practices into the fabric of their daily life, they
employed their core values and principles as cultural templates for modifying

and transforming these foreign goods and practices so that they would fit within the Indian community. The craftspeople at Metini were replacing obsidian with glass in the production of sharp edged tools and objects. At CA-SON-174 there was also an increasing recycling of glass to produce tools for village life, but there was a greater continuity in the use of obsidian than found at Metini. At both sites similar production methods (percussion techniques, some pressure flaking) as employed in the construction of expedient lithic tools were now used in the manufacture of glass objects. The increasing use of glass from sturdy alcohol bottles also allowed for greater use of expedient sharp edged glass sherds that could be used with little to no modification.

The residents of Metini Village and CA-SON-174 incorporated greater proportions of domesticated foods into their menu. However, there is little evidence that the beef and mutton cuts employed by the Kashaya Pomo were treated any differently from other large terrestrial game—they appear to have been cooked in underground ovens, mixed with gruel using the hot rocks method, or placed on embers in hearths. Similarly, the wheat and barley found at Metini Village was probably prepared and cooked in a similar fashion as other wild seeds that were processed by parching in baskets and grinding into a fine meal using hopper mortars. The vertebrate faunal remains from CA-SON-174 are a little more ambiguous since some of the remains may date to the later processing and consumption of animals by Carlos Call's household or the previous Call Ranch foreman. It is interesting that the deer from this site appear to have been butchered using a knife or other sharp object, while the beef cuts were processed using saws or choppers.

New forms of western dress appear to have been adopted by the residents of Metini Village, including possible work jeans and shirts with glass and ceramic buttons. Glass pane pieces and wrought and cut nails suggest that new architectural innovations may also have been incorporated at the village, and it is possible that new kinds of western building techniques were employed in the construction of some residential architecture. While new forms of architectural innovations were most certainly included in the village, the spatial layout of Metini Village, with its clear demarcation of the midden deposit and clean zone, appears to be built upon principles of settlement organization that have ancient roots in Kashaya Pomo cultural practices. Again the buttons, other clothing accessories, and architectural remains found at CA-SON-174 are more difficult to interpret as they might be associated with the Native laborers working at the Benitz Rancho or by later people associated with the Call Ranch.

There is some uncertainty about whether the dance house identified at Metini Village is a relatively new building innovation or the re-creation of an architectural form that has ancient roots among the Kashaya Pomo, but one which had not been seen in the local area for several decades since the coming of the Russian merchants. In either case, the dance house served as a centralized place where ceremonies, dances, feasts, and curing practices took place—cultural activities that have been employed among the Kashaya Pomo since ancient times (many of which no doubt occurred across the *Metini* region, the ancestral homeland of the tribal community). We believe the dance house would have played an important integrative function for the greater Kashaya Pomo community; periodic ceremonies and dances would have drawn together people from across the region for assemblies and communal gatherings. Location of such a structure at Metini Village is a tangible mark of the special and sacred nature of this specific place within the Kashaya's homeland at which the contemporary tribal community continues to gather and assemble.

We note that much of the archaeological site of CA-SON-175 is comprised of the clean zone and the large pit feature, places that exhibit little evidence for the daily domestic activities of residential living. Consequently, most of the residential space appears to be segregated to a strip of space along the eastern terrace edge. The functions of the three large surface depressions at CA-SON-174 are not clear at this time. They appear to be too small to be dance houses based on Barrett's (1975) ethnographic description though they may have served as sweat houses or some other special kind of architectural feature. It is interesting that the area around these structures is relatively clean based on the findings of our surface collection in 1988.

Given the relatively limited space for residential use at Metini Village it is hard to imagine that all 161 Indians counted in the 1848 census for the Benitz Rancho would have resided at Metini Village. No doubt some were living at CA-SON-174 and possibly other nearby locations, especially along the terrace edges of Fort Ross Creek beyond Metini Village or in the area of the North Wall Community.

The 1848 Presidio Ross census may provide some idea about the number of people residing at different settlements. The four chiefs in the census are listed separately followed by the names of single adults and couples with children. Our interpretation is that the chief is listed first followed by the people associated with that particular political leader. The breakdown of the census is as follows: Chief Tojon and his wife are listed with eight couples, one adult, and eight children for a total of 27 people. Chief Noportegi and his wife are listed with 12 couples, five adults, and 19 children for a total of 50 people. Chief Cojoto and his wife are listed with 11 couples, four adults, and seven children for a total of 35 people. Chief Kola-biscau and his wife are listed with 16 couples, two adults, and 13 children for a total of 49 people. Thus, the Benitz Rancho Indian workforce in 1848 (four chiefs and their wives, 47 couples, 12 single adults, and 47 children) appears to be separated into four groups ranging in size from 27 to 50 people. This finding suggests that Metini Village, CA-SON-174, and other places may have been populated by groups of 27 to 50 people, or combinations of these numbers if more than one chief and his people lived in a specific village or residential place.

In addition to the Indian workers and their families recorded in the 1848 Presidio Ross census who lived at CA-SON-174, CA-SON-175 and nearby, other Kashaya Pomo Indians probably continued to reside in the more distant hinterland. Given that the Kashaya Pomo people were probably dispersed across the regional landscape during the Benitz Rancho period, periodic gatherings and assemblies at the Metini Village dance house would have been crucial for keeping the larger Kashaya Pomo community together.

The critical role that religious practices have played in keeping the Kashaya Pomo integrated as a viable and vibrant Indian community has been masterfully penned by Mary Jean Kennedy (1955). She showed how later religious innovations, including the creation of the Bole-Maru ceremonies, led to the replacement of the semi-subterranean earth-covered dance houses with above-ground, redwood-planked round houses. These new religious practices, built upon the foundations of ancient beliefs among the Kashaya Pomo, involved women prophets (including Annie Jarvis and Essie Parrish) who were critical forces in keeping the Kashaya Pomo together as a united people during the difficult times of the early-to-mid 1900s. We believe that the dance or round house at Metini Village represents an earlier manifestation of this later religious revitalization created by the Kashaya Pomo, which confronted and ameliorated the long-term effects of sustained, settler colonialism.

Chapter 8

Conclusion

The archaeological investigation of Metini Village, funded by the National Science Foundation and supported by the California Department of Parks and Recreation and the Archaeological Research Facility at UC Berkeley, was a collaborative endeavor involving tribal elders and scholars of the Kashaya Pomo, archaeologists and rangers from California State Parks, and archaeologists and students from UC Berkeley. The primary goals of the archaeological investigation were twofold. One was to create an updated map and recording of the site that could be employed by managers at the Fort Ross State Historic Park to aid in the further protection and preservation of this important place. The other goal was to enhance the interpretative program at the park by highlighting the significance of Metini Village in the history of the region. Specifically, the study offered an exceptional opportunity to examine how the Kashaya Pomo negotiated, persisted, and survived sustained colonialism over many decades of close entanglements with two distinctive colonial settlements and regimes. Local Native peoples were thrown together with the Russian merchants of Colony Ross who unexpectedly showed up on their doorstep in 1812; with the abandonment of the region by the Russians in 1841, they then tangled with the creation of a successful rancho enterprise that reached its zenith in the 1850s and 1860s.

Fieldwork undertaken in 1998 and 1999 was specifically designed for the study of a sacred site that was protected and preserved in a California state park. Working closely with Kashaya Pomo elders and scholars and California State Park archaeologists, we employed a multi-phased field strategy that began with low-impact methods designed specifically to produce the least amount of disturbance to ancestral archaeological remains while gaining substantial knowledge about the extent and scope of Kashaya settlement at the site. The purpose of these initial investigations of surface and shallow surface deposits was to better understand the spatial layout and site structure of Metini Village. Based on the results of these low-impact field investigations, and in close consultation with members of our inclusive research team, we then focused our research on a few selected places where subsurface investigations, designed as surgically precise excavations, were initiated. Our multi-phased methodology, which included topographic mapping, geophysical survey (e.g., gradiometer, soil conductivity), intensive surface collection, and limited excavations (three 1-by-1 m units), produced a diverse assemblage of artifacts, including lithics (chipped stone, ground stone, and other lithic artifacts), glass objects (vessel glass, flat glass, glass beads), worked glass tools, ceramics, and metal objects, along with faunal specimens (shellfish, fish, mammals) and floral remains.

The findings from the laboratory analysis and spatial investigation of the archaeological materials from Metini Village were employed to address four research issues. In addressing the first issue concerning the chronology of CA-SON-175, we found that the primary occupation at Metini Village probably took place in the 1850s and 1860s, and was contemporaneous with the Benitz Rancho. It is possible that the site may also have been used in the 1830s and early 1840s in the latter phase of the Russian-American Company's tenure at Colony Ross, and then occasionally revisited and even reused by Kashaya Pomo people in the post-1873 period, when the Call family operated their ranching enterprise. We observed little archaeological evidence for earlier pre-colonial occupation of the site area.

The second research issue involved the spatial structure of Metini Village: How was the settlement laid out, where were domestic and religious structures situated, where did food processing and consumption take place, and where did different kinds of activities occur? The archaeological investigations identified three primary spatial components of the settlement: the large pit feature, the midden area, and the so-called "clean zone." Our interpretation of the large pit feature suggested that it was a small dance house, possibly constructed about 1857. We believe the building was employed as a communal structure for bringing the broader Kashaya Pomo community together for dances, spiritual prayers, and healing ceremonies. Significantly, the pit feature at Metini Village appears to have been the first dance house built in the local region in post-contact times, as no such structures were described during Russian colonial times. It is probable that earlier earth covered, semi-subterranean dance house structures were commonly used by the Kashaya Pomo in prehistoric times, and possibly even built in early historic times but beyond the reaches of the Russian-American Company; however, this question is beyond the scope of this volume. What is clear, however, is that more permanent dance houses were not observed in Indian villages near Colony Ross during Russian colonial times (1812–1841).

Our analysis of the midden area directly east of the dance house reveals that this space was probably used by Metini Village residents to perform many of their mundane domestic tasks (food processing, cooking, tool production) along the terrace edge facing Fort Ross Creek. We believe that terrestrial game, shellfish, and plant foods were cooked in hearths, earth ovens, and probably water tight baskets along this terrace edge. After the consumption of meals, discarded food and the contents of the hearths and ovens were dumped down the adjacent terrace slope. We also believe that the debitage from lithic and glass tool production was probably produced along the terrace edge and also discarded down the terrace slope. While we suspect these domestic activities took place near residential structures, we have found only circumstantial evidence (e.g., possible house pits recorded by Edward Gifford, nails, window glass) for the possible existence of structures near or along the terrace edge. If structures were built, we suspect that a diverse range of winter and summer architectural styles may have been employed.

The "clean zone" refers to the site area beyond the midden deposit and pit feature that was almost totally devoid of artifacts and faunal remains. We argue that this area may have been kept intentionally clean and that it may have been a sacred area associated with the dance house for outdoor dances and large gatherings of people. Our study suggests that Metini Village was not part of a larger archaeological manifestation that was once linked directly with the North Wall Community before being separated by the rerouting of Highway 1. The density of archaeological materials declines precipitously along the southern and northern edges of the Metini and North Wall Community sites, respectively, and both areas are characterized by distinctive chronologies and specific types of glass beads, obsidian/chert artifact ratios, and worked glass artifacts. We view the Metini Village and North Wall Community as distinctive places with diverse and independent occupational histories.

The third research issue explored how the Kashaya Pomo fared as colonial laborers. Our original intent was to compare the processes and outcomes of two different colonial enterprises on Metini Village occupants who served as laborers initially for the Russian-American Company and then later for the Benitz Rancho. However the proposed comparison was not possible given that the primary occupation of Metini Village dates to the 1850s and 1860s. The archaeological findings support written sources that suggest William Benitz provided his Indian workers with rations and possibly access to store-bought goods. Faunal remains recovered from the site suggest that live cattle may have been given to the workers, who then processed the animals on site and then cooked and consumed the meat at Metini Village. Other foods that may have been rationed to the workers include sheep/goat, wheat, barley, and possibly peas, which appear to have been processed and consumed on the site. The rationed goods were then supplemented with plants and animals gathered, hunted, and fished in the nearby environs for use as foods, medicines, and raw materials. The consistent finding of fragments of heavy-duty glass alcohol bottles on the site suggests that William Benitz may have also been providing his Indian laborers with alcohol, a practice suggested by an 1880 anonymous report cited by Kennedy (1955:77). It is also possible that some glass containers and ceramic vessels were provided to Metini residents, either as rations or as payment for work performed. Of course, some of these materials may have been second hand goods from the Benitz family that were either given to the laborers or were recycled from nearby rancho dumps. The discovery of glass and ceramic buttons and buttons from work clothes suggests that some western clothing may have been given to the Indian workers or that they had access to store-bought goods. Some archaeological finds, such as wrought and cut nails, fencing material, the iron ripper plow blade, and the shovel, may also be indicative of the tools used by the Indian workers on the Benitz Rancho.

Overall the archaeological findings do not dispute the written accounts that suggest William Benitz and his family treated the Native workers relatively well. It appears that he provided rationed goods to his laborers and allowed them to continue some of their traditional hunting and gathering practices while residing at Metini Village. The existence of the small dance house indicates that Benitz was tolerant of Native religious practices and periodic tribal gatherings at the village. In addition, the Native workers appear to have had access to some store-bought goods, such as western work clothes, glass containers, and ceramic vessels. Alcohol rations may also have been provided to the workers, though this practice is regarded by Kashaya elders and scholars as indicative of the ill treatment of Kashaya at the rancho. For example, tribal elders and scholars working on the archaeological project noted that their oral traditions indicated that some of their ancestors had been given alcohol to make them more subservient and dependent as colonial laborers. Tribal consultations emphasized that this colonial practice had a detrimental, long-term impact on many Indian families who experienced alcoholism and diseases resulting from alcohol dependency.

The final research issue addressed how the Kashaya Pomo maintained their core values and Indian community over the course of many decades of sustained colonialism. Our comparison of Metini Village with the North Wall Community, NAVS, Tomato Patch, and CA-SON-670—places where earlier colonial entanglements with the Russian enterprise played out—indicates both change and continuity in the life ways and cultural practices of the Kashaya Pomo who worked for the Benitz Rancho. Our comparison of Metini Village to CA-SON-174 provided an opportunity to examine the archaeological assemblage of a similarly aged Native village associated with the Benitz Rancho. In comparing the earlier pre-colonial and early colonial sites with Metini Village and CA-SON-174, we found that significant changes took place in the types of raw materials employed in the manufacture of tools and cultural objects, the kinds of plant and animal foods consumed, the items of dress that were worn, and even possibly the re-creation of new kinds of religious structures that had not been seen in the region for several decades. Many of these changes speak to the long-term, significant impacts of colonialism upon Kashaya exchange networks, mobility on the landscape, and increasing dependence upon European and American wage and labor economies. However, most of these material transformations were mediated and articulated through the cultural values and principles of the Kashaya Pomo.

New kinds of raw materials, such as glass, were now worked using methods that had been honed by the Kashaya Pomo for many centuries, such as in the production of stone tools. New foods, such as beef, mutton, wheat, and barley, were cooked using techniques and recipes that had been created and tasted by Kashaya chefs over many generations. While new artifacts (nails, window pane) and forms of architecture may have been incorporated into the settlement, the Kashaya employed age-old principles to integrate these elements into the overall village spatial organization.

We agree with Mary Jean Kennedy that a critical factor in how the Kashaya maintained their core cultural practices and sanity during the later years of colonialism was their religious practices and communal ceremonies. In recognizing the important role that women spiritual leaders played in keeping the Kashaya Pomo together as an Indian nation in the twentieth century, we argue that this process of religious integration in the face of sustained, settler colonialism may first be observed at Metini Village in 1850s and 1860s. We interpret the pit feature as a dance house whose architectural form had not been seen in the Colony Ross region for many decades until its construction in or about 1857. The building of the dance house may have represented a concerted effort to keep the Kashaya Pomo community together through periodic communal gatherings involving rituals, dances, singing, and feasts. It is very possible that the three large pit structures at CA-SON-174, which may have served as sweat houses, may have also played a similar integrative purpose. The importance of Metini Village as a religious place that had sacred significance to the Kashaya Pomo may be reflected in the possible reuse of this place for spiritual observances or even larger gatherings and ceremonies in post-1870 times, during the Call family ranching days, and later into the twentieth century.

Viewed from this perspective, Metini Village may represent a significant turning point in the history of the Kashaya Pomo people. Here, for the first time, we see the clear manifestation of a strategy that the Kashaya successfully employed to maintain their Indian community and cultural values in the face of European, Mexican, and American settler colonialism. This strategy involved a return to the basics of life, a spiritual renewal through the teachings of religious leaders, and periodic communal assemblies that would bring the entire community together. This strategy was first implemented during colonial times at Metini Village. It was later employed successfully by the Kashaya at Haupt's Ranch, and at their federally recognized Stewarts Point Rancheria under the spiritual guidance of Annie Jarvis and Essie Parrish. Maintaining this connection to both homeland and ancestral village endures into the present, as elders and community members continue to visit Metini Village and pass on the oral histories and oral traditions that bind them to this place. It also continues through various communal ceremonies, picnics, and gatherings that periodically bring together members of the Kashaya Pomo as a tribal community across their tribal territory, including Fort Ross.

References

Allan, James McGhie, III
2001   Forge and Falseworks: An Archaeological Investigation of the Russian American Company's Industrial Complex at Colony Ross. Ph.D dissertation, Department of Anthropology, University of California, Berkeley.

Ames, Kenneth M.
2005   *The North Coast Prehistory Project Excavations in Prince Rupert Harbour, British Columbia: The Artifacts.* British Archaeological Reports, International Series 1342, Oxford.

Andrefsky, William
1998   *Lithics: Macroscopic Approaches to Analysis.* New York: Cambridge University Press.

Atchley, Sara
1990   An Analysis of the Fort Ross Archaelogical Project Glass Trade Beads. Senior Honors Thesis, Department of Anthropology, University of California, Berkeley.

Ballard, Hannah S.
1995   Searching for Metini: Synthesis and Analysis of Unreported Archaeological Collections from Fort Ross State Historic Park, California. Senior Honors Thesis, Department of Anthropology, University of California, Berkeley.

1997   Ethnicity and Chronology at Metini, Fort Ross State Historic Park, California. In *The Archaeology of Russian Colonialism in the North and Tropical Pacific,* edited by P. R. Mills and A. Martinez, pp. 116–140. vol. 81. Kroeber Anthropological Society, Berkeley, California.

Barrett, Samuel A.
1908   *The Ethno-Geography of the Pomo and Neighboring Indians.* University of California Publications in American Archaeology and Ethnology 6. University of California, Berkeley, California.

1952   *Material Aspects of Pomo Culture, Part One and Two.* Bulletin of the Public Museum of the City of Milwaukee 20. Public Museum of the City of Milwaukee, Milwaukee, Wisconsin.

1975   Pomo Buildings. In *Seven Early Accounts of the Pomo Indians and Their Culture,* edited by R. F. Heizer, pp. 37–63. Archaeological Research Facility, University of California, Berkeley, California.

Beck, Horace C.
    1928   Classification and Nomenclature of Beads and Pendants. *Archaeologia* 77:1–76.

Benitz, Anthony
    1852   Letter Dated March 14, 1852. Copy of Letter on File, Bancroft Library, University of California, Berkeley. Benitz Family Letters 1852–1863, Banc MSS 76/58c.

Benitz, William
    1856   Letter Dated September 2, 1856. Copy of Letter on File, Bancroft Library, University of California, Berkeley. Benitz Family Letters 1852–1863, Banc MSS 76/58c.

Benitz, William
    1863   Letter Dated October 7, 1863. Copy of Letter on File, Bancroft Library, University of California, Berkeley. Benitz Family Letters 1852–1863, Banc MSS 76/58c.

Bennyhoff, James A. and Richard E. Hughes
    1987   Shell Bead and Ornament Exchange Networks Between California and the Western Great Basin. *Anthropological Papers of the American Museum of Natural History* 64(2):79–175.

Billeck, William T.
    2008   Red-on-White Drawn or Cornelian Beads: A 19th-Century Temporal Marker for the Plains. *Beads* 20:49–61.

Blair, Elliot H.
    2011   Appendix B: Report on Glass Beads Recovered from the North Wall Site at Fort Ross. In *Creating Trails from Traditions: The Kashaya Pomo Interpretive Trail at Fort Ross State Historic Park*, by Sara Lynae Gonzalez. Ph.D dissertation, Department of Anthropology, University of California, Berkeley.

Blair, Elliot H., Lorann S. A. Pendleton and Peter Francis, Jr.
    2009   The Beads of St. Catherines Island. In *Anthropological Papers of the American Museum of Natural History*, Vol. 89. American Museum of Natural History, New York.

Brackett, Claudia, Julia Kleyman and David McMahan
    2008   Exploring Russian American Trade Through Comparison of Chemical XRF Signatures of Glass from Colonial Russian Sites in Alaska and the *Tal'Tsinka* Factory in Central Siberia. Paper presented at the 9th International Conference on NDT of Art, Jerusalem, Israel.

Brill, Robert H.
    1964   Application of Fission-Track Dating to Historic and Prehistoric Glasses. *Archaeometry* 7(1):51–57.

Bychkov, Oleg V.
    1997   The Origin of Colonial Glass Production in Irkutsk Research Perspectives. *Kroeber Anthropological Society Papers* 81:42–49.

Castillo, Edward D.
  1978   The Impact of Euro-American Exploration and Settlement. In *Handbook of North American Indians: Volume 8, California*, edited by R. F. Heizer, pp. 99–127. Smithsonian Institution, Washington, D.C.

Cook, Sherburne F.
  1976   *The Conflict Between the California Indian and White Civilization.* University of California Press, Berkeley, California.

Corney, Peter
  1896   *Voyages in the Northern Pacific: Narratives of Several Trading Voyages from 1813 to 1818, between the Northwest Coast of America, the Hawaiian Islands and China, with a Description of the Russian Establishments on the Northwest Coast.* Thomas G. Thrum, Honolulu, Hawaii.

Crowell, Aron L.
  1997   *Archaeology and the Capitalist World System: A Study from Russian America.* Plenum Press, New York.

Cuthrell, Rob Q.
  2013   An Eco-Archaeological Study of Late Holocene Indigenous Foodways and Landscape Managment Practices at Quiroste Valley Cultural Preserve, San Mateo County, California. Ph.D dissertation, Department of Anthropology, University of California, Berkeley.

Darko, Emily M.
  2007   When Life Gives You Glass: An Analysis of Worked Glass Recovered from the Metini Village Site at Fort Ross State Historic Park. Senior Honors Thesis, Department of Anthropology, University of California, Berkeley.

Davis, M. K., T. L. Jackson, M. S. Shackley, T. Teague, and J. H. Hampel
  1998   Factors Affecting the Energy-Dispersive X-Ray Fluorescence (EDXRF) Analysis of Archaeological Obsidian. In *Archaeological Obsidian Studies: Method and Theory*, edited by M. S. Shackley, pp. 159–180. Plenum Press, New York.

Diamond, Joseph E.
  2009   Analysis of Historical Artifacts. In *Archaeological Laboratory Methods: An Introduction*, edited by M. Q. Sutton and B. S. Arkush, pp. 165–240. Kendall/Hunt Publishing Company, Dubuque, Iowa.

Dobyns, Henry F.
  1983   *Their Number Become Thinned: Native American Populations Dynamics in Eastern North America.* University of Tennessee Press, Knoxville, Tennessee.

  1991   New Native World: Links Between Demographic and Cultural Changes. In *Columbian Consequences: Volume 3, The Spanish Borderlands in Pan-American Perspective*, edited by D. H. Thomas, pp. 541–560. Smithsonian Institute Press, Washington, D.C.

Dovgalyuk, N. P. and L. V. Tataurova
  2010   Glass Beads from Russian Villages in the Middle Irtysh Area with Reference to the Trade Links of Russian Settlers in 17th–18th Century Siberia. *Archaeology, Ethnology and Anthropology of Eurasia* 38(2):37–45.

Dunnell, Robert C.

    1991   Methodological Impacts of Catastrophic Depopulation on American Archaeology and Ethnology. In *Columbian Consequences: Volume 3, The Spanish Borderlands in Pan-American Perspective*, edited by D. H. Thomas, pp. 561–580. Smithsonian Institute Press, Washington, D.C.

Eschmeyer, William N., E. S. Herald and H. Hamman

    1983   A Field Guide to Pacific Coast Fishes of North America. Houghton Mifflin Co., Boston, Massachusetts.

Farris, Glenn J.

    1981   *Preliminary Report of the 1981 Excavations of the Fort Ross Warehouse.* Manuscript on file, California Department of Parks and Recreation, Sacramento, California.

    1983   *Archaeological Excavations Related to the Construction of the Fort Ross Visitor's Center, Fort Ross State Historic Park, Sonoma County, California.* Manuscript on file, California Department of Parks and Recreation, Sacramento, California.

    1986   *Cultural Resource Survey at the Fort Ross Campground, Sonoma County, California.* Manuscript on file, California Department of Parks and Recreation, Sacramento, California.

    1989   The Russian Imprint on the Colonization of California. In *Columbian Consequences, Volume 1: Archaeological and Historical Perspectives on the Spanish Borderlands West*, edited by D. H. Thomas, pp. 481–498. Smithsonian Institution Press, Washington, D.C.

    1990   Archaeology of the Old "Magasin" at Ross Counter, California. *Proceedings of the Second International Conference on Russian America.* Sitka, Alaska.

    1992   Russian Trade Beads Made in Irkutsk, Siberia. *The Bead Forum* 21:2–3.

    1997   Historical Archaeology of the Native Alaskan Village Site. In *The Archaeology and Ethnohistory of Fort Ross, California. Volume 2: The Native Alaskan Neighborhood: A Multiethnic Community at Colony Ross*, edited by K. G. Lightfoot, A. M. Schiff and T. A. Wake, pp. 129–135. Contributions of the University of California Archaeological Research Facility No. 55. Archaeological Research Facility, Berkeley, California.

    2012a   *So Far From Home: Russians in Early California.* Heyday, Berkeley, California

    2012b   Cyrille Pierre-Théodore Laplace's Visit to Bodega Bay and Fort Ross (1839). In *So Far From Home: Russians in Early California*, edited by G. J. Farris, pp. 235–267. Heyday, Berkeley, California.

Fenner, Morgan

    2002   An Analysis of the Occupants of CA-SON-670/H at Fort Ross State Historic Park. Senior Honors Thesis, Department of Anthropology, University of California, Berkeley.

Francis, Peter, Jr.
1994   Beads at the Crossroads of Continents. In *Anthropology of the North Pacific Rim*, edited by W. W. Fitzhugh and V. Chaussonnet, pp. 281–305. Smithsonian Institution Press, Washington D.C.

Fredrickson, David A.
1989   Spatial and Temporal Patterning of Obsidian Materials in the Geysers Region. In *Current Directions in California Obsidian Studies*, edited by R. Hughes, pp. 95–110. Contributions of the University of California Archaeological Research Facility No. 48. Archaeological Research Facility, Berkeley, California.

Fredrickson, David A. and Thomas M. Origer
2002   Obsidian Hydration in the Borax Lake Basin, Lake County, California. In *Essays in California Archaeology: A Memorial to Franklin Fenenga*, edited by W. J. Wallace and F. A. Riddell, pp. 148–165. Contributions of the University of California Archaeological Research Facility No. 60. Archaeological Research Facility, Berkeley, California.

Gibson, James R.
1976   *Imperial Russia in Frontier America: The Changing Geography of Supply of Russian America, 1784–1867*. Oxford University Press, New York.

Gibson, Robert O.
1992   An Introduction to the Study of Aboriginal Beads from California. Pacific Coast Archaeological Society Quarterly 28(3)1–45.

Gifford, Edward W.
1947   California Shell Artifacts. *Anthropological Records* 9(1):1–132. University of California Press, Berkeley, Callifornia.

1967   Ethnographic Notes on the Southwestern Pomo. *University of California Anthropological Records* 25:1–48. University of California Press, Berkeley, Callifornia.

Gobalet, Kenneth W.
1997   Fish Remains from the Early 19th Century Native Alaskan Habitation at Fort Ross. In *The Archaeology and Ethnohistory of Fort Ross, California. Volume 2: The Native Alaskan Neighborhood: A Multiethnic Community at Colony Ross*, edited by K. G. Lightfoot, A. M. Schiff and T. A. Wake, pp. 319–327. Contributions of the University of California Archaeological Research Facility No. 55. Archaeological Research Facility, Berkeley, California.

Goldstein, Lynne
2012   The Cemetery at Fort Ross: What Does it Tell Us About Those Who Lived Here? *Proceedings of the Society for California Archaeology* 26:234–242.

Goldstein, Lynne and Robert A. Brinkmann
2003[2008]   The Context of the Cemetery at Fort Ross: Multiple Lines of Evidence, Multiple Research Questions. *Pacific Coast Archaeological Society Quarterly* 39(4):1–21.

Golovnin, Vasilli M.

1979   *Around the World on the Kamchatka 1817–1819.* Translated by E. L. Wiswell. The Hawaiian Historical Society and The University Press of Hawaii, Honolulu, Hawaii.

Gonzalez, Sara L., Darren Modzelewski, Lee M. Panich and Tsim D. Schneider

2006   Archaeology for the Seventh Generation. *American Indian Quarterly* 30(3/4):388–415.

Gonzalez, Sara L.

2011   Creating Trails From Tradition: The Kashaya Pomo Interpretive Trail at Fort Ross State Historic Park. Ph.D dissertation, Department of Anthropology, University of California, Berkeley.

2016   Indigenous Values and Methods in Archaeological Practice: Low-Impact Archaeology through the Kashaya Pomo Interpretive Trail Project. *American Antiquity* 81(3):533–549.

Grayson, Donald K.

1978   Minimum Numbers and Sample Size in Vertebrate Faunal Analysis. *American Antiquity* 43(1):53–65.

Halpern, Abraham M.

1988   *Southeastern Pomo Ceremonials: The Kuksu Cult and its Successors.* Anthropological Records 29. University of California Press, Berkeley, California.

Hart, Siobhan M.

2012   Decolonizing through Heritage Work in the Pocumtuck Homeland of Northeastern North America. In *Decolonizing Indigenous Histories: Exploring Prehistoric/Colonial Transitions in Archaeology*, edited by M. Oland, S. M. Hart and L. Frink, pp. 86–109. University of Arizona Press, Tucscon, Arizona.

Heizer, Robert F. and Alan F. Almquist

1971   *The Other Californians: Prejudice and Discrimination under Spain, Mexico, and the United States to 1920.* University of California Press, Berkeley.

Henley, Thomas J.

1857   No. 100 Office of Superintendent Indians Affairs. In *Report of the Commissoner of Indian Affairs, Accompanying the Annual Report of the Secretary of the Interior for the Year 1856*, edited by H. G. W. Manypenny, pp. 236–246. A.O.P Nicholson, Printer, Washington, D.C.

Holmes, W. H.

1975   Pomo Reservation, Mendocino County (1902). In *Seven Early Accounts of the Pomo Indians and their Culture*, edited by R. F. Heizer, pp. 21–23. Archaeological Research Facility, University of California, Berkeley, California.

Jackson, Robert H.

1984   Gentile Recruitment and Population Movements in the San Francisco Bay Missions. *Journal of California and Great Basin Anthropology* 6(2):225–239.

Jackson, Thomas L.
 1989   Late Prehistoric Obsidian Production and Exchange in the North Coast Ranges, California. In *Current Directions in California Obsidian Studies*, edited by R. Hughes, pp. 79–94. Contributions of the University of California Archaeological Research Facility No. 48. Archaeological Research Facility, Berkeley, California.

Kalani, Lyn and Sarah Sweedler
 2004   *Images of America: Fort Ross and the Sonoma Coast*. Arcadia Publishing, Charleston, South Carolina.

Karklins, Karlis
 2012[1982]   Guide to the Description and Classification of Glass Beads. *Beads* 24:62–90.

Kennedy, Mary Jean
 1955   Culture Contact and Acculturation of the Southwestern Pomo. Ph.D. dissertation, Department of Anthropology, University of California, Berkeley.

Khlebnikov, Kirill
 1990   *The Khlebnikov Archive: Unpublished Journal (1800–1837) and Travel Notes (1820, 1822, and 1824)*. Translated by J. Bisk. University of Alaska Press, Fairbanks, Alaska.

Kidd, Kenneth E. and Martha Ann Kidd
 2012[1970]   A Classification System for Glass Beads for the use of Field Archaeologists. *Beads* 24:39–61.

Kniffen, Fred
 1939   Pomo Geography. *University of California Publications in American Archaeology and Ethnology* 36(6).

Kostromitinov, P.
 1974   Notes on the Indians in Upper California. In *Ethnographic Observations on the Coast Miwok and Pomo by Contre-Admiral F. P. Von Wrangell and P. Kostromitinov of the Russian Colony Ross, 1839*, edited by F. Stross and R. Heizer, pp. 7–18. Archaeological Research Facility, University of California, Berkeley, California.

Kotzebue, Otto Von
 1830   *A New Voyage Round the World, in the Years 1823, 24, 25, and 26*. Vols. 1 and 2. Henry Colburn and Richard Bentley, London, England.

Langhamer, Antonín
 2003   *The Legend of Bohemian Glass: A Thousand Years of Glassmaking in the Heart of Europe*. Tigris Spol.S.R.O., Holešov, Czech Republic.

Laplace, Cyrille
 2006   Visit of Cyrille Pierre-Theodore Laplace to Fort Ross ad Bodega Bay in August 1839. Translated by Glenn Farris. Fort Ross Interpretive Association, Fort Ross.

Lightfoot, Kent G., Antoinette Martinez and Ann M. Schiff
 1998   Daily Practice and Material Culture in Pluralistic Social Settings: An Archaeological Study of Culture Change and Persistence from Fort Ross, California. *American Antiquity* 63(2):199–222.

Lightfoot, Kent G.

1993   Native Responses to the Russian Mercantile Colony of Fort Ross, Northern California. *Journal of Field Archaeology* 20(2):159–175.

1995   Culture Contact Studies: Redefining the Relationship between Prehistoric and Historical Archaeology. *American Antiquity* 60(2):199–217.

1999   *The Archaeological Investigation of the North Wall of the Fort Ross Stockade. Archaeological Fieldwork Involved in the Reconstruction of the North Stockade Wall in the Fort Ross State Historic Park, Sonoma County, California.* On file, California Department of Parks and Recreation, Russian River/Mendocino District, P.O. Box 123, Duncans Mills, California.

2005   *Indians, Missionaries, and Merchants: The Legacy of Colonial Encounters on the California Frontiers.* University of California Press, Berkeley, California.

2006   Missions, Furs, Gold and Manifest Destiny: Rethinking an Archaeology of Colonialism for Western North America. In *Historical Archaeology*, edited by M. Hall and S. W. Silliman, pp. 272–292. Blackwell Publishing, Malden, Massachusetts.

2008   Collaborative Research Programs: Implications for the Practice of North American Archaeology. In *Collaborating at the Trowel's Edge: Teaching and Learning in Indigenous Archaeology*, edited by S. W. Silliman, pp. 211–227. University of Arizona Press, Tucson, Arizona.

Lightfoot, Kent G., Otis Parrish, Roberta A. Jewett, E. Breck Parkman and Daniel F. Murley

2001   The Metini Village Project: Collaborative Research in the Fort Ross State Historic Park. *Society for California Archaeology Newsletter* 35(2):1, 23–26.

Lightfoot, Kent G., Ann M. Schiff, Antoinette Martinez, Thomas A. Wake, Stephen Silliman, Peter Mills and Lisa Holm

1997   Culture Change and Persistence in the Daily Lifeways of Interethnic Households. In *The Archaeology and Ethnohistory of Fort Ross, California. Volume 2: The Native Alaskan Neighborhood: A Multiethnic Community at Colony Ross*, edited by K. G. Lightfoot, A. M. Schiff and T. A. Wake, pp. 355–419. Contributions of the University of California Archaeological Research Facility No. 55. Archaeological Research Facility, Berkeley, California.

Lightfoot, Kent G., Ann M. Schiff and Thomas A. Wake (editors)

1997   *The Archaeology and Ethnohistory of Fort Ross, California. Volume 2: The Native Alaskan Neighborhood: A Multiethnic Community at Colony Ross.* Contributions of the University of California Archaeological Facility No. 55. Archaeological Research Facility, Berkeley, California.

Lightfoot, Kent G. and Stephen W. Silliman

1997   Chronology of Archaeological Deposits from the Fort Ross Beach and Native Alaskan Village Sites. In *The Archaeology and Ethnohistory of Fort Ross, California. Volume 2: The Native Alaskan Neighborhood: A Multiethnic Community at Colony Ross*, edited by K. G. Lightfoot, A. M. Schiff and T. A. Wake, pp. 337–354. Contributions of the University of California Archaeological Research Facility No. 55. Archaeological Research Facility, Berkeley, California.

Lightfoot, Kent G., Thomas A. Wake and Ann M. Schiff
1991   *The Archaeology and Ethnohistory of Fort Ross, California, Volume 1: Introduction.* Contributions of the University of California Archaeological Research Facility No. 49. Archaeological Research Facility, Berkeley, California.

Lightfoot, Kent G., Lee M. Panich, Tsim D. Schneider, Sara L. Gonzalez, Matthew A. Russell, Darren Modzelewski, Theresa Molino and Elliot H. Blair
2013   The Study of Political Economies and Colonialism in Native California: Implications for Contemporary Tribal Groups and Federal Recognition. *American Antiquity* 78(1):89–104.

Lindsay, Brendan C.
2012   *Murder State: California's Native American Genocide, 1846–1873.* University of Nebraska Press, Lincoln.

Loeb, Edwin M.
1926   Pomo Folkways. *University of California Publications in American Archaeology and Ethnology* 19(2). University of California Press, Berkeley, California.

Luscomb, Sally C.
1992   The Collector's Encyclopedia of Buttons. Schiffer Book for Collectors. Schiffer Publishing, Ltd., West Chester, PA.

Lütke, Fedor P.
1989   September 4–28, 1818. From the Diary of Fedor P. Lütke during his Circumnavigation Aboard the Sloop Kamchatka, 1817–1819: Observations on California. In *The Russian American Colonies Three Centuries of Russian Eastward Expansion 1798–1867. Volume 3: A Documentary Record,* edited by B. Dmytryshyn, E. A. P. Crownhart-Vaughan and T. Vaughan, pp. 257–285. Oregon Historical Society Press, Portland, Oregon.

Lyman, R. L.
1991   *Prehistory of the Oregon Coast: The Effects of Excavation Strategies and Assemblage Size on Archaeological Inquiry.* Academic Press, San Diego, California.

Martinez, Antoinette
1997   View from the Ridge: The Kashaya Pomo in a Russian-American Company Context. In *The Archaeology of Russian Colonialism in the North and Tropical Pacific,* edited by P. R. Mills and A. Martinez, pp. 141–156. vol. 81. Kroeber Anthropological Association, Berkeley, California.

1998   An Archaeological Study of Change and Continuity in the Material Remains, Practices and Cultural Identities of Native California Women in a Nineteenth Century Pluralistic Context. Ph.D. dissertation, Department of Anthropology, University of California, Berkeley.

Mattewson, R. C.
1859   *Plat Map and Field Notes of the Muniz Rancho Finally Confirmed to Manuel Torres.* Copy on File, California Department of Parks and Recreation, Sacramento, California.

McKenzie, John
　　1963　*Historic Resources and Indian Sites at Fort Ross State Historic Park as Identified by John McKenzie, August 20, 1963.* Manuscript on file, California Department of Parks and Recreation, Sacramento.

Meighan, Clement W.
　　1967　Appendix: Comparative Notes on Two Historic Village Sites. In *Ethnographic Notes on the Southwestern Pomo,* edited by E. W. Gifford. *Anthropological Records* 25:46–47. University of California Press, Berkeley, California.

　　1985　Glass Beads. In *Excavations at Mission San Antonio, 1976–1978,* edited by Robert L. Hoover and Julia G. Costello, pp. 56–63. Institute of Archaeology, University of California, Los Angeles.

　　n.d.　Glass Trade Beads in California.

Milner, Allyson L.
　　2009　Mixing Material and Culture at Metini: A Close Look at Lithic and Glass Collections. Senior Honors Thesis, Department of Anthropology, University of California, Berkeley.

Motz, Lee
　　1979　Fort Ross Glass Trade Bead Analysis. Manuscript on file, California Department of Parks and Recreation, Sacramento.

Mrozowski, S. A., H. Herbster, D. Brown and K. L. Priddy
　　2009　Magunkaquog Materiality, Federal Recognition, and the Search for Deeper Meaning. *International Journal of Historical Archaeology* 13:430–463.

Nelson, Peter
　　2015　Engaged Research, Management and Planning at Tolay Lake Regional Park. Paper presented at the 80th Annual Meeting of the Society for American Archaeology, San Francisco, California.

Newquist, Ingrid
　　2002　Kashaya in Post-Russian Times: Analysis of Archaeological Materials from a Multi-Occupation Site at Fort Ross, California. Senior Honors Thesis, Department of Anthropology, University of California, Berkeley.

Newland, Michael D. and Michael D. Meyer
　　2003　*Archaeological Excavations of the Old and New Russian Magazins, Fort Ross State Historic Park, Sonoma County, California.* Manuscript on file, California Department of Parks and Recreation, Sacramento.

Origer, Thomas M.
　　1987　*Temporal Control in the Southern North Coast Ranges of California: The Application of Obsidian Hydration Analysis.* Papers in Northern California Anthropology 1. Northern California Anthropological Group, Berkeley.

　　1989　Hydration Analysis of Obsidian Flakes Produced by Ishi During the Historic Period. In *Current Directions in California Obsidian Studies,* edited by R. E. Hughes, pp. 69–77. Contributions of the University of California Archaeological Research Facility No. 48. Archaeology Research Facility, Berkeley, California.

Osborn, Sannie Kenton
    1997   Death in the Daily Life of the Ross Colony: Mortuary Behavior in
    Frontier Russian America. Ph.D dissertation, Department of Anthropology,
    University of Wisconsin-Milwaukee, Milwaukee.

Oswalt, Robert L.
    1964   *Kashaya Texts*. University of California Publications in Linguistics
    36. University of California Press, Berkeley, California.

Panich, Lee M.
    2010   Missionization and the Persistence of Native Identity on the Colo-
    nial Frontier of Baja California. *Ethnohistory* 57(2):225–262.

    2013   Archaeologies of Persistence: Reconsidering the Legacies of Colo-
    nialism in Native North America. *American Antiquity* 78(1):105–122.

    2014   Native American Consumption of Shell and Glass Beads at Mis-
    sion Santa Clara de Asís. *American Antiquity* 79(4):730–748.

Popper, Virginia S.
    2006   Macrobotanical Analysis of Soil Samples from Metini Village
    (CA-SON-175), Sonoma County, California. Manuscript on file, Califor-
    nia Archaeology Laboratory, University of California, Berkeley.

Powers, Stephen
    1976   *Tribes of California*. University of California Press, Berkeley, Cali-
    fornia.

Presidio Ross Census
    1848   *Lists of Indians at Present Time, January 8, 1848*. Manuscript on
    file, Bancroft Library, University of California, Berkeley. Vallejo Papers,
    Banc MSS C-B 12, Documents 326, 327.

Ritter, Eric W.
    1972   *Preliminary Report on Archaeological Investigations at Fort Ross*. Man-
    uscript on file, California Department of Parks and Recreation, Sacramento,
    California.

Ross, Lester A.
    1990   Trade Beads from Hudson's Bay Company Fort Vancouver
    (1829–1860), Vancouver, Washington. *Beads* 2:29–67.

    1997   Glass and Ceramic Trade Beads from the Native Alaskan Neigh-
    borhood. In *The Archaeology and Ethnohistory of Fort Ross, California.
    Volume 2: The Native Alaskan Neighborhood: A Multiethnic Community at
    Colony Ross*, edited by K. G. Lightfoot, A. M. Schiff and T. A. Wake, pp.
    179–212. Contributions of the University of California Archaeological
    Research Facility No. 55. Archaeological Research Facility, Berkeley, Cali-
    fornia.

    1998   Appendix A: Glass Beads from Two Early Nineteenth Century
    Kashaya Pomo Village Sites (Tomato Patch Village Site and Ridge Village
    Site), Sonoma County, California. In *An Archaeological Study of Change and*

Continuity in the Material Remains, Practices, and Cultural Identities of Native Californian Women in a Nineteenth Century Pluralistic Context, edited by Antoinette Martinez, pp. 201–223, Ph.D dissertation, Department of Anthropology, University of California, Berkeley.

Schiff, Ann M.

1997   Shellfish Remains at the Fort Ross Beach and Native Alaskan Village Sites. In *The Archaeology and Ethnohistory of Fort Ross, California. Volume 2: The Native Alaskan Neighborhood: A Multiethnic Community at Colony Ross,* edited by K. G. Lightfoot, A. M. Schiff and T. A. Wake, pp. 328–336. Contributions of the University of California Archaeological Research Facility No. 55. Archaeological Research Facility, Berkeley, California.

Schneider, Tsim D.

2010   Placing Refuge: Shell Mounds and the Archaeology of Colonial Encounters in the San Francisco Bay Area, California. Ph.D dissertation, Department of Anthropology, University of California, Berkeley.

Shackley, M. Steven

1998   Geochemical Differentiation and Prehistoric Procurement of Obsidian in the Mount Taylor Volcanic Field, Northwest New Mexico. *Journal of Archaeological Science* 25:1073–1082.

Silliman, Stephen W.

1997   European Origins and Native Destinations: Historical Artifacts from the Native Alaskan Village and Fort Ross Beach Sites. In *The Archaeology and Ethnohistory of Fort Ross, California. Volume 2: The Native Alaskan Neighborhood: A Multiethnic Community at Colony Ross,* edited by K. G. Lightfoot, A. M. Schiff and T. A. Wake, pp. 136–178. Contributions of the University of California Archaeological Research Facility No. 55. Archaeological Research Facility, Berkeley, California.

2000   Colonial Worlds, Indigenous Practices: The Archaeology of Labor on a 19th Century California Rancho. Ph.D dissertation, Department of Anthropology, University of California, Berkeley.

2004   *Lost Laborers in Colonial California: Native Americans and the Archaeology of Rancho Petaluma.* University of Arizona Press, Tucson, Arizona.

2005a   Culture Contact or Colonialism? Challenges in the Archaeology of Native North America. *American Antiquity* 70(1):55–74.

2005b   Obsidian Studies and the Archaeology of 19th-Century California. *Journal of Field Archaeology* 30(1):75–94.

2009   Change and Continuity, Practice and Memory: Native American Persistence in Colonial New England. *American Antiquity* 74(2):211–230.

Simons, Dwight D.

1997   Bird Remains at the Fort Ross Beach and Native Alaskan Village Sites. In *The Archaeology and Ethnohistory of Fort Ross, California. Volume 2: The Native Alaskan Neighborhood: A Multiethnic Community at Colony Ross,* edited by K. G. Lightfoot, A. M. Schiff and T. A. Wake, pp. 310–318. Contributions of the University of California Archaeological Research Facility No. 55. Archaeological Research Facility, Berkeley, California.

Sleeper-Smith, Susan
 2001   *Indian Women and French Men: Rethinking Cultural Encounter in the Western Great Lakes.* University of Massachusetts Press, Amherst.

Smart, T. L. and E. S. Hoffman
 1988   Environmental Interpretation of Archaeological Charcoal. In *Current Paleoethnobotany: Analytical Methods and Cultural Interpretations of Archaeological Plant Remains,* edited by C. A. Hastorf and V. S. Popper, pp. 167–205. University of Chicago Press, Chicago.

Smith, Janice Christina
 1974   Pomo and Promyshlenniki: Time and Trade Goods at Fort Ross. M.A. Thesis, Department of Anthropology, UCLA, Los Angeles.

Sprague, Roderick
 2002   China or Prosser Button Identification and Dating. *Historical Archaeology* 36(2):111–127.

Stahl, Ann B.
 2012   When Does History Begin? Material Continuity and Change in West Africa. In *Decolonizing Indigenous Histories: Exploring Prehistoric/Colonial Transitions in Archaeology,* edited by M. Oland, S. M. Hart and L. Frink, pp. 158–177. The University of Arizona Press, Tucson.

Stewart, Omer C.
 1943   Notes on Pomo Ethnogeography. *University of California Publications in American Archaeology and Ethnology* 40(2):29–62.

Stillinger, Robert
 1975   *A Preliminary Analysis of Sonoma S.D.A.-1 (CA-SON-67).* Manuscript on file, Manuscript No. S-6295, Northwest Information Center, Sonoma State University, Rohnert Park, California.

Stone, Lyle M.
 1974   *Fort Michilimackinac 1715–1781: An Archaeological Perspective on the Revolutionary Frontier.* Publications of the Museum, Anthropological Series Vol. 2, Michigan State University, East Lansing.

Swiden, Christina
 1986   Appendix A. Analysis of Shellfish Remains from SON-1455. In *Cultural Resource Survey at the Fort Ross Campground, Sonoma County, California,* edited by G. J. Farris, pp. 55–64. Manuscript on file, California Department of Parks and Recreation, Sacramento, California.

Thomas, David H. (editor)
 1989   *Columbian Consequences: Volume 1, Archaeological and Historical Perspectives on the Spanish Borderlands West.* Smithsonian Institution Press, Washington D.C.

 1990   *Columbian Consequences: Volume 2, Archaeological and Historical Perspectives on the Spanish Borderlands East.* Smithsonian Institution Press, Washington D.C.

 1991   *Columbian Consequences: Volume 3, The Spanish Borderlands in Pan-American Perspective.* Smithsonian Institution, Washington D.C.

Tomlin, Kaye

1993   *The Caretakers: After the Russian-American Company.* Fort Ross Interpretive Association, Inc., Fort Ross, California.

Treganza, Adan E.

1954   Fort Ross: A Study in Historical Archaeology. *Reports of the University of California Archaeological Survey* 23:1–26.

Tremaine, Kim

1989   Obsidian as a Time Keeper: An Investigation in Absolute and Relative Dating. M.A. Thesis, Sonoma State University.

Tremaine, Kim and David Fredrickson

1988   Induced Obsidian Hydration Experiments: An Investigation in Relative Dating. *Materials Research Society Symposium Proceedings* 123:271–278.

van der Sleen, W. G. N.

1973   *A Handbook on Beads.* Halbart, Liege.

Verano, J. W. and D. H. Ubelaker (editors)

1992   *Disease and Demography in the Americas.* Smithsonian Institution Press, Washington, D.C.

Vizenor, Gerald

2008   *Survivance: Narratives of Native Presence.* University of Nebraska Press, Lincoln.

Wake, Thomas A.

1995   Mammal Remains from Fort Ross: A Study in Ethnicity and Culture Change. Ph.D dissertation, Department of Anthropology, University of California, Berkeley.

1997a   Bone Artifacts and Tool Production in the Native Alaskan Neighborhood. In *The Archaeology and Ethnohistory of Fort Ross, California. Volume 2: The Native Alaskan Neighborhood: A Multiethnic Community at Colony Ross,* edited by K. G. Lightfoot, A. M. Schiff and T. A. Wake, pp. 248–278. Contributions of the University of California Archaeological Research Facility No. 55. Archaeological Research Facility, Berkeley, California.

1997b   Mammal Remains from the Native Alaskan Neighborhood. In *The Archaeology and Ethnohistory of Fort Ross, California. Volume 2: The Native Alaskan Neighborhood: A Multiethnic Community at Colony Ross,* edited by K. G. Lightfoot, A. M. Schiff and T. A. Wake, pp. 279–309. Contributions of the University of California Archaeological Research Facility No. 55. Archaeological Research Facility, Berkeley, California.

Wrangell, F. P. Von

1969   Russia in California, 1833, Report of Governor Wrangel. Translation and Editing of Original 1833 Report by James R. Gibson. *Pacific Northwest Quarterly* 60:205–215.

1974 Some Remarks on the Savages on the Northwest Coast of America: The Indians in Upper California. In *Ethnographic Observations on the Coast Miwok and Pomo by Contre-Admiral F. P. Von Wrangell and P. Kostromitinov of the Russian Colony Ross, 1839*, edited by F. Stross and R. Heizer, pp. 1–6. Archaeological Research Facility, University of California, Berkeley, California.

Appendices

Keys to codes used in these appendices appear on the last page of each appendix.

Metini #	Unit #	Level	Material Category	Artifact Class	Raw Material	Edge Mod.	Count
ME-4/29/99-04-LI-02	20S 21E	1 (0-10 CM)	LF	FS	CH	No	1
ME-4/29/99-04-LI-03	20S 21E	1 (0-10 CM)	LF	BF	CH	EM	1
ME-4/29/99-05-LI-01	0N 10W	1 (0-10 CM)	LF	SH	CH	No	1
ME-5/01/99-02-LI-01	15S 4E	1 (0-10 CM)	LF	SH	CH	EM	2
ME-5/01/99-02-LI-02	15S 4E	1 (0-10 CM)	LF	CP	CH	EM	1
ME-5/01/99-02-LI-06	15S 4E	1 (0-10 CM)	LF	CF	CH	No	1
ME-4/29/99-06-LI-08	20S 21E	2 (10-20 CM)	LF	SH	CH	No	1
ME-4/30/99-01-LI-01	0N 10W	2 (10-20 CM)	LF	SH	OB	No	1
ME-4/30/99-01-LI-02	0N 10W	2 (10-20 CM)	LF	BF	CH	EM	1
ME-5/01/99-11-LI-01	15S 4E	2 (10-20 CM)	LF	SH	CH	No	3
ME-5/01/99-11-LI-02	15S 4E	2 (10-20 CM)	LF	SH	CH	No	2
ME-5/01/99-11-LI-03	15S 4E	2 (10-20 CM)	LF	FS	OB	EM	1
ME-4/29/99-06-LI-02	20S 21E	2 (10-20CM)	LF	FS	OB	No	2
ME-4/29/99-06-LI-03	20S 21E	2 (10-20CM)	LF	FS	CH	No	2
ME-4/29/99-06-LI-04	20S 21E	2 (10-20CM)	LF	SH	CH	No	11
ME-4/29/99-06-LI-05	20S 21E	2 (10-20CM)	LF	FS	QZ	No	1
ME-5/01/99-02-LI-05	15S 4E	3 (20-27 CM)	LF	SH	CH	No	2
ME-5/02/99-03-LI-01	15S 4E	3 (20-27 CM)	LF	PX	QZ	No	1
ME-4/30/99-12-LI-01	20S 21E	3 (20-30 CM)	LF	FS	CA	No	1
ME-4/30/99-12-LI-02	20S 21E	3 (20-30 CM)	LF	SH	CH	No	1
ME-4/30/99-12-LI-04	20S 21E	3 (20-30 CM)	LF	SH	CH	No	1
ME-4/30/99-07-LI-01	0N 10W	3 (20-30CM)	LF	SH	OB	No	1
ME-4/30/99-07-LI-02	0N 10W	3 (20-30CM)	LF	FS	CH	EM	1
ME-4/30/99-07-LI-03	0N 10W	3 (20-30CM)	LO	RO	RO	RO	7
ME-4/30/99-07-LI-04	0N 10W	3 (20-30CM)	LF	SH	CH	No	1
ME-5/01/99-07-LI-01A	20S 21E	4 (30-40 CM)	LF	CP	CH	No	1
ME-5/01/99-07-LI-01B	20S 21E	4 (30-40 CM)	LF	FS	CH	No	1
ME-5/01/99-08-LI-01	20S 21E	5 (40-50 CM)	LF	UN	CH	EM	1
ME-4/16/99-01-LI-02	23S 23E	Surface	LF	PX	OB	EM	1
ME-4/16/99-01-LI-03	23S 23E	Surface	LF	SH	CH	No	2
ME-4/16/99-05-LI-01	26S 28E	Surface	LF	CP	OB	No	1
ME-4/16/99-06-LI-01	29S 36E	Surface	LF	FS	OB	No	1
ME-4/17/99-01-LI-01	29S 21E	Surface	LF	SH	CH	EM	1
ME-4/17/99-01-LI-02	29S 21E	Surface	LF	SH	CH	No	3
ME-4/17/99-05-LI-01	35S 28E	Surface	LF	SH	CH	No	2
ME-4/17/99-06-LI-01	34S 36E	Surface	LF	FS	CH	No	1
ME-4/17/99-08-LI-01	39S 37E	Surface	LF	FS	QZ	No	1
ME-4/17/99-08-LI-02	39S 37E	Surface	LF	SH	CH	EM	1
ME-4/17/99-10-LI-01	36S 22E	Surface	LF	SH	CH	No	2
ME-4/17/99-10-LI-02	36S 22E	Surface	LF	CF	CH	No	1
ME-4/21/99-01-LI-02	1N 35E	Surface	LF	SH	CH	No	1
ME-4/21/99-01-LI-03	1N 35E	Surface	LF	CP	CH	No	1
ME-4/21/99-02-LI-01A	5N 38E	Surface	LF	FS	CH	No	1
ME-4/21/99-02-LI-01B	5N 38E	Surface	LF	SH	CH	No	1
ME-4/21/99-02-LI-02	5N 38E	Surface	LF	SH	CH	No	1
ME-4/21/99-04-LI-01	7N 28E	Surface	LF	SH	CH	No	1
ME-4/21/99-07-LI-01	11N 30E	Surface	LF	CP	CH	No	1
ME-4/28/99-02-LI-01	19N 22E	Surface	LO	RO	RO	RO	1
ME-4/29/99-01-LI-01A	6S 43E	Surface	LF	FS	CH	No	1

Metini #	Unit #	Level	Material Category	Artifact Class	Raw Material	Edge Mod.	Count
ME-4/29/99-01-LI-01B	6S 43E	Surface	LF	SH	CH	No	2
ME-4/29/99-01-LI-02A	6S 43E	Surface	LF	BF	OB	EM	1
ME-4/29/99-01-LI-02B	6S 43E	Surface	LF	BF	CH	EM	1
ME-4/29/99-01-LI-03	6S43E	Surface	LF	CF	CH	No	1
ME-4/29/99-02-LI-01A	11S 41E	Surface	LF	CP	CH	No	1
ME-4/29/99-02-LI-01B	11S 41E	Surface	LF	FS	CH	No	1
ME-4/29/99-02-LI-02	11S 41E	Surface	LF	CP	CA	EM	1
ME-4/29/99-07-LI-01	1N 40E	Surface	LF	SH	CH	No	1
ME-4/29/99-07-LI-02	1N 40E	Surface	LF	SH	CH	No	1
ME-4/30/99-04-LI-01	4S 40E	Surface	LF	CP	CH	No	1
ME-4/30/99-05-LI-01	35S 43E	Surface	LF	SH	CH	No	1
ME-4/30/99-05-LI-02	35S 43E	Surface	LF	FS	OB	No	1
ME-4/30/99-06-LI-02	38S 41E	Surface	LF	SH	CH	No	2
ME-4/30/99-06-LI-03	38S 41E	Surface	LF	CF	CH	No	1
ME-4/30/99-11-LI-01	27N 29E	Surface	LF	SH	CH	EM	1
ME-6/05/98-06-LI-01	13N 20W	Surface	LF	SH	CH	No	1
ME-6/13/98-02-LI-01	7S 11W	Surface	LF	SH	CH	No	1
ME-6/13/98-03-LI-01	2S 15W	Surface	LF	SH	CH	No	1
ME-6/17/98-01-LI-01	13S 18W	Surface	LF	SH	CH	No	1
ME-6/17/98-03-LI-01	17S 18W	Surface	LF	FS	CH	EM	1
ME-6/18/98-01-LI-01	36S 2W	Surface	LO	RO	RO	RO	1
ME-6/18/98-02-LI-01	21S 18W	Surface	LO	RO	RO	RO	1
ME-6/18/98-03-LI-01	38S 7W	Surface	LO	RO	RO	RO	1
ME-6/18/98-07-LI-01	6S 6E	Surface	LF	CP	OB	EM	1
ME-6/19/98-03-LI-01A	16S 7E	Surface	LF	CP	OB	EM	1
ME-6/19/98-03-LI-01B	16S 7E	Surface	LF	FS	OB	EM	1
ME-6/20/98-02-LI-01	13S 14E	Surface	LF	UF	OB	EM	1
ME-6/20/98-02-LI-02	13S 14E	Surface	LF	FS	CH	EM	1
ME-6/20/98-03-LI-01	10S 14E	Surface	LF	SH	CH	EM	1
ME-6/20/98-06-LI-02	6S 18E	Surface	LF	SH	CH	No	2
ME-6/20/98-06-LI-03A	6S 18E	Surface	LF	SH	CH	No	1
ME-6/20/98-06-LI-03B	6S 18E	Surface	LF	CP	CH	No	1
ME-6/20/98-06-LI-03C	6S 18E	Surface	LF	FS	CH	EM	1
ME-6/20/98-06-LI-04	6S 18E	Surface	LF	CP	CA	No	1
ME-6/20/98-06-LI-05	6S 18E	Surface	LO	RO	RO	RO	1
ME-6/20/98-06-LI-06	6S 18E	Surface	LO	RO	RO	RO	1
ME-6/24/98-01-LI-01	31S 3E	Surface	LF	SH	CH	No	1
ME-6/24/98-03-LI-01	32S 5E	Surface	LF	FS	CH	No	1
ME-6/24/98-04-LI-01	40S 0E	Surface	LF	FS	CH	EM	1
ME-6/25/98-07-LI-01	6N 2E	Surface	LF	SH	CH	No	1
ME-6/25/98-08-LI-01	8N 5E	Surface	LF	SH	CH	No	1
ME-6/26/98-03-LI-01	8S 22E	Surface	LF	FS	CH	No	1
ME-6/26/98-05-LI-01	5S 33E	Surface	LF	CF	CH	No	1
ME-6/26/98-05-LI-02	5S 33E	Surface	LF	SH	CH	EM	1
ME-6/26/98-08-LI-01	10S 37E	Surface	LF	SH	CH	No	1
ME-6/26/98-09-LI-01	18S 22E	Surface	LF	SH	CH	No	1
ME-6/26/98-09-LI-02A	18S 22E	Surface	LF	PX	OB	EM	1
ME-6/26/98-09-LI-02B	18S 22E	Surface	LF	SH	OB	EM	1
ME-6/26/98-10-LI-01	16S 26E	Surface	LF	BF	OB	EM	1

Metini #	Unit #	Level	Material Category	Artifact Class	Raw Material	Edge Mod.	Count
ME-6/26/98-10-LI-02	16S 26E	Surface	LF	CP	CH	No	1
ME-6/26/98-10-LI-03	16S 26E	Surface	LF	FS	CH	No	1
ME-6/26/98-11-LI-01	20S 30E	Surface	LF	SH	CH	No	1
ME-9/12/98-02-LI-01	2S 5E	Surface	LF	SH	CH	EM	1
ME-9/12/98-03-LI-01	15S 21E	Surface	LF	PX	CH	EM	1
ME-5/02/99-01-LI-01	15S 4E	TOP OF LEVEL 3 ~20 CM	LF	SH	CH	EM	1
ME-5/02/99-01-LI-02	15S 4E	TOP OF LEVEL 3 ~20 CM	LF	FS	OB	No	1

KEY TO CODES

Appendix 1: Chipped Stone Artifacts

Material Category: LF=Lithic Flake Stone

Artifact Class:	BI=Biface	CO=Core
	PP=Projectile Point	PF=Projectile Point Frag.
	UN=Uniface	EM= Edge-Modified Flake
	CP=Complete Flake	PX=Proximal Flake
	FS=Flake Shatter	SH=Angular Shatter
	RO=Rock (non-artifact)	

Raw Material:	CH=Chert	OB=Obsidian
	BA=Basalt	QZ=Quartzite
	CA=Chalcedony	SA=Sandstone

Edge-Modified:	EM=Edge-Modified	NO=Not Modified
	RO=Rock (non-artifact)	

Appendix 2: Geochemical and Hydration Analysis of Obsidian Artifacts

Catalog #	P #	New P #	Site	Unit #	Surf EW	Surf NS	Level	Artifact Class	Edge Modification	Rb	Sr	Y	Zr	Nb	Ba	Source	Hydration Measurements	Mean Hydration Measurement	Temaine's Comparison Constant	Count	Hydration Comments
ME-4/16/99-01-LL-02	P1190-412	P1190-220	Metini	23S 23E	23	-23	Surface	FS	EM	153	56	53	292	13	670	Annadel	1.0,1.0,1.0,1.0,1.0,1.0	1	1	1	none
ME-4/16/99-05-LL-01	P1190-414	P1190-222	Metini	26S 28E	28	-26	Surface	CP	No	141	53	49	290	12	620	Annadel	1.6,1.6,1.6,1.6,1.7	1.6	1.6	1	weathered
ME-4/16/99-06-LL-01	P1190-415	P1190-223	Metini	29S 36E	36	-29	Surface	FS	No	145	59	49	279	13	642	Annadel	1.5,1.5,1.5,1.6,1.6,1.6	1.6	1.6	1	none
ME-4/30/99-05-LL-02	P1190-458	P1190-267	Metini	35S 43E	43	-35	Surface	FS	No	139	50	48	283	12	575	Annadel	0.9,0.9,1.0,1.0,1.0,1.0	1	1	1	none
ME-6/18/98-07-LL-01	P1190-074	P1190-183	Metini	6S 6E	6	-6	Surface	CP	EM	196	11	46	249	12	447	Napa	5.3,5.4,5.4,5.5,5.5,5.5	5.4	4.2	1	none
ME-6/19/98-03-LL-01	P1190-075	P1190-184	Metini	16S 7E	7	-16	Surface	CP	EM	185	10	44	235	11	424	Napa	0.9,1.0,1.0,1.0,1.0,1.1	1	0.77	1	none
ME-6/20/98-02-LL-01	?	P1190-185	Metini	13S 14E	14	-13	Surface	FS	EM	185	9	47	243	11	411	Napa	4.0,4.1,4.1,4.2,4.3,4.3	4.2	3.2	1	none
ME-6/26/98-09-LL-02-A	P1190-101	P1190-211	Metini	18S 22E	22	-18	Surface	PX	EM	143	54	50	286	12	605	Annadel	0.8,0.8,0.9,0.9,0.9	0.9	0.9	1	weathered
ME-6/26/98-09-LL-02-B	P1190-101	P1190-211	Metini	18S 22E	22	-18	Surface	PX	EM	142	8	32	179	9	365	Napa*	0.9,0.9,1.0,1.0,1.0,1.0	1	0.77	1	none
ME-4/30/99-01-LL-01	P1190-452	P1190-261	Metini	0N 10W	-10	0	2 (10-20 CM)	SH	No	149	35	28	183	19	231	Annadel	2.3,2.3,2.4,2.5,2.5,2.5	2.4	2.4	1	none
ME-4/30/99-07-LL-01	P1190-464	P1190-272	Metini	0N 10W	-10	0	3 (20-30 CM)	SH	No	80	29	23	143	13	543	Annadel*	1.1,1.3,1.3,1.3,1.3,1.4	1.3	1.3	1	none
ME-5/1/99-2-LL-2	P1190-474	P1190-474	Metini	1S 4E	4	-15	1 (0-10 CM)	CP	EM	186	12	44	242	12	436	Napa	diffuse hydration			1	weathered
ME-5/2/99-1-LL-2			Metini	1S 4E	4	-15	TOP OF L3 20 CM	FS	No								not analyzed			1	
ME-4/29/99-06-LL-02-A	P1190-443	P1190-251	Metini	20S 21E	21	-20	2 (10-20 CM)	FS	No	128	48	46	264	11	518	Annadel	1.5,1.5,1.5,1.5,1.6,1.7	1.6	1.6	1	none
ME-4/29/99-06-LL-02-B	P1190-443	P1190-251	Metini	20S 21E	21	-20	2 (10-20 CM)	FS	No	95	34	28	167	9	533	Annadel	0.9,0.9,0.9,0.9,1.0,1.0	0.9	0.9	1	none
RGM-1										145	100	24	216	9	752	Standard					

*These samples were below the minimum size for confident analyses. Source assignment was made by the pattern of the elemental concentrations.

KEY TO CODES

Appendix 2: Geochemical and Hydration Analysis of Obsidian Artifacts

Artifact Class:
CP=Complete Flake   FS=Flake Shatter
PX=Proximal Flake   SH=Angular Shatter

163

Appendix 3: Other Lithic Artifacts

Metini #	Unit #	Level	Artifact Category	Material Category	Lithic Class	Use Wear	Raw Material	Count
ME-5/01/99-02-LI-03	15S 4E	1 (0-10 CM)	LI	LG	GO	Grinding	SA	1
ME-5/01/99-02-LI-04	15S 4E	1 (0-10 CM)	LI	LG	MHS	Pecking/ Grinding	SA	1
ME-4/29/99-06-LI-01	20S 21E	2 (10-20 CM)	LI	LG	OT	Striations	SL	1
ME-4/29/99-06-LI-06	20S 21E	2 (10-20 CM)	LI	LG	GO		SA	1
ME-4/29/99-06-LI-07	20S 21E	2 (10-20 CM)	LI	LG	FC		SA	3
ME-4/29/99-06-LI-09	20S 21E	2 (10-20 CM)	LI	LG	MO	Pecking/ Grinding	SA	1
ME-5/01/99-11-LI-04	15S 4E	2 (10-20 CM)	LI	LG	PEF	Pecking/ Grinding	SA	1
ME-5/01/99-11-LI-05	15S 4E	2 (10-20 CM)	LI	LG	GO	Pecking/ Grinding	SA	1
ME-5/01/99-21-LI-01	15S 4E	2 (10-20 CM)	LI	LG	FC		SA	2
ME-4/30/99-12-LI-03	20S 21E	3 (20-30 CM)	LI	LG	GO	Pecking/ Grinding	SA	1
ME-4/16/99-01-LI-01	23S 23E	Surface	LI	LG	FC		SA	2
ME-4/17/99-01-LI-03	29S 21E	Surface	LI	LG	GO	Grinding	BA	1
ME-4/17/99-04-LI-01	35S 21E	Surface	LI	LG	GO	Grinding	BA	1
ME-4/17/99-07-LI-01	36S 32E	Surface	LI	LG	GO	Grinding	BA	1
ME-4/21/99-01-LI-01	1N 35E	Surface	LI	LG	FC		SA	1
ME-4/29/99-07-LI-03	1N 40E	Surface	LI	LO	OT		QZ	1
ME-4/30/99-02-LI-01	19S 43E	Surface	LI	LG	GO		SA	1
ME-4/30/99-03-LI-01	27S 42E	Surface	LI	LG	FC		SA	1
ME-4/30/99-05-LI-03	35S 43E	Surface	LI	LG	GO		SA	1
ME-4/30/99-06-LI-04	38S 41E	Surface	LI	LG	GO		SA	1
ME-4/30/99-08-LI-01	14N 42E	Surface	LI	LG	FC		SA	1
ME-4/30/99-08-LI-02	14N 42E	Surface	LI	LG	FC		OT	1
ME-6/05/98-04-LI-01	7N 14W	Surface	LI	LG	FC		SA	1
ME-6/06/98-02-Li-01	29N 18W	Surface	LI	LG	OT	Striations	SL	1
ME-6/20/98-06-LI-01	6S 18E	Surface	LI	LG	FC		SA	2
ME-6/20/98-07-LI-01	17S 16E	Surface	LI	LG	FC		OT	2
ME-6/20/98-07-LI-02	17S 16E	Surface	LI	LG	MHS		SA	1
ME-6/25/98-05-LI-01	13N 10E	Surface	LI	LG	FC	Grinding	GR	1
ME-6/26/98-01-LI-01	5S 24E	Surface	LI	LG	FC	Grinding	IG	1
ME-6/26/98-06-LI-01	5S 36E	Surface	LI	LG	FC		SA	5
ME-6/26/98-07-LI-01	7S 30E	Surface	LI	LG	FC		SA	1

KEY TO CODES

Appendix 3: Other Lithic Artifacts

Material Category: LG=Lithic Ground Stone

Artifact Class: MHS=Milling Handstone   PEF=Pestle Fragment
MO=Mortar   GO=Ground Stone Other
FC=Fire-Cracked Rock   OT=Other

Raw Material: SA=Sandstone   BA=Basalt
IG=Igneous Rock   GR=Granite
SL=Slate   QZ=Quartz
UN=Unidentified

Appendix 4: Ceramic Artifacts

Metini #	Unit #	Level	Artifact Category	Class	Ware Group	Type/Decoration	Vessel Form	Date	Count
ME-4/29/99-04-HC-01	20S 21E	1 (0-10 CM)	HC	Refined earthenware	Ironstone	Undecorated		1840-1900	2
ME-5/01/99-02-HC-01	15S 4E	1 (0-10 CM)	HC	Refined earthenware	Whiteware	Handpainted blue edge, underglaze	Rim, plate	1835-1870	1
ME-4/29/99-06-HC-01A	20S 21E	2 (10-20 CM)	HC	Refined earthenware	Ironstone	Undecorated		1840-1900	1
ME-4/29/99-06-HC-01B	20S 21E	2 (10-20 CM)	HC	Porcelain	White	Overglaze, handpainted edge	Rim, saucer	1790+	1
ME-4/29/99-06-HC-02	20S 21E	2 (10-20 CM)	HC	Kaolin	Tobacco pipe	Undecorated white kaolin			1
ME-5/01/99-11-HC-01	15S 4E	2 (10-20 CM)	HC	Refined earthenware	Whiteware	Transferprint flow blue, underglaze, double-sided	Hollow form	1835-1870	1
ME-5/01/99-09-HC-01	20S 21E	North Wall Profile	HC	Refined earthenware	Hotelware	Handpainted overglaze (ghost)	Rim, bowl	1880	1
ME-4/16/99-01-HC-01	23S 23E	Surface	HC	Kaolin	Tobacco pipe	Undecorated	Pipe stem		1
ME-4/16/99-02-HC-01	21S 29E	Surface	HC	Porcelain	Non-white	Handpainted overglace, red		1730-1830	1
ME-4/16/99-04-HC-01	23S 38E	Surface	HC	Refined earthenware	Ironstone	Undecorated	Bowl, shoulder frag	1840-1900	1
ME-4/16/99-05-HC-01A	26S 28E	Surface	HC	Refined earthenware	Ironstone	Undecorated (molded faceted ext.)	Rim, cup	1840-1900	1
ME-4/16/99-05-HC-01B	26S 28E	Surface	HC	Refined earthenware	Whiteware	Underglaze hand-painted blue, broadstroke		1820-1875	1
ME-4/16/99-06-HC-01	29S 36E	Surface	HC	Refined earthenware	Ironstone	Undecorated		1840-1900	1
ME-4/17/99-01-HC-01	29S 21E	Surface	HC	Refined earthenware	Ironstone	Undecorated, (molded decoration)	Rim, bowl	1840-1900	1
ME-4/17/99-03-HC-01	31S 33E	Surface	HC	Refined earthenware	Ironstone	Underglaze blue handpainted edge, scalloped edge	Rim, plate	1800-1860	1
ME-4/17/99-06-HC-01A	34S 36E	Surface	HC	Porcelain	White	Undecorated	Hollow form		1
ME-4/17/99-06-HC-01B	34S 36E	Surface	HC	Refined earthenware	Ironstone	Molded shell-edge decoration, blue	Rim, plate	1840-1900	1
ME-4/17/99-10-HC-01A	36S 22E	Surface	HC	Refined earthenware	Ironstone	Undecorated	Hollow form, probably bowl	1840-1900	1
ME-4/17/99-10-HC-01B	36S 22E	Surface	HC	Refined earthenware	Ironstone	Unkown	Rim, plate	1840-1900	1
ME-4/17/99-10-HC-02	36S 22E	Surface	HC	Kaolin	Tobacco pipe	Undecorated white kaolin	Pipe bowl		2
ME-4/29/99-01-HC-01	6S 43E	Surface	HC	Porcelain	Non-white	Handpainted overglaze, (orange), earth tone sprigged		1790-1825	1
ME-4/29/99-03-HC-01	20S 21E	Surface	HC	Porcelain	White	Decal (ghost), overglaze	Rim, lid	1880+	1
ME-4/29/99-07-HC-01	1N 40E	Surface	HC	Refined earthenware	Whiteware	Undecorated	Base	1820-1900	1
ME-4/30/99-05-HC-01	35S 43E	Surface	HC	Refined earthenware	Ironstone	Transferprint blue, underglaze, double-sided	Hollow form	1800-1860	1
ME-6/20/98-01-HC-01	5S 16E	Surface	HC	Porcelain	Non-white	Underglaze blue painted	Rim, saucer	1660-1850	1
ME-6/20/98-04-HC-01	12S 17E	Surface	HC	Refined earthenware	Whiteware	Handpainted underglaze blue		1820-1875	1
ME-6/20/98-05-HC-01	17S 14E	Surface	HC	Refined earthenware	Pearlware	Transferprint blue, double sided transfer	Base, cup	1785-1830	1
ME-6/20/98-06-HC-01	6S 18E	Surface	HC	Porcelain	Non-white	Underglaze blue painted		1660-1850	1
ME-6/20/98-07-HC-01A	17S 16E	Surface	HC	Porcelain	Non-white				1
ME-6/20/98-07-HC-01B	17S 16E	Surface	HC	Refined earthenware	Ironstone	Transferprint blue, double sided transfer		1800-1860	1
ME-6/20/98-07-HC-02	17S 16E	Surface	HC	Kaolin	Tobacco pipe	Undecorated	Pipe stem		1
ME-6/24/98-03-HC-01	32S 5E	Surface	HC	Porcelain	Non-white	Handpainted overglaze, color unknown		1730-1850	1
ME-6/24/98-06-HC-01	36S 18E	Surface	HC	Refined earthenware	Ironstone	Undecorated	Rim	1840-1900	1
ME-6/26/98-10-HC-01	16S 26E	Surface	HC	Kaolin	Tobacco pipe	Undecorated	Pipe bowl		1

KEY TO CODES

Appendix 4: Ceramic Artifacts

Artifact Category: HC=Historic Ceramic

Basic Categories:
PO-WH=Porcelain-White   RE-WW=Refined Earthenware-Whiteware   RE-PW=Refined Earthenware-Pearlware
PO-NW=Porcelain-Non-White   RE-IS=Refined Earthenware-Ironstone   RE-HW= Refined Earthenware-Hotel Ware
KP=Kaolinite Pipe Stem or Bowl

Appendix 5: Glass Artifacts (Non-Worked or Modified) / *page 1*

Metini #	Unit #	Level	Basic Group	Artifact Category	Vessel Type	Molding	Color	Vessel Part	Date	Form	Tint	Count
ME-4/29/99-04-GL-01A	20S 21E	1 (0-10 CM)	EA	GL	VS	DP	DG					1
ME-4/29/99-04-GL-01B	20S 21E	1 (0-10 CM)	EA	GL	VS	DP	DG					2
ME-4/29/99-04-GL-01C	20S 21E	1 (0-10 CM)	EA	GL	FG	FG	CO					1
ME-4/29/99-04-GL-01D	20S 21E	1 (0-10 CM)	EA	GL	FG	FG	CO					1
ME-4/29/99-05-GL-01	0N 10W	1 (0-10 CM)	EA	GL	VS	UN	GR					1
ME-5/01/99-02-GL-01A	15S 4E	1 (0-10 CM)	EA	GL	VS	DP	DG					5
ME-5/01/99-02-GL-01B	15S 4E	1 (0-10 CM)	EA	GL	VS	MO	DG					6
ME-5/01/99-02-GL-01C	15S 4E	1 (0-10 CM)	EA	GL	VS	MO	CO					2
ME-5/01/99-02-GL-01D	15S 4E	1 (0-10 CM)	EA	GL	VS	MO	CO					4
ME-4/29/99-06-GL-01A	20S 21E	2 (10-20 CM)	EA	GL	VS	DP	DG					8
ME-4/29/99-06-GL-01B	20S 21E	2 (10-20 CM)	EA	GL	VS	DP	DG					1
ME-4/29/99-06-GL-01C	20S 21E	2 (10-20 CM)	EA	GL	VS	MO	DG					2
ME-4/29/99-06-GL-01D	20S 21E	2 (10-20 CM)	EA	GL	VS	MO	DG					3
ME-4/29/99-06-GL-01E	20S 21E	2 (10-20 CM)	EA	GL	VS	MO	BR					1
ME-4/29/99-06-GL-01F	20S 21E	2 (10-20 CM)	EA	GL	VS	MO	CO			Medicinal bottle, square flat-sided	Aqua tint	1
ME-4/29/99-06-GL-01G	20S 21E	2 (10-20 CM)	EA	GL	FG	FG	CO				Aqua tint	3
ME-4/29/99-06-GL-01H	20S 21E	2 (10-20 CM)	EA	GL	FG	FG	CO				Aqua tint	3
ME-4/29/99-06-GL-01I	20S 21E	2 (10-20 CM)	EA	GL	FG	FG	CO					4
ME-5/01/99-11-GL-01A	15S 4E	2 (10-20 CM)	EA	GL	VS	DP	DG					6
ME-5/01/99-11-GL-01B	15S 4E	2 (10-20 CM)	EA	GL	VS	DP	DG			Case bottle		1
ME-5/01/99-11-GL-01C	15S 4E	2 (10-20 CM)	EA	GL	VS	UN	DG					5
ME-5/01/99-11-GL-01D	15S 4E	2 (10-20 CM)	EA	GL	MI	MI	CO			Mirror		1
ME-5/01/99-11-GL-01E	15S 4E	2 (10-20 CM)	EA	GL	VS	UN	CO					1
ME-5/01/99-11-GL-01F	15S 4E	2 (10-20 CM)	EA	GL	VS	MO	CO					5
ME-5/01/99-20-GL-01	15S 4E	2 (10-20 CM)	EA	GL	VS	UN	CO					1
ME-4/30/99-07-GL-01	0N 10W	3 (20-30 CM)	EA	GL	VS	MO	DG					2
ME-4/30/99-12-GL-01A	20S 21E	3 (20-30 CM)	EA	GL	VS	DP	DG					1
ME-4/30/99-12-GL-01B	20S 21E	3 (20-30 CM)	EA	GL	FG	FG	CO					1

Metini #	Unit #	Level	Basic Group	Artifact Category	Vessel Type	Molding	Color	Vessel Part	Date	Form	Tint	Count
ME-4/30/99-12-GL-01C	20S 21E	3 (20-30 CM)	EA	GL	VS	MO	CO					3
ME-4/30/99-12-GL-01D	20S 21E	3 (20-30 CM)	EA	GL	FG	FG	CO					2
ME-4/16/99-01-GL-01A	23S 23E	Surface	EA	GL	VS	MO	DG					3
ME-4/16/99-01-GL-01B	23S 23E	Surface	EA	GL	VS	MO	CO					3
ME-4/16/99-02-GL-01	21S 29E	Surface	EA	GL	VS	DP	BR		1730-1870	Case bottle		1
ME-4/16/99-03-GL-01	22S 32E	Surface	EA	GL	VS	DP	DG		1730-1870			1
ME-4/16/99-05-GL-01A	26S 28E	Surface	EA	GL	VS	DP	DG		1730-1870			1
ME-4/16/99-05-GL-01B	26S 28E	Surface	EA	GL	VS	DP	DG	Bottle base				1
ME-4/16/99-06-GL-01	29S 36E	Surface	EA	GL	FG	FG	CO				Aqua tint	1
ME-4/17/99-01-GL-01A	29S 21E	Surface	EA	GL	VS	UN	DG					1
ME-4/17/99-01-GL-01B	29S 21E	Surface	EA	GL	FG	FG	CO					1
ME-4/17/99-02-GL-01	30S34E	Surface	EA	GL	VS	DP	GR					1
ME-4/17/99-05-GL-01A	35S 28E	Surface	EA	GL	VS	PM	CO		1867-1920		Aqua tint	1
ME-4/17/99-05-GL-01B	35S 28E	Surface	EA	GL	LA	LA	CO	Rim, lamp				1
ME-4/17/99-07-GL-01	36S 32E	Surface	EA	GL	VS	DP	DG					1
ME-4/17/99-09-GL-01A	40S 26E	Surface	EA	GL	VS	UN	CO				Aqua tint	1
ME-4/17/99-09-GL-01B	40S 26E	Surface	EA	GL	VS	BL	CO			Patent or perfume bottle		1
ME-4/21/99-01-GL-01A	1N 35E	Surface	EA	GL	VS	DP	DG		1730-1867			1
ME-4/21/99-01-GL-01B	1N 35E	Surface	EA	GL	FG	FG	CO					1
ME-4/21/99-02-GL-01A	5N 38E	Surface	EA	GL	VS	DP	DG		1730-1867			1
ME-4/21/99-02-GL-01B	5N 38E	Surface	EA	GL	VS	DP	DG		1730-1867	Case bottle		1
ME-4/29/99-01-GL-01A	6S 43E	Surface	EA	GL	FG	FG	CO					2
ME-4/29/99-01-GL-01B	6S 43E	Surface	EA	GL	FG	FG	CO					2
ME-4/29/99-02-GL-01A	11S 41E	Surface	EA	GL	VS	MO	BR			Square, flat-sided bottle		1
ME-4/29/99-02-GL-01B	11S 41E	Surface	EA	GL	VS	MO	CO					1
ME-4/29/99-07-GL-01A	1N 40E	Surface	EA	GL	VS	DP	DG		1730-1867		Aqua tint	1
ME-4/29/99-07-GL-01B	1N 40E	Surface	EA	GL	VS	MO	CO					1
ME-4/29/99-08-GL-01	20S 21E	Surface	EA	GL	VS	UN	CO					1

Appendix 5: Glass Artifacts (Non-Worked or Modified) / *page 3*

Metini #	Unit #	Level	Basic Group	Artifact Category	Vessel Type	Molding	Color	Vessel Part	Date	Form	Tint	Count
ME-4/30/99-04-GL-01A	4S 40E	Surface	EA	GL	VS	MM	CO	Prescription lip	1889+	Mineral water bottle		1
ME-4/30/99-04-GL-01B	4S 40E	Surface	EA	GL	VS	DP	DG		1730-1870+			1
ME-4/30/99-04-GL-01C	4S 40E	Surface	EA	GL	FG	FG	CO				Aqua tint	1
ME-4/30/99-05-GL-01A	35S 43E	Surface	EA	GL	VS	UN	DG					1
ME-4/30/99-05-GL-01B	35S 43E	Surface	EA	GL	VS	MO	CO			Flat-sided panel bottle		1
ME-4/30/99-05-GL-01C	35S 43E	Surface	EA	GL	VS	MO	CO	Finish frag				1
ME-4/30/99-06-GL-01	38S 41E	Surface	EA	GL	VS	DP	DG					1
ME-4/30/99-08-GL-01	14N 42E	Surface	EA	GL	VS	MO	DG					1
ME-4/30/99-11-GL-01	27N 29E	Surface	EA	GL	VS	DP	DG		1730-1867	Case bottles		2
ME-6/06/98-01-GL-01	16N 4W	Surface	EA	GL	VS	UN	DG			Bubbles		2
ME-6/20/98-02-GL-01A	13S 14E	Surface	EA	GL	VS	DP	DG					3
ME-6/20/98-02-GL-01B	13S 14E	Surface	EA	GL	FG	FG	CO				Light blue tint	1
ME-6/20/98-03-GL-01	10S 14E	Surface	EA	GL	VS	BL	CO			Pharmaceutical		1
ME-6/20/98-04-GL-01	12S 17E	Surface	EA	GL	VS	MO	CO				Aqua tint	1
ME-6/20/98-05-GL-01A	17S 14E	Surface	EA	GL	VS	DP	DG					2
ME-6/20/98-05-GL-01B	17S 14E	Surface	EA	GL	VS	DP	DG	Bottle neck				1
ME-6/20/98-05-GL-01C	17S 14E	Surface	EA	GL	FG	FG	CO				Aqua tint	4
ME-6/20/98-07-GL-01A	17S 16E	Surface	EA	GL	VS	PM	CO			Patent bottle side panel	Aqua tint	1
ME-6/20/98-07-GL-01B	17S 16E	Surface	EA	GL	VS	DP	DG		1867-1920			1
ME-6/20/98-07-GL-01C	17S 16E	Surface	EA	GL	VS	MO	CO			Hexagonal panelled container. Could be portrait glass or a ketchup bottle.		1
ME-6/20/98-07-GL-01D	17S 16E	Surface	EA	GL	VS	MO	CO					1
ME-6/20/98-07-GL-01E	17S 16E	Surface	EA	GL	FG	FG	CO				Aqua tint	1
ME-6/20/98-08-GL-01	4S 10E	Surface	EA	GL	VS	DP	GR		1730-1870	Case bottle, bubbles		1
ME-6/23/98-01-GL-01	25S 2E	Surface	EA	GL	VS	DP	DG		1730-1870 (2)	Bubbles		2
ME-6/23/98-03-GL-01	30S 8E	Surface	EA	GL	VS	MO	DG					1
ME-6/26/98-01-GL-01	5S 24E	Surface	EA	GL	VS	MO	DG					1

Appendix 5: Glass Artifacts (Non-Worked or Modified) / page 4

Metini #	Unit #	Level	Basic Group	Artifact Category	Vessel Type	Molding	Color	Vessel Part	Date	Form	Tint	Count
ME-6/26/98-02-GL-01	2S 25E	Surface	EA	GL	VS	MO	DG					1
ME-6/26/98-03-GL-01A	8S 22E	Surface	EA	GL	VS	UN	DG					1
ME-6/26/98-03-GL-01B	8S 22E	Surface	EA	GL	VS	MO	CO					2
ME-6/26/98-05-GL-01	5S 33E	Surface	EA	GL	VS	DP	DG		1730-1870	Bubbles		1
ME-6/26/98-06-GL-01A	5S 36E	Surface	EA	GL	VS	UN	CO					1
ME-6/26/98-06-GL-01B	5S 36E	Surface	EA	GL	VS	MO	DG					1
ME-6/26/98-08-GL-01A	10S 37E	Surface	EA	GL	VS	DP	BR		1730-1870 (2)			2
ME-6/26/98-08-GL-01B	10S 37E	Surface	EA	GL	VS	MO	GR					1
ME-6/26/98-09-GL-01A	18S 22E	Surface	EA	GL	VS	DP	DG		1730-1870 (3)			3
ME-6/26/98-09-GL-01B	18S 22E	Surface	EA	GL	LA	LA	CO					1
ME-6/26/98-09-GL-01C	18S 22E	Surface	EA	GL	VS	MO	CO					1
ME-6/26/98-09-GL-01D	18S 22E	Surface	EA	GL	VS	MO	CO					1
ME-6/26/98-10-GL-01A	16S 26E	Surface	EA	GL	VS	MO	CO					1
ME-6/26/98-10-GL-01B	16S 26E	Surface	EA	GL	FG	FG	CO	Bottle shoulder				1
ME-6/26/98-12-GL-01	19S 38E	Surface	EA	GL	VS	MO	CO				Solarized	1
ME-9/12/98-03-GL-01	15S 21E	Surface	EA	GL	VS	DP	DG		1730-1870			1
ME-9/12/98-04-GL-01	11S 28E	Surface	EA	GL	VS	MO	DG					1
ME-9/12/98-05-GL-01	12S 33E	Surface	EA	GL	VS	MO	DG					1
ME-5/02/99-06-GL-01	15S 4E	West Wall above Feature 1	EA	GL	VS	MO	CO					1

KEY TO CODES

Appendix 5: Glass Artifacts (Non-Worked or Modified)

Artifact Category: GL=Glass

Vessel Type:
VS=Vessel   FG=Flat Glass
LG=Lamp/Globe   MI=Mirror

Molding:
BL=Free Blown Glass   DP=Dip Molding
MM=Machine Molding   PM=Plate Molding
MO=Molded Glass   UN=Unidentifiable Manufacture Method

Color:
GR=Light Green   DG=Dark Green   BG=Blue-Green
YG=Yellow-Green   AQ=Aqua   BR=Brown   CO=Colorless

Metini #	Unit	Level	Basic Group	Artifact Category	Worked Glass Class	EM	Max Length (cm)	Max Width (cm)	Max Thickness (cm)	Weight (g)	Vessel Type	Molding	Color	Tint	Ves Part	Date	Form	Count
ME-6/20/98-05-LI-01	17S 14E	Surface	EA	WG	FS	EM	-	-	-	-	VS	UN	DG					1
ME-9/12/98-05-LI-01	12S 33E	Surface	EA	WG	SH	No	-	-	-	-	VS	UN	DG					1
ME-6/04/98-01-WG-01	2N 10W	Surface	EA	WG	GS	EM	-	-	-	-	VS	DP	DG					1
ME-6/20/98-01-WG-01	5S 16E	Surface	EA	GL	GS	No	27.52	26.38	3.79	3.22	VS	UN	DG					1
ME-6/20/98-04-WG-01A	12S 17E	Surface	EA	GL	GS	No	15.18	14.22	1.44	0.36	FG	FG	CO					1
ME-6/20/98-04-WG-01A	12S 17E	Surface	EA	GL	GS	No	17.17	8.7	2.02	0.51	VS	MO	CO					1
ME-6/20/98-04-WG-01C	12S 17E	Surface	EA	GL	GS	No	23.45	17.53	3.35	1.91	VS	DP	DG					1
ME-6/20/98-04-WG-01D	12S 17E	Surface	EA	WG	GS	EM	17.06	11.07	2.99	0.77	VS	DP	DG					1
ME-6/20/98-04-WG-01E	12S 17E	Surface	EA	GL	GS	No	28.22	25.05	2.73	2.05	VS	DP	DG					1
ME-6/20/98-04-WG-02A	12S 17E	Surface	EA	WG	PX	EM	14.5	13.63	4.09	0.42	VS	DP	DG					1
ME-6/20/98-04-WG-02B	12S 17E	Surface	EA	WG	FS	EM	13.01	6.77	2.18	0.13	VS	DP	DG					1
ME-6/20/98-04-WG-02C	12S 17E	Surface	EA	WG	PX	EM	16.53	14.48	3.5	0.77	VS	DP	DG					1
ME-6/20/98-04-WG-03	12S 17E	Surface	EA	WG	GS	EM	35.32	31.2	4.44	5.14	VS	MO	DG				Lettered Plate	1
ME-6/20/98-04-WG-04	12S 17E	Surface	EA	GL	CP	No	22.96	11.43	6.5	1.85	VS	DP	DG					1
ME-6/20/98-04-WG-05	12S 17E	Surface	EA	WG	GS	EM	44.2	42.68	20.63	18.5	VS	DP	DG		Base of bottle		Case bottle	1
ME-6/20/98-05-WG-01	17S 14E	Surface	EA	GL	GS	No	30.38	15.28	3.03	2.33	VS	DP	DG					1
ME-6/20/98-06-WG-01A	6S 18E	Surface	EA	WG	GS	EM	41.85	37.41	4.65	8.59	VS	DP	DG			1730-1870+		1
ME-6/20/98-06-WG-01B	6S 18E	Surface	EA	WG	GS	EM	27.31	24.78	4.75	2.26	VS	BL	GR		Bottle neck			1
ME-6/20/98-06-WG-02	6S 18E	Surface	EA	WG	CP	EM	30.58	14.25	6.48	1.9	VS	DP	DG			1730-1870+		1
ME-6/20/98-07-WG-01A	17S 16E	Surface	EA	WG	GS	EM	30.8	19.95	14.44	6.18	VS	DP	DG		Bottle base			1
ME-6/20/98-07-WG-01B	17S 16E	Surface	EA	GL	GS	No	14.59	8.22	4.73	1.01	VS	MO	DG					1
ME-6/20/98-07-WG-01C	17S 16E	Surface	EA	GL	GS	No	30.78	20.04	7.31	4.81	VS	MM	GR		Bottle base		Beer bottle	1
ME-6/20/98-07-WG-02A	17S 16E	Surface	EA	WG	FS	EM	16.11	8.73	5.08	0.74	VS	MO	GR					1
ME-6/20/98-07-WG-02B	17S 16E	Surface	EA	WG	FS	EM	21.49	15.87	6.87	1.85	VS	DP	DG		Bottle base			1
ME-6/20/98-07-WG-03A	17S 16E	Surface	EA	WG	CP	EM	21.9	14.91	3.5	1.37	VS	MO	DG					1
ME-6/20/98-07-WG-03B	17S 16E	Surface	EA	WG	CP	No	15.68	9.87	2.7	0.37	VS	DP	DG		Exterior bottle cortex			1
ME-6/20/98-07-WG-04A	17S 16E	Surface	EA	WG	FS	EM	16.01	9.8	3.62	0.58	VS	MO	DG					1
ME-6/20/98-07-WG-04B	17S 16E	Surface	EA	WG	CP	EM	16.33	13.77	3.29	0.65	VS	DP	DG					1
ME-6/23/98-02-WG-01	22S 6E	Surface	EA	WG	PX	EM	17.32	8.6	3.49	0.54	VS	DP	DG			1730-1870+		1
ME-6/23/98-02-WG-01	25S 11E	Surface	EA	WG	GS	EM	29.92	22.15	4.59	4.08	VS	DP	DG			1730-1870+		1
ME-6/23/98-02-WG-02	25S 11E	Surface	EA	WG	GS	EM	26.26	15.18	5.86	1.98	VS	DP	DG			1730-1870		1
ME-6/24/98-02-WG-01	22S 19E	Surface	EA	WG	GS	EM	42.83	23.19	4.58	5.75	VS	MO	AQ				Panelled bottle	1
ME-6/24/98-02-WG-02	22S 19E	Surface	EA	WG	SH	EM	31.02	23.55	5.1	3.35	VS	DP	DG			1730-1870+		1
ME-6/24/98-05-WG-01	39S 13E	Surface	EA	WG	SH	EM	24.28	23.28	8.92	2.85	VS	DP	DG		Down tooled lip, champagne finish	1730-1870+		1
ME-6/25/98-03-WG-01	11N 1E	Surface	EA	WG	GS	EM	18.87	13.45	3.48	0.8	VS	MO	CO				Panelled bottle, case bottle	1
ME-6/25/98-05-WG-01	13N 10E	Surface	EA	WG	GS	EM	36.85	29.08	3.98	5.95	VS	DP	DG					1
ME-6/26/98-01-WG-01	5S 24E	Surface	EA	WG	CP	No	12.53	6.54	2.51	0.16	VS	DP	DG			1730-1870+		1
ME-6/26/98-01-WG-02A	5S 24E	Surface	EA	WG	FS	EM	24.73	11.92	9.51	1.77	VS	DP	DG		Bottle base	1730-1870+		1
ME-6/26/98-01-WG-02B	5S 24E	Surface	EA	WG	FS	No	14.45	13.11	2.01	0.31	VS	DP	DG					1
ME-6/26/98-01-WG-03	5S 24E	Surface	EA	WG	CO	No	28.79	15.86	9.22	6.33	VS	DP	CO		Bottle base	1730-1870+		1
ME-6/26/98-03-WG-01A	8S 22E	Surface	EA	WG	GS	EM	52.79	49.39	10.94	26.9	VS	UN	DG					1
ME-6/26/98-03-WG-01B	8S 22E	Surface	EA	GL	GS	No	17.46	14.07	3.33	0.9	VS	MO	DG					1
ME-6/26/98-03-WG-01C	8S 22E	Surface	EA	GL	GS	No	19.26	11.67	2.23	0.61	VS	MO	CO					1
ME-6/26/98-03-WG-02	8S 22E	Surface	EA	WG	PPF	No	28.59	15.88	5.93	2.14	VS	UN	DG					1
ME-6/26/98-03-WG-03	8S 22E	Surface	EA	WG	CF	No	30.9	18.45	12.1	6.55	VS	DP	DG		Bottle base	1730-1870+		1
ME-6/26/98-03-WG-04	8S 22E	Surface	EA	WG	FS	EM	15.86	9.97	4.86	0.71	VS	MO	DG					1
ME-6/26/98-03-WG-05	8S 22E	Surface	EA	WG	SH	No	13.72	8.75	2.09	0.28	VS	MO	DG					1
ME-6/26/98-04-WG-01A	7S 27E	Surface	EA	GL	GS	No	28.08	27.07	2.89	2.69	VS	DP	DG					1
ME-6/26/98-04-WG-01B	7S 27E	Surface	EA	WG	GS	EM	51.97	25.11	4.71	6.02	VS	DP	DG					1
ME-6/26/98-04-WG-01C	7S 27E	Surface	EA	WG	GS	EM	30.29	27.98	6.07	5.18	VS	DP	DG					1
ME-6/26/98-04-WG-02A	7S 27E	Surface	EA	WG	PX	No	23.02	12.27	5.56	1.08	VS	DP	DG			1730-1870+		1
ME-6/26/98-04-WG-02B	7S 27E	Surface	EA	WG	FS	No	10.42	6.95	2.42	0.13	VS	DP	DG					1
ME-6/26/98-05-WG-01A	5S 33E	Surface	EA	WG	GS	EM	72.82	29.81	5.4	13.18	VS	DP	DG			1730-1870+		1
ME-6/26/98-05-WG-01B	5S 33E	Surface	EA	GL	GS	No	27.05	16.72	2.72	1.46	VS	DP	DG			1730-1870+		1
ME-6/26/98-05-WG-01C	5S 33E	Surface	EA	GL	GS	No	19.04	12.83	2.1	0.78	VS	UN	AQ					1
ME-6/26/98-05-WG-02	5S 33E	Surface	EA	WG	FS	EM	37.31	17.44	4.05	3.06	VS	DP	DG			1730-187+		1
ME-6/26/98-06-WG-01A	5S 36E	Surface	EA	GL	GS	No	21.54	16.92	3.97	2.15	VS	UN	DG					1

Metini #	Unit	Level	Basic Group	Artifact Category	Worked Glass Class	EM	Max Length (cm)	Max Width (cm)	Max Thickness (cm)	Weight (g)	Vessel Type	Molding	Color	Tint	Ves Part	Date	Form	Count
ME-6/26/98-06-WG-01B	5S 36E	Surface	EA	WG	SH	No	18.35	13.74	4.7	1.41	VS	DP	GR			1730-1870+	Case bottle	1
ME-6/26/98-07-WG-01	7S 30E	Surface	EA	WG	FS	No	20.94	9.44	3.89	0.37	VS	MO	DG					1
ME-6/26/98-08-WG-01	10S 37E	Surface	EA	WG	SH	No	5.23	4.58	2.11	0.06	VS	UN	DG					1
ME-6/26/98-08-WG-02	10S 37E	Surface	EA	WG	GS	EM	36.33	24.54	3.98	6.55	VS	DP	DG			1730-1870+		1
ME-6/26/98-09-WG-01	18S 22E	Surface	EA	WG	CF	EM	27	19.2	8.92	3.98	VS	DP	DG		Bottle base	1730-1870+		1
ME-6/26/98-09-WG-02A	18S 22E	Surface	EA	GL	GS	No	50.75	27.53	5.03	9.84	VS	DP	BR					1
ME-6/26/98-09-WG-02B	18S 22E	Surface	EA	GL	GS	No	11.35	4.7	2.68	0.18	VS	DP	DG					1
ME-6/26/98-09-WG-02C	18S 22E	Surface	EA	GL	GS	No	13.23	9.03	1.77	0.43	VS	DP	GR					1
ME-6/26/98-09-WG-02D	18S 22E	Surface	EA	WG	GS	EM	22.32	12.47	3.33	1.32	VS	DP	BR				Case bottle	1
ME-6/26/98-09-WG-03A	18S 22E	Surface	EA	WG	CP	No	8.97	5.66	1.2	0.05	VS	UN	DG					1
ME-6/26/98-09-WG-03B	18S 22E	Surface	EA	WG	CP	No	8.14	4.63	1.03	0.02	VS	UN	DG					1
ME-6/26/98-09-WG-04	18S 22E	Surface	EA	WG	SH	No	7.07	6.95	1.36	0.08	VS	DP	DG					1
ME-6/26/98-10-WG-01	16S 26E	Surface	EA	WG	SH	No	25.13	22.49	8.8	6.54	VS	DP	DG		Lip and rim, champagne finish			1
ME-6/26/98-10-WG-02	16S 26E	Surface	EA	GL	GS	No	23.18	13.73	2.78	1.2	VS	DP	DG					1
ME-6/26/98-11-WG-01	20S 30E	Surface	EA	WG	CO	EM	41.93	35.43	23.12	27.52	VS	DP	DG		Bottle kickup			1
ME-6/26/98-12-WG-01	19S 38E	Surface	EA	WG	GS	EM	54.96	39.05	3.45	11.06	VS	DP	DG		Bottle shoulder with seam			1
ME-6/26/98-12-WG-02	19S 38E	Surface	EA	WG	GS	EM	26.31	19.15	6.27	3.32	VS	DP	DG		Bottle base			1
ME-9/12/98-03-WG-01A	15S 21E	Surface	EA	WG	GS	EM	27.48	25.55	2.06	2.53	VS	MO	BR					1
ME-9/12/98-03-WG-01B	15S 21E	Surface	EA	GL	GS	No	26.74	19.72	4.71	3.6	FG	FG	CO					1
ME-9/12/98-03-WG-02A	15S 21E	Surface	EA	WG	GS	EM	32.73	22.74	5.26	4.83	VS	MO	DG					1
ME-9/12/98-03-WG-02B	15S 21E	Surface	EA	WG	FS	EM	25.77	7.04	3.13	0.64	VS	MO	DG					1
ME-9/12/98-04-WG-01	11S 28E	Surface	EA	WG	SH	EM	37.16	20.36	3.31	2.8	VS	DP	DG			1730-1870+		1
ME-9/12/98-04-WG-02A	11S 28E	Surface	EA	WG	GS	EM	27.2	7.7	3.93	1.5	VS	DP	DG					1
ME-9/12/98-04-WG-02B	11S 28E	Surface	EA	GL	GS	No	32.17	15.72	3.35	1.77	VS	DP	DG					1
ME-9/12/98-04-WG-02C	11S 28E	Surface	EA	GL	GS	No	25.99	10.63	3.45	1.73	VS	DP	DG					1
ME-9/12/98-05-WG-01A	12S 33E	Surface	EA	WG	GS	EM	11.6	11.09	2.75	0.62	VS	MO	GR					1
ME-9/12/98-05-WG-01B	12S 33E	Surface	EA	WG	GS	EM	41.75	35.1	7.39	10.7	VS	DP	DG		Bottle base (kick up)			1
ME-9/12/98-05-WG-02	12S 33E	Surface	EA	WG	CO	No	32.45	32.07	14.8	11.38	VS	DP	DG		Bottle base (kick up)			1
ME-9/12/98-06-WG-01A	13S 36E	Surface	EA	WG	SH	EM	28.65	22.19	6.96	7.61	VS	MO	DG		Bottle lip (stopper type finish)			1
ME-9/12/98-06-WG-01B	13S 36E	Surface	EA	WG	GS	No	39.7	19.08	4.87	4.9	VS	MO	DG		Metallic patina			1
ME-9/12/98-06-WG-01C	13S 36E	Surface	EA	WG	GS	No	24.72	15.42	3.24	1.21	VS	PM	CO	Aqua			Patent bottle; partial letters "ier" or "ifr"	1
ME-9/12/98-06-WG-01D	13S 36E	Surface	EA	WG	GS	EM	25.53	15.7	3.43	2.3	VS	DP	BR					1
ME-9/12/98-06-WG-01E	13S 36E	Surface	EA	WG	GS	No	34.06	19.17	3.77	4.2	VS	DP	BR					1
ME-4/16/99-01-WG-01A	23S 23E	Surface	EA	GL	GS	No	14.21	13.97	1.91	0.68	VS	MO	GR					1
ME-4/16/99-01-WG-01B	23S 23E	Surface	EA	WG	GS	EM	48.27	41.46	2.39	7.93	VS	DP	DG		Bottle shoulder			1
ME-4/16/99-01-WG-02	23S 23E	Surface	EA	WG	CP	EM	14.25	16.56	1.83	0.45	VS	UN	DG					1
ME-4/16/99-02-WG-01	21S 29E	Surface	EA	GL	GS	No	29.08	17.17	3.74	2.34	VS	DP	DG					1
ME-4/16/99-03-WG-01	22S 32E	Surface	EA	WG	GS	EM	51.09	39.1	5.66	17.16	VS	DP	DG					1
ME-4/16/99-04-WG-01A	23S 38E	Surface	EA	WG	GS	EM	32.72	24.41	3.51	3.52	VS	MO	DG				Case bottle - embossed "OH" or "HO"	1
ME-4/16/99-04-WG-01B	23S 38E	Surface	EA	WG	GS	EM	30.83	27.17	3.3	5.11	VS	MO	DG					1
ME-4/16/99-04-WG-02A	23S 38E	Surface	EA	WG	PX	EM	30.94	20.29	5.01	2.82	VS	DP	DG					1
ME-4/16/99-04-WG-02B	23S 38E	Surface	EA	WG	FS	EM	10.32	16.26	5.62	0.63	VS	MO	DG					1
ME-4/16/99-04-WG-02A	23S 38E	Surface	EA	GL	GS	No	28.35	28.07	2.73	2.93	VS	MO	DG					1
ME-4/16/99-04-WG-02B	23S 38E	Surface	EA	WG	GS	EM	34.76	25.21	4.94	4.77	VS	MO	DG					1
ME-4/16/99-04-WG-02C	23S 38E	Surface	EA	WG	GS	EM	21.8	10.57	3.35	1.15	VS	DP	DG					1
ME-4/16/99-04-WG-02D	23S 38E	Surface	EA	GL	GS	No	17.36	10.88	2.49	0.85	VS	UN	CO	Aqua				1
ME-4/16/99-04-WG-02E	23S 38E	Surface	EA	WG	GS	EM	26.59	12.42	2.8	1.29	VS	MO	GR					1
ME-4/16/99-05-WG-01A	26S 28E	Surface	EA	WG	SH	EM	17.85	11.42	3.26	0.92	VS	DP	DG					1
ME-4/16/99-05-WG-01B	26S 28E	Surface	EA	WG	SH	EM	32.69	9.08	6.76	2.48	VS	DP	DG					1
ME-4/16/99-05-WG-01C	26S 28E	Surface	EA	WG	FS	No	7.72	5.85	2.47	0.09	VS	DP	DG					1
ME-4/16/99-05-WG-02	26S 28E	Surface	EA	GL	GS	No	25.81	17.22	2.88	1.91	VS	UN	DG					1

Metini #	Unit	Level	Basic Group	Artifact Category	Worked Glass Class	EM	Max Length (cm)	Max Width (cm)	Max Thickness (cm)	Weight (g)	Vessel Type	Molding	Color	Tint	Ves Part	Date	Form	Count
ME-4/16/99-06-WG-01	29S 36E	Surface	EA	WG	FS	EM	13.65	16.54	1.8	0.44	VS	DP	DG					1
ME-4/17/99-01-WG-01	29S 21E	Surface	EA	WG	CF	No	28.37	14.69	12.71	4.17	VS	DP	DG		Bottle base			1
ME-4/17/99-01-WG-02	29S 21E	Surface	EA	WG	FS	No	5.36	6.62	1.26	0.05	VS	DP	DG					1
ME-4/17/99-01-WG-03	29S 21E	Surface	EA	WG	FS	EM	12.95	12.54	1.69	0.38	VS	MO	CO					1
ME-4/17/99-01-WG-04A	29S 21E	Surface	EA	GL	GS	No	16.7	12.26	3.21	0.82	VS	MO	CO		Tumbler rim			1
ME-4/17/99-01-WG-04B	29S 21E	Surface	EA	WG	GS	EM	19.84	19.6	2.78	1.89	VS	DP	DG					1
ME-4/17/99-01-WG-04C	29S 21E	Surface	EA	WG	GS	EM	16.58	8.59	1.99	0.38	VS	DP	DG					1
ME-4/17/99-01-WG-04D	29S 21E	Surface	EA	GL	GS	No	27.77	19.44	1.96	1.41	VS	DP	DG					1
ME-4/17/99-02-WG-01	30S 34E	Surface	EA	WG	GS	EM	29.65	29.72	3.14	5.59	VS	DP	DG					1
ME-4/17/99-03-WG-01	31S 33E	Surface	EA	WG	FS	No	15.26	9.38	4.6	0.58	VS	UN	DG					1
ME-4/17/99-03-WG-02A	31S 33E	Surface	EA	WG	GS	EM	21.56	20.86	2.79	2.48	VS	DP	DG					1
ME-4/17/99-03-WG-02B	31S 33E	Surface	EA	WG	GS	EM	18.93	14.96	2.26	1.05	VS	DP	GR					1
ME-4/17/99-04-WG-01	35S 21E	Surface	EA	WG	GS	EM	32.06	26.49	5.87	6.26	VS	MO	AQ		Bottle base		Panelled bottle	1
ME-4/17/99-04-WG-02	35S 21E	Surface	EA	WG	GS	EM	29.93	16.09	4.17	2.41	VS	MO	GR					1
ME-4/17/99-05-WG-01A	35S 28E	Surface	EA	WG	CP	EM	21.62	9.73	2.96	0.63	VS	DP	DG					1
ME-4/17/99-05-WG-01B	35S 28E	Surface	EA	WG	FS	No	9.34	7.88	1.18	0.05	VS	DP	DG					1
ME-4/17/99-05-WG-02A	35S 28E	Surface	EA	WG	GS	EM	23.15	11.01	1.71	0.65	VS	DP	DG					1
ME-4/17/99-05-WG-02B	35S 28E	Surface	EA	WG	GS	EM	30.16	22.47	3.54	3.67	VS	MO	BR				Embossed "UD"	1
ME-4/17/99-06-WG-01A	34S 36E	Surface	EA	WG	CF	EM	23.93	17.74	13.87	4.53	VS	DP	DG		Bottle base			1
ME-4/17/99-06-WG-01B	34S 36E	Surface	EA	GL	GS	No	12.1	8.59	2.08	0.46	VS	UN	GR					1
ME-4/17/99-06-WG-02	34S 36E	Surface	EA	WG	CP	EM	9.52	11.01	3.33	0.23	VS	DP	DG					1
ME-4/17/99-07-WG-01	36S 32E	Surface	EA	WG	GS	EM	24.58	19.01	4.64	3.78	VS	DP	DG					1
ME-4/17/99-07-WG-02	36S 32E	Surface	EA	WG	SH	No	16.45	13.78	6.49	1.79	VS	DP	DG					1
ME-4/17/99-08-WG-01A	39S 37E	Surface	EA	GL	GS	No	14.64	13.01	2.89	0.61	VS	MO	DG					1
ME-4/17/99-08-WG-01B	39S 37E	Surface	EA	WG	SH	EM	13.82	14.1	2.02	0.61	VS	MO	DG					1
ME-4/17/99-08-WG-01C	39S 37E	Surface	EA	WG	SH	No	16.12	7.51	2.39	0.33	VS	MO	DG					1
ME-4/17/99-09-WG-01	40S 26E	Surface	EA	WG	FS	EM	22.99	12.59	3.67	1.29	VS	UN	GR		Bottle base fragment			1
ME-4/17/99-10-WG-01	36S 22E	Surface	EA	WG	GS	EM	16.2	14.25	2.65	0.84	VS	DP	DG					1
ME-4/21/99-01-WG-01	1N 35E	Surface	EA	WG	GS	EM	44.84	23.35	5.33	6.84	VS	DP	DG					1
ME-4/21/99-01-WG-02	1N 35E	Surface	EA	WG	FS	EM	44.99	24.06	5.35	7.67	VS	DP	DG					1
ME-4/21/99-02-WG-01A	5N 38E	Surface	EA	WG	CF	No	53.28	43.64	9.12	28.04	VS	DP	DG		Bottle base			1
ME-4/21/99-02-WG-01B	5N 38E	Surface	EA	WG	GS	EM	34.92	20.72	3.54	4.65	VS	MO	CO	Aqua				1
ME-4/21/99-02-WG-02	5N 38E	Surface	EA	WG	FS	No	8.83	10.16	1.31	0.09	VS	DP	DG					1
ME-4/21/99-02-WG-03	5N 38E	Surface	EA	WG	CP	EM	15.12	17.15	2.73	0.63	VS	DP	DG					1
ME-4/21/99-02-WG-04A	5N 38E	Surface	EA	WG	GS	EM	14.52	7.53	2.37	0.45	VS	DP	DG					1
ME-4/21/99-02-WG-04B	5N 38E	Surface	EA	GL	GS	No	27.72	30.95	4.44	4.64	VS	DP	DG					1
ME-4/21/99-02-WG-04C	5N 38E	Surface	EA	GL	GS	No	34.04	26.94	2.82	3.43	VS	DP	BG					1
ME-4/21/99-02-WG-04D	5N 38E	Surface	EA	WG	GS	EM	36.48	29.36	4.68	6.12	VS	DP	DG					1
ME-4/21/99-02-WG-04E	5N 38E	Surface	EA	GL	GS	No	39.49	15.71	3.79	3.37	VS	DP	DG					1
ME-4/21/99-02-WG-04F	5N 38E	Surface	EA	WG	GS	EM	60.15	20.1	7.75	19.3	VS	DP	DG					1
ME-4/21/99-02-WG-05	5N 38E	Surface	EA	WG	SH	No	13.74	19.85	8.73	3.38	VS	DP	DG		Bottle base			1
ME-4/21/99-03-WG-01	0N 28E	Surface	EA	GL	GS	No	29.55	30	2.44	4.1	VS	DP	DG					1
ME-4/21/99-06-WG-01	8N 24E	Surface	EA	WG	GS	EM	20.51	16.68	3.73	2.09	VS	DP	DG					1
ME-4/21/99-08-WG-01	13N 35E	Surface	EA	WG	SH	EM	21.34	15.51	5.31	2.16	VS	DP	DG				Case bottle; embossed (unreadable)	1
ME-4/29/99-01-WG-01A	6S 43E	Surface	EA	WG	CP	EM	27.33	13.85	7.67	2.16	VS	DP	DG					1
ME-4/29/99-01-WG-01B	6S 43E	Surface	EA	WG	CP	EM	15.46	9.56	2.97	0.42	VS	UN	DG					1
ME-4/29/99-01-WG-01C	6S 43E	Surface	EA	WG	FS	No	12.14	8.17	1.29	0.14	VS	UN	DG					1
ME-4/29/99-01-WG-02	6S 43E	Surface	EA	GL	GS	No	23.31	11.46	3.34	1.27	VS	DP	DG				Case bottle	1
ME-4/29/99-01-WG-03	6S 43E	Surface	EA	WG	FS	No	14.85	7.08	5.3	0.43	VS	UN	DG					1
ME-4/29/99-01-WG-04	6S 43E	Surface	EA	WG	FS	No	11.89	5.83	2.31	0.18	VS	UN	DG					1
ME-4/29/99-02-WG-01	11S 41E	Surface	EA	WG	CF	EM	31.66	28.47	10.68	10.94	VS	DP	DG		Bottle base			1
ME-4/29/99-02-WG-02	11S 41E	Surface	EA	WG	GS	EM	49.92	34.46	3.28	7.66	VS	DP	GR				Mineral bottle	1
ME-4/29/99-02-WG-03A	11S 41E	Surface	EA	WG	GS	EM	32.2	14.85	5.11	2.63	VS	DP	AQ				Case bottle, mineral water	1
ME-4/29/99-02-WG-03B	11S 41E	Surface	EA	GL	GS	No	41.76	24.83	4.8	5.63	VS	MO	CO				Flattened bottle	1
ME-4/29/99-02-WG-04	11S 41E	Surface	EA	WG	SH	No	12.81	6.87	5.29	0.52	VS	DP	DG					1
ME-4/29/99-07-WG-01A	1N 40E	Surface	EA	WG	CF	EM	29.12	24.74	12.01	6.76	VS	DP	DG		Bottle base			1
ME-4/29/99-07-WG-01B	1N 40E	Surface	EA	WG	GS	EM	28.78	15.96	2.72	2	VS	DP	DG					1

Metini #	Unit	Level	Basic Group	Artifact Category	Worked Glass Class	EM	Max Length (cm)	Max Width (cm)	Max Thickness (cm)	Weight (g)	Vessel Type	Molding	Color	Tint	Ves Part	Date	Form	Count
ME-4/29/99-07-WG-01C	1N 40E	Surface	EA	WG	GS	EM	12.23	7.82	2.21	0.29	VS	DP	DG					1
ME-4/29/99-07-WG-02	1N 40E	Surface	EA	WG	FS	EM	14.2	7.44	1.9	0.23	VS	MO	CO					1
ME-4/30/99-02-WG-01	19S 43E	Surface	EA	WG	GS	EM	35.88	24.49	3.86	5.89	VS	DP	DG					1
ME-4/30/99-04-WG-01A	4S 40E	Surface	EA	WG	GS	EM	28.92	32.92	5.1	7.24	VS	DP	DG					1
ME-4/30/99-04-WG-01B	4S 40E	Surface	EA	WG	GS	EM	4.07	13.2	3.05	0.96	VS	DP	DG					1
ME-4/30/99-04-WG-01C	4S 40E	Surface	EA	WG	GS	EM	19.14	31.84	6.41	3.35	VS	MO	AQ		Prescription lip, bottle finish			1
ME-4/30/99-04-WG-02	4S 40E	Surface	EA	WG	PX	EM	16.64	14.09	2.57	0.78	VS	DP	DG					1
ME-4/30/99-04-WG-03	4S 40E	Surface	EA	WG	CO	EM	41.43	18.61	13.88	10.3	VS	DP	DG		Bottle base			1
ME-4/30/99-05-WG-01A	35S 43E	Surface	EA	WG	GS	EM	8.62	8.51	1.54	0.2	VS	DP	DG					1
ME-4/30/99-05-WG-01B	35S 43E	Surface	EA	WG	GS	EM	23.43	13.73	3.69	1.97	VS	DP	DG				Case bottle, embossed	1
ME-4/30/99-05-WG-02	35S 43E	Surface	EA	WG	SH	No	15.01	13.9	6.27	1.1	VS	DP	DG					1
ME-4/30/99-05-WG-03	35S 43E	Surface	EA	WG	GS	EM	27.44	20.82	3.4	2.45	VS	DP	DG					1
ME-4/30/99-06-WG-01	38S 41E	Surface	EA	WG	GS	EM	44.1	29.22	3.41	7.97	VS	DP	GR					1
ME-4/30/99-09-WG-01	6N 41E	Surface	EA	WG	SH	No	7.53	6.13	1.96	0.07	VS	UN	GR					1
ME-4/30/99-010-WG-01	19N 42E	Surface	EA	GL	GS	No	26.12	19.38	3.8	2.51	VS	MO	CO					1
ME-5/01/99-01-WG-01	22N 38E	Surface	EA	WG	GS	EM	-	-	-	-	VS	DP	DG					1
ME-4/30/99-01-WG-01A	0N 10W	2 (10-20 CM)	EA	WG	SH	EM	11.65	8.21	3.88	0.69	VS	DP	GR					1
ME-4/30/99-01-WG-01B	0N 10W	2 (10-20 CM)	EA	WG	GS	EM	5.5	6.77	2.5	0.18	VS	DP	DG					1
ME-4/30/99-01-WG-01C	0N 10W	2 (10-20 CM)	EA	WG	FS	EM	12.18	11.55	4.03	0.45	VS	DP	GR					1
ME-4/30/99-01-WG-01D	0N 10W	2 (10-20 CM)	EA	WG	SH	No	7.49	6.46	3.74	0.24	VS	DP	GR					1
ME-5/01/99-02-WG-01A	15S 4E	1 (0-10 CM)	EA	WG	CP	EM	38.86	20.63	6.26	4.82	VS	DP	DG					1
ME-5/01/99-02-WG-01B	15S 4E	1 (0-10 CM)	EA	WG	PX	EM	24.33	15.7	4.65	1.44	VS	DP	DG					1
ME-5/01/99-02-WG-01C	15S 4E	1 (0-10 CM)	EA	WG	PX	EM	16.92	12.24	2.61	0.6	VS	UN	DG					1
ME-5/01/99-02-WG-01D	15S 4E	1 (0-10 CM)	EA	WG	FS	No	8.23	9.89	3.16	0.17	VS	UN	BR					1
ME-5/01/99-02-WG-01E	15S 4E	1 (0-10 CM)	EA	WG	SH	No	4.66	2.72	0.71	0.01	VS	UN	DG					1
ME-5/01/99-02-WG-01F	15S 4E	1 (0-10 CM)	EA	WG	FS	No	9.48	8.82	1.2	0.07	VS	UN	DG					1
ME-5/01/99-02-WG-02A	15S 4E	1 (0-10 CM)	EA	WG	GS	EM	14.82	15.52	3.06	1	VS	DP	DG					1
ME-5/01/99-02-WG-02B	15S 4E	1 (0-10 CM)	EA	WG	GS	EM	14.73	16.42	2.38	1.02	VS	DP	DG					1
ME-5/01/99-02-WG-03	15S 4E	1 (0-10 CM)	EA	WG	GS	EM	19.02	15.77	3.48	1.52	VS	DP	DG					1
ME-5/01/99-11-WG-01A	15S 4E	2 (10-20 CM)	EA	WG	GS	EM	73.94	47.01	5.39	31.99	VS	DP	DG				Case bottle, embossed partial "C" and "S"	1
ME-5/01/99-11-WG-01B	15S 4E	2 (10-20 CM)	EA	WG	SH	EM	37.25	24.5	5.58	7.11	VS	DP	DG				Case bottle	1
ME-5/01/99-11-WG-01C	15S 4E	2 (10-20 CM)	EA	WG	GS	EM	40.18	20.53	5.06	6.39	VS	MO	CO	Aqua	Bottle base			1
ME-5/01/99-11-WG-01D	15S 4E	2 (10-20 CM)	EA	WG	GS	EM	29.9	23.55	2.6	3.22	VS	DP	DG					1
ME-5/01/99-11-WG-01E	15S 4E	2 (10-20 CM)	EA	WG	GS	EM	16.77	19.09	3.29	1.48	VS	DP	DG					1
ME-5/01/99-11-WG-01F	15S 4E	2 (10-20 CM)	EA	WG	SH	No	9.46	6.72	2.34	0.19	VS	DP	DG					1
ME-5/01/99-11-WG-02A	15S 4E	2 (10-20 CM)	EA	WG	CP	EM	19.05	17.61	4.52	1.07	VS	DP	DG				Case bottle	1
ME-5/01/99-11-WG-02B	15S 4E	2 (10-20 CM)	EA	WG	CP	EM	14.73	17.91	2.66	0.58	VS	DP	DG					1
ME-5/01/99-11-WG-02C	15S 4E	2 (10-20 CM)	EA	WG	FS	No	5.75	5.73	1.91	0.05	VS	UN	GR					1
ME-5/01/99-11-WG-02D	15S 4E	2 (10-20 CM)	EA	WG	CP	EM	25.22	21.12	3.7	2.15	VS	DP	DG					1
ME-5/01/99-11-WG-03A	15S 4E	2 (10-20 CM)	EA	WG	GS	EM	18.34	10.45	2.18	0.53	VS	MO	DG					1
ME-5/01/99-11-WG-03B	15S 4E	2 (10-20 CM)	EA	WG	GS	EM	30.74	13.36	2.31	1	VS	MO	DG					1
ME-5/01/99-11-WG-03C	15S 4E	2 (10-20 CM)	EA	GL	GS	No	20.89	8.98	1.61	0.48	VS	MO	GR					1
ME-5/01/99-11-WG-03D	15S 4E	2 (10-20 CM)	EA	GL	GS	No	15.36	10.33	1.1	0.3	VS	MO	GR					1
ME-5/01/99-11-WG-03E	15S 4E	2 (10-20 CM)	EA	GL	GS	No	13.2	4.9	3.28	0.31	VS	MO	GR					1
ME-5/01/99-11-WG-03F	15S 4E	2 (10-20 CM)	EA	WG	GS	EM	22.51	7.44	1.38	0.35	VS	MO	GR					1
ME-5/01/99-11-WG-03G	15S 4E	2 (10-20 CM)	EA	WG	SH	No	16.52	5.33	3.83	0.41	VS	MO	DG					1
ME-5/01/99-11-WG-03H	15S 4E	2 (10-20 CM)	EA	WG	GS	EM	13.68	8.67	2.45	0.38	VS	MO	DG					1
ME-5/01/99-11-WG-04A	15S 4E	2 (10-20 CM)	EA	WG	CP	EM	17.6	7.59	2.19	0.3	VS	DP	DG				Case bottle	1
ME-5/01/99-11-WG-04B	15S 4E	2 (10-20 CM)	EA	WG	FS	EM	17.1	8.31	3.06	0.5	VS	MO	CO					1
ME-5/01/99-11-WG-05	15S 4E	2 (10-20 CM)	EA	WG	PX	EM	8.49	13.04	2.75	0.32	VS	DP	DG					1
ME-5/01/99-11-WG-06	15S 4E	2 (10-20 CM)	EA	WG	SH	No	20.17	6.79	4.58	0.74	VS	DP	DG				Case bottle	1
ME-5/01/99-11-WG-07	15S 4E	2 (10-20 CM)	EA	WG	SH	No	9.71	5.4	2.51	0.09	VS	DP	DG				Case bottle	1
ME-5/02/99-01-WG-01	15S 4E	TOP OF Level 3, ~20CM	EA	GL	GS	No	17.52	14.73	1.54	0.49	VS	MO	DG					1
ME-5/02/99-01-WG-02A	15S 4E	TOP OF Level 3, ~20CM	EA	WG	FS	No	10.15	7.24	1.35	0.1	VS	UN	DG					1

Metini #	Unit	Level	Basic Group	Artifact Category	Worked Glass Class	EM	Max Length (cm)	Max Width (cm)	Max Thickness (cm)	Weight (g)	Vessel Type	Molding	Color	Tint	Ves Part	Date	Form	Count
ME-5/02/99-01-WG-02B	15S 4E	TOP OF Level 3, ˜20CM	EA	WG	FS	EM	7.17	7.29	1.59	0.1	VS	MO	CO					1
ME-5/02/99-03-WG-02	15S 4E	3 (20-27 CM)	EA	WG	CP	No	7.95	9.49	1.45	0.09	VS	DP	DG					1
ME-5/22/99-06-WG-01A	15S 4E	WEST WALL ABOVE FEATURE 1	EA	WG	CP	No	16.1	8.24	1.3	0.17	VS	MO	BR					1
ME-5/22/99-06-WG-01B	15S 4E	WEST WALL ABOVE FEATURE 1	EA	WG	FS	No	7.31	9.06	1.33	0.1	VS	MO	BR					1
ME-5/02/99-03-WG-01	15S 4E	3 (20-27 CM)	EA	WG	FS	EM	28.1	21.48	5.43	3.66	VS	DP	DG				Case bottle	1
ME-4/29/99-03-WG-01	20S 21E	Surface	EA	WG	GS	EM	26.97	16.07	2.89	2.07	VS	DP	DG					1
ME-4/29/99-04-WG-01A	20S 21E	1 (0-10 CM)	EA	WG	SH	EM	26.58	15.91	6.92	3.24	VS	DP	DG		Bottle base			1
ME-4/29/99-04-WG-01B	20S 21E	1 (0-10 CM)	EA	WG	FS	No	9.73	5.33	3.19	0.08	VS	DP	DG					1
ME-4/29/99-04-WG-02A	20S 21E	1 (0-10 CM)	EA	WG	SH	EM	27.7	16.48	3.96	1.96	VS	DP	DG					1
ME-4/29/99-04-WG-02B	20S 21E	1 (0-10 CM)	EA	WG	CP	EM	23.87	19.05	4	1.81	VS	DP	DG					1
ME-4/29/99-04-WG-02C	20S 21E	1 (0-10 CM)	EA	WG	SH	EM	11.71	8.4	2.59	0.35	VS	DP	DG					1
ME-4/29/99-04-WG-02D	20S 21E	1 (0-10 CM)	EA	WG	FS	No	10.16	6.56	2	0.11	VS	DP	DG					1
ME-4/29/99-04-WG-03A	20S 21E	1 (0-10 CM)	EA	GL	GS	No	22.74	11.79	3.79	1.14	VS	UN	DG					1
ME-4/29/99-04-WG-03B	20S 21E	1 (0-10 CM)	EA	WG	GS	EM	14.68	9.65	2.36	0.7	VS	UN	DG					1
ME-4/29/99-04-WG-03C	20S 21E	1 (0-10 CM)	EA	WG	FS	No	12.63	3.56	3.23	0.19	VS	MO	AQ					1
ME-4/29/99-04-WG-04	20S 21E	1 (0-10 CM)	EA	WG	FS	No	4.51	5.3	0.83	0.03	VS	UN	DG					1
ME-4/29/99-06-WG-01A	20S 21E	2 (10-20 CM)	EA	WG	CP	EM	10.08	15.45	6.54	0.77	VS	DP	DG					1
ME-4/29/99-06-WG-01B	20S 21E	2 (10-20 CM)	EA	WG	CP	EM	27.36	24.18	3.31	2.41	VS	DP	DG					1
ME-4/29/99-06-WG-01C	20S 21E	2 (10-20 CM)	EA	WG	CP	EM	30.81	14.48	2.92	1.37	VS	DP	DG					1
ME-4/29/99-06-WG-01D	20S 21E	2 (10-20 CM)	EA	WG	FS	EM	16.49	12.63	4.38	1.05	VS	DP	DG					1
ME-4/29/99-06-WG-01E	20S 21E	2 (10-20 CM)	EA	WG	FS	No	11.01	8.21	2.38	0.24	VS	DP	DG					1
ME-4/29/99-06-WG-01F	20S 21E	2 (10-20 CM)	EA	WG	FS	EM	21.66	7.16	4.1	0.99	VS	DP	DG					1
ME-4/29/99-06-WG-01G	20S 21E	2 (10-20 CM)	EA	WG	FS	EM	27.28	19.34	4.54	3.03	VS	MO	AQ		Bottle neck			1
ME-4/29/99-06-WG-01H	20S 21E	2 (10-20 CM)	EA	WG	FS	No	10.9	9.67	1.03	0.08	VS	MO	DG					1
ME-4/29/99-06-WG-01I	20S 21E	2 (10-20 CM)	EA	WG	SH	No	6.75	6	2.21	0.12	VS	MO	DG					1
ME-4/29/99-06-WG-01J	20S 21E	2 (10-20 CM)	EA	WG	SH	No	29.79	14.87	4.52	2.34	VS	MO	DG					1
ME-4/29/99-06-WG-01K	20S 21E	2 (10-20 CM)	EA	WG	SH	No	18.82	9.26	6.42	0.88	VS	MO	DG					1
ME-4/29/99-06-WG-01L	20S 21E	2 (10-20 CM)	EA	WG	FS	No	9.93	8.14	2.02	0.14	VS	MO	DG					1
ME-4/29/99-06-WG-02A	20S 21E	2 (10-20 CM)	EA	WG	GS	EM	23.82	21.85	2.55	2.29	VS	DP	DG					1
ME-4/29/99-06-WG-02B	20S 21E	2 (10-20 CM)	EA	WG	GS	EM	16.61	8.45	2.44	0.43	VS	DP	DG					1
ME-4/29/99-06-WG-02C	20S 21E	2 (10-20 CM)	EA	WG	GS	EM	38.31	28.31	5.52	8.7	VS	MO	DG				Case bottle embossed "L and E" or "H"	1
ME-4/29/99-06-WG-02D	20S 21E	2 (10-20 CM)	EA	GL	GS	No	37.65	20.27	3.59	2.53	VS	MO	YG				Molded "A" and "N"	1
ME-4/29/99-06-WG-02E	20S 21E	2 (10-20 CM)	EA	WG	GS	EM	30.81	26.05	1.96	2.46	VS	DP	DG					1
ME-4/29/99-06-WG-02F	20S 21E	2 (10-20 CM)	EA	WG	GS	EM	22.96	18.34	4.76	2.79	VS	DP	DG					1
ME-4/29/99-06-WG-02G	20S 21E	2 (10-20 CM)	EA	WG	GS	EM	55.33	18.68	3.36	6.48	VS	DP	DG					1
ME-4/29/99-06-WG-02H	20S 21E	2 (10-20 CM)	EA	WG	GS	EM	53.92	29.19	5.34	8.26	VS	DP	DG					1
ME-4/29/99-06-WG-02I	20S 21E	2 (10-20 CM)	EA	WG	GS	EM	28.91	17.68	4.13	3.35	VS	DP	DG					1
ME-4/29/99-06-WG-02J	20S 21E	2 (10-20 CM)	EA	WG	GS	EM	22.5	14.72	2.41	1.07	VS	DP	DG					1
ME-4/29/99-06-WG-02K	20S 21E	2 (10-20 CM)	EA	WG	GS	EM	20.84	9.02	2.34	0.73	VS	DP	DG					1
ME-4/29/99-06-WG-03	20S 21E	2 (10-20 CM)	EA	WG	CO	No	29.73	39.15	11.45	14.25	VS	DP	DG					1
ME-4/29/99-06-WG-04A	20S 21E	2 (10-20 CM)	EA	WG	SH	EM	36.64	19.05	6.27	4.26	VS	DP	BR					1
ME-4/29/99-06-WG-04B	20S 21E	2 (10-20 CM)	EA	WG	SH	EM	36.88	22.33	9.6	8.65	VS	DP	DG		Bottle base			1
ME-4/29/99-06-WG-04C	20S 21E	2 (10-20 CM)	EA	WG	SH	EM	23.79	31.88	8.19	4.84	VS	DP	DG					1
ME-4/29/99-06-WG-04D	20S 21E	2 (10-20 CM)	EA	WG	GS	EM	17.79	14.5	3.47	1.81	VS	DP	DG					1
ME-4/29/99-06-WG-05	20S 21E	2 (10-20 CM)	EA	WG	FS	No	12.36	8.4	2.74	0.26	VS	DP	DG					1
ME-4/29/99-06-WG-06	20S 21E	2 (10-20 CM)	EA	WG	SH	No	12.1	4.18	3.26	0.17	VS	DP	DG					1
ME-4/30/99-12-WG-01A	20S 21E	3 (20-30 CM)	EA	WG	FS	EM	14.36	15.81	4.76	0.79	VS	DP	DG					1
ME-4/30/99-12-WG-01B	20S 21E	3 (20-30 CM)	EA	WG	FS	No	8.68	8.04	1.64	0.12	VS	DP	DG					1
ME-4/30/99-12-WG-01C	20S 21E	3 (20-30 CM)	EA	WG	CP	EM	16.06	10.19	1.48	0.32	VS	DP	GR					1
ME-4/30/99-12-WG-01D	20S 21E	3 (20-30 CM)	EA	WG	FS	No	12.93	4.97	2.69	0.14	VS	DP	DG					1
ME-4/30/99-12-WG-01E	20S 21E	3 (20-30 CM)	EA	WG	FS	No	7	8.8	2.54	0.14	VS	DP	DG					1
ME-4/30/99-12-WG-01F	20S 21E	3 (20-30 CM)	EA	WG	CP	EM	15.13	7.96	2.13	0.29	VS	DP	DG					1
ME-4/30/99-12-WG-01G	20S 21E	3 (20-30 CM)	EA	WG	PX	EM	13.08	7.7	0.85	0.1	VS	UN	DG					1
ME-4/30/99-12-WG-02	20S 21E	3 (20-30 CM)	EA	WG	FS	No	8.89	7.76	1.41	0.07	VS	UN	CO					1
ME-4/30/99-12-WG-03	20S 21E	3 (20-30 CM)	EA	WG	SH	No	14.47	8.26	3.05	0.43	VS	UN	CO					1

Metini #	Unit	Level	Basic Group	Artifact Category	Worked Glass Class	EM	Max Length (cm)	Max Width (cm)	Max Thickness (cm)	Weight (g)	Vessel Type	Molding	Color	Tint	Ves Part	Date	Form	Count
ME-4/30/99-12-WG-04	20S 21E	3 (20-30 CM)	EA	WG	SH	No	5.5	7.2	1.45	0.03	VS	UN	DG					1
ME-4/30/99-12-WG-05	20S 21E	3 (20-30 CM)	EA	GL	GS	No	21.89	10.32	2.51	0.77	VS	MO	BR					1
ME-5/01/99-07-WG-01	20S 21E	4 (30-40 CM)	EA	WG	FS	No	6.73	6.11	0.87	0.04	VS	MO	BR					1
ME-5/02/99-04-WG-01	15S 4E	4 (27-52 CM)	EA	WG	FS	Artifact is missing and could not be analyzed												0

KEY TO CODES

Appendix 6: Worked Glass Artifacts

Artifact Category: WG=Worked Glass

Worked Glass Class:
- CP=Complete Flake
- FS=Flake Shatter
- CO=Core
- PF=Projectile Point Frag.
- BI=Biface

- PX=Proximal Flake
- SH=Angular Shatter
- CF=Core Fragment
- UN=Uniface
- GS=Glass Sherd

EM:
- EM=Edge-Modified
- No=Edge Not Modified

Vessel Type:
- VS=Vessel
- LG=Lamp/Globe

- FG=Flat Glass
- MI=Mirror

Molding:
- BL=Free Blown Glass
- MM=Machine Molding
- MO=Molded Glass

- DP=Dip Molding
- PM=Plate Molding
- UN=Unidentifiable Manufacture Method

Color:
- GR=Light Green
- BR=Brown
- BG=Blue-Green
- AQ=Aqua

- DG=Dark Green
- CO=Colorless
- YG=Yellow-Green

Appendix 7: Glass Bead Artifacts / *page 1*

Metini #	Unit #	Level	Material	Manufacture	Construction	Finishing Characteristics	Shape	Diameter (mm)	Length (mm)	Color	Diaphanaeity	Kidd and Kidd (1970) Type	Ross (1997) Type	Ross (1997) Variety	Comments
ME-6/20/9802-BE01A	13S 14E	Surface	Glass	Wound	Simple	N/A	Oblate	6.6	5.8	White	Opaque	WIb2	W/MSU	-	
ME-6/20/9804-BE01A	12S 17E	Surface	Glass	Drawn	Compound	Heat rounded	Rounded tube	7.4	6.1	White over white	Opaque	IVa	D/PCHU	-	
ME-6/20/9804-BE01B	12S 17E	Surface	Glass	Drawn	Compound	Heat rounded	Torus/Suboblate	4.4	2.6	White over off-white	Opaque	IVa13	D/PCHU	1	
ME-6/20/9804-BE01C	12S 17E	Surface	Glass	Drawn	Compound	Heat rounded	Torus/Suboblate	4.0	2.8	Red over white	Translucent over opaque	IVa3	D/PCHU	56	Cornaline de Alleppo
ME-6/20/9802-BE01A	25S 11E	Surface	Glass	Drawn	Compound	Heat rounded	Short barrel	6.7	7.4	White over white	Opaque	IVa	D/PCHU	-	
ME-6/20/9802-BE01B	25S 11E	Surface	Glass	Drawn	Compound	Heat rounded	Suboblate	4.2	3.7	White over white	Opaque	IVa13	D/PCHU	1	
ME-6/25/9808-BE01A	8N 5E	Surface	Glass	Drawn	Simple	Ground Facets	Hexagonal Tube	8.1	8.4	Blue	Translucent	If	D/MM2CDf	-	"Russian" Blue
ME-6/26/9801-BE01A	5S 24E	Surface	Glass	Wound	Compound	N/A	Broken tube	10.0	-	White over white	Translucent over opaque	-	-	-	Broken
ME-6/26/9803-BE01A	8S 22E	Surface	Glass	Wound	Simple	N/A	Tube	11.1	18.3	White	Opaque	WIa3	-	-	Broken
ME-6/26/9803-BE01B	8S 22E	Surface	Glass	Drawn	Simple	Heat rounded	Suboblate	6.8	4.6	White	Opaque	IIa13	D/MCHU	-	
ME-6/26/9803-BE01C	8S 22E	Surface	Glass	Drawn	Compound	Heat rounded	Oblate	6.2	4.5	Red over white	Opaque	IVa2	D/PCHU	56	Cornaline de Alleppo
ME-6/26/9805-BE01A	5S 33E	Surface	Glass	Wound	Simple	N/A	Oblate	6.6	6.5	White	Opaque	WIb2	W/MSU	-	
ME-6/26/9805-BE01B	5S 33E	Surface	Glass	Drawn	Simple	Heat rounded	Short tube	9.5	9.2	White	Opaque	IIa	D/MCHU	-	
ME-6/26/9805-BE01C	5S 33E	Surface	Glass	Drawn	Simple	UNK	Oblate	8.1	6.1	Blue	Opaque	IIa13	D/MCHU	-	
ME-6/26/9808-BE01A	10S 37E	Surface	Glass	Drawn	Simple	Heat rounded	Suboblate	8.7	5.4	White	Opaque	IIa13	D/MCHU	-	Fragment
ME-6/26/9808-BE01B	10S 37E	Surface	Glass	Drawn	Compound	Ground facets	Hexagonal tube	9.8	8.1	Clear over white	Transparent over opaque	IIIf1	D/PM2CDf	-	
ME-6/26/9809-BE01A	18S 22E	Surface	Glass	Drawn	Simple	Heat rounded	Rounded tube	8.3	7.6	White	Opaque	IIa13	D/MCHU	-	
ME-4/16/9906-BE01A	29S 36E	Surface	Glass	Drawn	Compound	Heat rounded	Suboblate	4.9	3.1	White over white	Opaque	IVa13	D/PCHU	1	
ME-4/17/9901-BE01A	29S 21E	Surface	Glass	Wound	Simple	N/A	Oblate	6.2	4.9	White	Opaque	WIb2	W/MSU	-	Fragment
ME-4/21/9903-BE01A	0N 28E	Surface	Glass	Drawn	Simple	UNK	UNK			White	Opaque			-	
ME-4/29/9902-BE01A	11S 41E	Surface	Glass	Drawn	Simple	Heat rounded	Oblate/Rounded tube	10.5	9.2	White	Opaque	IIa13	D/MCHU	-	
ME-4/29/9902-BE01B	11S 41E	Surface	Glass	Drawn	Compound	Ground facets	Hexagonal tube	7.7	7.4	Clear over white	Transparent over opaque	IIIf1	D/PM2CDf	-	
ME-4/29/9902-BE01C	11S 41E	Surface	Glass	Drawn	Compound	Heat rounded	Oblate	6.3	5.0	White over white	Opaque	IVa	D/PCHU	-	"Crackled" exterior
ME-4/29/9902-BE01D	11S 41E	Surface	Glass	Drawn	Compound	Heat rounded	Oblate	4.3	3.2	White over white	Opaque	IVa13	D/PCHU	1	
ME-4/29/9904-BE01A	20S 21E	1 (0-10 CM)	Glass	Drawn	Compound	Heat rounded	Oblate	7.9	5.9	White over white	Opaque	IVa	D/PCHU	-	
ME-4/29/9904-BE01B	20S 21E	1 (0-10 CM)	Glass	Drawn	Simple	Heat rounded	Oblate	6.3	4.8	white	Opaque	IIa13	D/MCHU	-	
ME-4/29/9906-BE01A	20S 21E	2 (10-20 CM)	Glass	Drawn	Simple	Heat rounded	Oblate	7.6	6.8	white	Opaque	IIa13	D/MCHU	-	
ME-4/29/9906-BE01B	20S 21E	2 (10-20 CM)	Glass	Drawn	Simple	Heat rounded	Oblate	8.7	6.7	White	Opaque	IIa13	D/MCHU	-	
ME-4/29/9906-BE01C	20S 21E	2 (10-20 CM)	Glass	Drawn	Compound	Heat rounded	Oblate	7.2	5.0	white over white	Opaque	IVa13	D/PCHU	-	
ME-4/29/9906-BE01D	20S 21E	2 (10-20 CM)	Glass	Drawn	Compound	Heat rounded	Oblate	5.9	4.3	white over white	Opaque	IVa13	D/PCHU	-	
ME-4/29/9906-BE01E	20S 21E	2 (10-20 CM)	Glass	Drawn	Compound	Heat rounded	Suboblate	5.9	4.1	White over white	Opaque	IVa13	D/PCHU	-	

Appendix 7: Glass Bead Artifacts / *page 2*

Metini #	Unit #	Level	Material	Manufacture	Construction	Finishing Characteristics	Shape	Diameter (mm)	Length (mm)	Color	Diaphanaeity	Kidd and Kidd (1970) Type	Ross (1997) Type	Ross (1997) Variety	Comments
ME-4/29/99-06-BE-01F	20S 21E	2 (10-20 CM)	Glass	Drawn	Compound	Heat rounded	Suboblate	6.0	3.6	white over white	Opaque	IVa13	D/PCHU	-	
ME-4/29/99-06-BE-01G	20S 21E	2 (10-20 CM)	Glass	Drawn	Compound	Heat rounded	Suboblate	4.9	3.8	White over white	Opaque	IVa13	D/PCHU	-	
ME-4/30/99-12-BE-01A	20S 21E	3 (20-30 CM)	Glass	Drawn	Compound	Heat rounded	Oblate	3.4	2.6	White over white	Opaque	IVa13	D/PCHU	45	
ME-5/01/99-02-BE-01A	15S 4E	1 (0-10 CM)	Glass	Drawn	Simple	Ground facets	Hexagonal tube	7.3	5.5	Light green	transparent	If	D/MM2CDf	-	
ME-5/01/99-02-BE-01B	15S 4E	1 (0-10 CM)	Glass	Drawn	Compound	Ground facets	Hexagonal tube	6.7	6.1	Clear over white	Transparent over opaque	IIIf1	D/PM2CDf	-	
ME-5/01/99-02-BE-01C	15S 4E	1 (0-10 CM)	Glass	Drawn	Compound	Heat rounded	Suboblate	4.8	3.5	White over white	Opaque	IVa13	D/PCHU	-	
ME-5/01/99-02-BE-01D	15S 4E	1 (0-10 CM)	Glass	Drawn	Simple	heat rounded	Oblate	2.6	1.9	Blue	Opaque	IIa36	D/MCHU	53	
ME-5/01/99-02-BE-01E	15S 4E	1 (0-10 CM)	Glass	Drawn	Compound	Heat rounded	Oblate	3.9	3.8	red over white	opaque	IVa2	D/PCHU	56	Cornaline de Alleppo
ME-5/01/99-07-BE-01A	20S 21E	4 (30-40 CM)	Glass	Drawn	Compound	Heat rounded	Oblate	3.7	3.4	White over white	Opaque	IVa13	D/PCHU	-	
ME-5/01/99-11-BE-01A	15S 4E	2 (10-20 CM)	Glass	Drawn	Simple	Heat rounded	Oblate	6.3	5.3	White	Opaque	IIa13	D/MCHU	-	
ME-5/01/99-11-BE-01B	15S 4E	2 (10-20 CM)	Glass	Drawn	Compound	Heat rounded	Oblate	3.9	2.9	White over white	Opaque	IVa13	D/PCHU	1	
ME-5/01/99-11-BE-01C	15S 4E	2 (10-20 CM)	Glass	Drawn	Compound	Heat rounded	Oblate	4.1	3.5	White over white	Opaque	IVa13	D/PCHU	1	
ME-5/01/99-11-BE-01D	15S 4E	2 (10-20 CM)	Glass	Drawn	Compound	Heat rounded	Suboblate	4.9	3.4	Red over green	Opaque over translucent	IVa6	D/PCHU	3	Green Heart
ME-5/02/99-03-BE-01A	15S 4E	3 (20-27 CM)	Glass	Drawn	Simple	Heat rounded	UNK	-	-	Blue				-	3 fragments

Appendix 8: Button Artifacts

Metini #	Unit #	Level	Artifact Cat.	Material	Color	Form	Manufacture Method	Diameter	Count
ME-6/05/98-01-BU-01	5.1N 35E	Surface	BU	Bone		5 hole (center and 4 holes)	Carved/cut	16 mm	1
ME-6/20/98-04-BU-01	12S 17E	Surface	BU	Glass	Opaque white	4 hole	Molded	11 mm	1
ME-9/12/98-04-BU-01	11S 28E	Surface	BU	Glass	Opaque white	4 hole	Molded	10 mm	2
ME-4/16/99-06-BU-01	29S 36E	Surface	BU	Glass	Opaque white	4 hole	Molded	20 mm	1
ME-4/17/99-05-BU-01	35S 28E	Surface	BU	Glass	Opaque white	4 hole	Molded	10 mm	1
ME-4/21/99-02-BU-01	5N 38E	Surface	BU	Iron	Corroded	Snap fastner or pull through button type	Cast/molded	16 mm	1
ME-4/16/99-04-ME-02	23S 38E	Surface	ME	Brass		Button cover	Cast/molded	3.4 cm	1
ME-5/02/99-03-BU-01	15S 4E	3 (20-27 CM)	BU	Glass	Opaque white	4 hole	Molded	11 mm	1
ME-4/29/99-04-BU-01	20S 21E	1 (0-10 CM)	BU	Brass	Corroded	Single hole (post manufactured)	Cast/molded	17 mm	1
ME-4/29/99-06-BU-01A	20S 21E	2 (10-20 CM)	BU	Glass	Opaque white	4 hole	Molded	11 mm	1
ME-4/29/99-06-BU-01B	20S 21E	2 (10-20 CM)	BU	Glass	Opaque blue	4 hole	Molded	10 mm	2

KEY TO CODES

Appendix 8: Button Artifacts

Artifact Category: BU=Button

Metini #	Unit #	Level	Material Type	Artifact Class	Form	Size	Count	Comments
ME-6/20/98-02-ME-01	13S 14E	Surface	Iron	Wrought stapel		L = 7.7cm; W = 2.8 cm	1	U-shaped, possible fence staple.
ME-6/20/98-06-ME-01	6S 18E	Surface	Iron	Cut nail	Stock and head, square head	L = 10.cm	1	Corroded, large cut nail or spike with square head; looks like bent railroad spike.
ME-6/24/98-06-ME-01	36S 18E	Surface	Iron	Wrought nail	Stock	L = 11.2cm	1	Very corroded, bent into hook (clinched nail or used as hook?); 1 stock hook-shaped piece exfoliating.
ME-6/26/98-03-ME-01	8S 22E	Surface	Iron	Cut nail	Stock and head, square head	Fragment	1	Tack or nail (shaped head).
ME-6/26/98-04-ME-01A	7S 27E	Surface	Iron	Wrought nail	Stock and head, rose head	L = 9.1cm	1	Rose head, bent.
ME-6/26/98-04-ME-01B	7S 27E	Surface	Iron	Wrought nail	Stock and head, rose head	Fragment	1	Rose head, badly corroded, fragment.
ME-6/26/98-04-ME-01C	7S 27E	Surface	Copper	Spring		D = 11mm	1	Wire spring; diameter = 11mm, length 21 mm.
ME-6/26/98-04-ME-01D	7S 27E	Surface	Copper	Constricted sem-sphere		D = 15mm	1	Height = 9mm, opening diameter = 11-12 mm, diameter of artifact = 15 mm; bell or button? round capsule (like an acorn top - button?).
ME-6/26/98-04-ME-01E	7S 27E	Surface	Lead/white metal	Sheet trimming		W = 0.6 cm	1	Scap metal.
ME-6/26/98-04-ME-01F	7S 27E	Surface	Iron	Strip			1	Can fragment (seam).
ME-6/26/98-09-ME-01	18S 22E	Surface	Lead/white metal	Disk with 4 pierced holes		3.9 cm by 4.1 cm	1	Circular object w/4 drill holes; drill holes alternate directions; stria visible on top & bottom surface; possible fishing net weight, weaving/spinning weight or button?
ME-9/12/98-05-ME-01	12S 33E	Surface	Tin, galvanized sheet metal	Sheet metal scrap			1	Corrugated sheet metal fragment.
ME-4/16/99-04-ME-01	23S 38E	Surface	Brass	Thimble		Height = 18mm, opening width = 16-18 mm	1	Thimble, palmer analysis indicates brass, slightly bent.
ME-4/16/99-04-ME-03	23S 38E	Surface	Iron	Cut nail	Stock and head	Fragment	1	Nail; rect. head/stock, fragment.
ME-4/17/99-02-ME-01	30S 34E	Surface	Iron	Cut nail	Stock and head	L = 8cm,	1	"Square nail," rectangular head/stock, bent.
ME-4/29/99-01-ME-01	6S 43E	Surface	Iron	Sheet scrap			2	Flat scrap.

Appendix 9: Metal Artifacts / *page 2*

Metini #	Unit #	Level	Material Type	Artifact Class	Form	Size	Count	Comments
ME-4/29/99-02-ME-01	11S 41E	Surface	Brass	Clothing fastner		7 mm x 5 cm (width)	1	"S" shaped, jewelry part? Palmer analysis hook and eye clothing fastener.
ME-4/29/99-07-ME-01	1N 40E	Surface	Iron	Cut nail	Stock and head	Fragment	1	Nail/track, rectangular head/stock.
ME-4/29/99-05-ME-01	0N 10W	1 (0-10 CM)	Iron	Wire fencing			1	Corroded, fencing fragment, possibly barbed wire?.
ME-4/30/99-01-ME-01	0N 10W	2 (10-20 CM)	Iron	Wragment		Fragment	1	Scrap.
ME-5/01/99-03-ME-01	0N 10W	PP	Iron	Square spike	Head and stock	L = 15.3 cm, width = 1.8 cm	1	100cm n, 78cm e, 26cm bd; large cut spike; sq head sq stock, additional fragments.
ME-5/01/99-11-ME-01A	15S 4E	2 (10-20 CM)	Iron	Cut nail	Head and stock		1	T head.
ME-5/01/99-11-ME-01B	15S 4E	2 (10-20 CM)	Iron	Cut nail	Head and stock	L = 3.7 cm	1	
ME-5/01/99-11-ME-01C	15S 4E	2 (10-20 CM)	Iron	Cut nail	Head and stock	Fragment	1	Fragment.
ME-5/01/99-11-ME-01D	15S 4E	2 (10-20 CM)	Iron	Cut nail	Stock		1	Stock fragment, pointed end, most likely fragment from originally bagged fragments.
ME-5/01/99-11-ME-01E	15S 4E	2 (10-20 CM)	Iron	Sheet fragments			3	Possibly part of shovel from Feature 1, curved fragments.
ME-5/01/99-18-ME-01	15S 4E	2 (10-20 CM)	Iron	Shovel handle			1	Shovel handle; Feature 1.
ME-4/29/99-06-ME-01	20S 21E	2 (10-20 CM)	Iron	Cut nail	Headless stock	L = 6.9 cm	1	Long nail, rect. stock/ no head.
ME-4/29/99-06-ME-02A	20S 21E	2 (10-20 CM)	Iron	Fencing or wire frag			1	Fencing or other wire fragment.
ME-4/29/99-06-ME-02B	20S 21E	2 (10-20 CM)	Iron	Sheet fragment			1	Flat sheet iron scrap or trimming.
ME-5/02/99-05-ME-01	15S 4E	2 (10-20 CM); 3 (20-30 CM)	Iron	Shovel head			1	Shovel head; Feature 1.
ME-5/02/99-01-ME-01	15S 4E	TOP OF L3 20 CM	Iron	Sheet fragment			1	NW 1/4 of unit with Feature 1; flat.
ME-5/02/99-03-ME-01	15S 4E	3 (20-27 CM)	Iron	Sheet fragments			2	Feature 1; scraps, possibly part of shovel.
ME-4/30/99-12-ME-01A	20S 21E	3 (20-30 CM)	Iron	Cut nail	Head and stock	L = 5.3cm	1	Narrow in-stock head (not added to stock).
ME-4/30/99-12-ME-01B	20S 21E	3 (20-30 CM)	Brass	Sheet fragments			2	Sheet fragments; one with shaped corner; covering plate, possibly for gun, box, etc...

Metini #	Unit #	Level	Taxa	Diagnostic Element	Counts
ME-4/29/99-04-MO-01	20S 21E	1 (0-10 CM)	MU	UM, FG	1
ME-4/29/99-04-MO-02	20S 21E	1 (0-10 CM)	CH	PL, FG	2
ME-4/29/99-04-MO-03	20S 21E	1 (0-10 CM)	SN	CO, FG	5
ME-4/29/99-04-MO-04	20S 21E	1 (0-10 CM)	BA	FG	1
ME-4/29/99-04-MO-05	20S 21E	1 (0-10 CM)	AB	FG	1
ME-4/29/99-04-MO-06	20S 21E	1 (0-10 CM)	SN	WH, CO, FG	3
ME-4/29/99-04-MO-07	20S 21E	1 (0-10 CM)	UN	FG	1
ME-4/29/99-06-MO-01	20S 21E	2 (10-20 CM)	OL	WH	1
ME-4/29/99-06-MO-02	20S 21E	2 (10-20 CM)	GC	PL, FG	0.5
ME-4/29/99-06-MO-03	20S 21E	2 (10-20 CM)	CH	PL	18
ME-4/29/99-06-MO-04	20S 21E	2 (10-20 CM)	MU	UM, FG	3
ME-4/29/99-06-MO-05	20S 21E	2 (10-20 CM)	AB	FG	1
ME-4/29/99-06-MO-06	20S 21E	2 (10-20 CM)	LI	CA	1
ME-4/29/99-06-MO-07	20S 21E	2 (10-20 CM)	BA	FG	10
ME-4/29/99-06-MO-08	20S 21E	2 (10-20 CM)	SN	WH, FG	2
ME-4/29/99-06-MO-09	20S 21E	2 (10-20 CM)	ND	FG	1
ME-5/01/99-11-MO-01	15S 4E	2 (10-20 CM)	AB	FG	1
ME-5/01/99-11-MO-02	15S 4E	2 (10-20 CM)	UN	FG	1
ME-4/30/99-12-MO-01	20S 21E	3 (20-30 CM)	SN	CO	4
ME-4/30/99-12-MO-02	20S 21E	3 (20-30 CM)	MU	UM, FG	1
ME-4/30/99-12-MO-03	20S 21E	3 (20-30 CM)	CH	PL	2
ME-4/30/99-12-MO-04	20S 21E	3 (20-30 CM)	GC	PL	1
ME-4/30/99-12-MO-05	20S 21E	3 (20-30 CM)	AB	FG	1
ME-4/30/99-12-MO-06	20S 21E	3 (20-30 CM)	UN	FG	1
ME-5/01/99-07-MO-01	20S 21E	4 (30-40 CM)	SN	FG	1
ME-4/16/99-01-MO-01	23S 23E	Surface	MU	UM	1
ME-4/16/99-01-MO-02	23S 23E	Surface	GC	PL, FG	1
ME-4/16/99-01-MO-03	23S 23E	Surface	BA	FG	2
ME-4/16/99-01-MO-04	23S 23E	Surface	CH	PL	5
ME-4/16/99-01-MO-05	23S 23E	Surface	AB	FG	1
ME-4/16/99-01-MO-06	23S 23E	Surface	SN	WH	1
ME-4/16/99-01-MO-07	23S 23E	Surface	ND	FG	1
ME-4/16/99-02-MO-01	21S 29E	Surface	AB	FG	1
ME-4/16/99-02-MO-02	21S 29E	Surface	BA	FG	5
ME-4/16/99-02-MO-03	21S 29E	Surface	MU	UM, FG	1
ME-4/16/99-02-MO-04	21S 29E	Surface	GC	PL, FG	0.5
ME-4/16/99-02-MO-05	21S 29E	Surface	CH	PL	4
ME-4/16/99-02-MO-06	21S 29E	Surface	SN	CO, FG	2
ME-4/16/99-02-MO-07	21S 29E	Surface	ND	FG	1
ME-4/16/99-03-MO-01	22S 32E	Surface	BA	FG	4

Metini #	Unit #	Level	Taxa	Diagnostic Element	Counts
ME-4/16/99-03-MO-02	22S 32E	Surface	CH	PL	4.5
ME-4/16/99-03-MO-03	22S 32E	Surface	AB	FG	1
ME-4/16/99-03-MO-04	22S 32E	Surface	SN	WH, FG	1
ME-4/16/99-03-MO-05	22S 32E	Surface	MU	UM, FG	10
ME-4/16/99-03-MO-06	22S 32E	Surface	ND	FG	1
ME-4/16/99-03-MO-07	22S 32E	Surface	LI	CA	1
ME-4/16/99-04-MO-01	23S 38E	Surface	BA	FG	12
ME-4/16/99-04-MO-02	23S 38E	Surface	LI	CA	4
ME-4/16/99-04-MO-03	23S 38E	Surface	AB	FG	1
ME-4/16/99-04-MO-04	23S 38E	Surface	CH	PL	10
ME-4/16/99-04-MO-05	23S 38E	Surface	SN	CO, WH, FG	3
ME-4/16/99-04-MO-06	23S 38E	Surface	MU	UM, FG	10
ME-4/16/99-04-MO-07	23S 38E	Surface	WH	WH	1
ME-4/16/99-04-MO-08	23S 38E	Surface	ND	FG	1
ME-4/16/99-04-MO-09	23S 38E	Surface	GC	PL, FG	1.5
ME-4/16/99-05-MO-01	26S 28E	Surface	AB	FG	1
ME-4/16/99-05-MO-02	26S 28E	Surface	CH	PL	2
ME-4/16/99-05-MO-03	26S 28E	Surface	MU	FG	1
ME-4/16/99-05-MO-04	26S 28E	Surface	BA	FG	3
ME-4/16/99-05-MO-05	26S 28E	Surface	ND	FG	1
ME-4/16/99-06-MO-01	29S 36E	Surface	MU	UM, FG	1
ME-4/16/99-06-MO-02	29S 36E	Surface	AB	FG	1
ME-4/16/99-06-MO-03	29S 36E	Surface	SN	FG	1
ME-4/16/99-06-MO-04	29S 36E	Surface	BA	FG	1
ME-4/16/99-06-MO-05	29S 36E	Surface	CH	PL	0.5
ME-4/16/99-06-MO-06	29S 36E	Surface	CH	FG	1
ME-4/17/99-01-MO-01	29S 21E	Surface	AB	FG	1
ME-4/17/99-01-MO-02	29S 21E	Surface	SN	FG	1
ME-4/17/99-01-MO-03	29S 21E	Surface	SN	CO, FG	2
ME-4/17/99-01-MO-04	29S 21E	Surface	GC	PL, FG	1.5
ME-4/17/99-01-MO-05	29S 21E	Surface	CH	PL	28.5
ME-4/17/99-01-MO-06	29S 21E	Surface	BA	FG	9
ME-4/17/99-01-MO-07	29S 21E	Surface	LI	CA	2
ME-4/17/99-01-MO-08	29S 21E	Surface	WH	WH	1
ME-4/17/99-01-MO-09	29S 21E	Surface	MU	UM, FG	33
ME-4/17/99-01-MO-10	29S 21E	Surface	ND	FG	1
ME-4/17/99-02-MO-01	30S 34E	Surface	SN	FG	1
ME-4/17/99-02-MO-02	30S 34E	Surface	MU	UM, FG	1
ME-4/17/99-02-MO-03	30S 34E	Surface	AB	FG	1
ME-4/17/99-02-MO-04	30S 34E	Surface	CH	PL, FG	3

Metini #	Unit #	Level	Taxa	Diagnostic Element	Counts
ME-4/17/99-02-MO-05	30S 34E	Surface	UN	FG	1
ME-4/17/99-02-MO-06	30S 34E	Surface	OL	WH	1
ME-4/17/99-03-MO-01	31S 33E	Surface	SN	FG	1
ME-4/17/99-03-MO-02	31S 33E	Surface	AB	WO, FG	1
ME-4/17/99-03-MO-03	31S 33E	Surface	CH	PL	5
ME-4/17/99-03-MO-04	31S 33E	Surface	BA	FG	2
ME-4/17/99-03-MO-05	31S 33E	Surface	LI	CA	1
ME-4/17/99-03-MO-06	31S 33E	Surface	MU	UM, FG	2
ME-4/17/99-03-MO-07	31S 33E	Surface	UN	FG	1
ME-4/17/99-03-MO-08	31S 33E	Surface	GC	PL	2
ME-4/17/99-04-MO-01	35S 21E	Surface	OL	WH	1
ME-4/17/99-04-MO-02	35S 21E	Surface	MU	UM, FG	5
ME-4/17/99-04-MO-03	35S 21E	Surface	BA	FG	4
ME-4/17/99-04-MO-04	35S 21E	Surface	CH	PL	3
ME-4/17/99-04-MO-05	35S 21E	Surface	GC	PL	0.5
ME-4/17/99-04-MO-06	35S 21E	Surface	SN	CO, FG	1
ME-4/17/99-04-MO-07	35S 21E	Surface	UN	FG	1
ME-4/17/99-05-MO-01	35S 28E	Surface	AB	FG	1
ME-4/17/99-05-MO-02	35S 28E	Surface	BA	FG	13
ME-4/17/99-05-MO-03	35S 28E	Surface	MU	UM, FG	8
ME-4/17/99-05-MO-04	35S 28E	Surface	CH	PL	20.5
ME-4/17/99-05-MO-05	35S 28E	Surface	SN	FG	1
ME-4/17/99-05-MO-06	35S 28E	Surface	LI	CA, FG	3
ME-4/17/99-05-MO-07	35S 28E	Surface	ND	FG	1
ME-4/17/99-05-MO-08	35S 28E	Surface	GC	PL, FG	1
ME-4/17/99-06-MO-01	34S 36E	Surface	BA	FG	3
ME-4/17/99-06-MO-02	34S 36E	Surface	AB	FG	1
ME-4/17/99-06-MO-03	34S 36E	Surface	LI	CA, FG	1
ME-4/17/99-06-MO-04	34S 36E	Surface	CH	PL	7
ME-4/17/99-06-MO-05	34S 36E	Surface	SN	FG	1
ME-4/17/99-06-MO-06	34S 36E	Surface	SN	WH, FG	0
ME-4/17/99-06-MO-07	34S 36E	Surface	MU	UM, FG	4
ME-4/17/99-06-MO-08	34S 36E	Surface	UN	FG	1
ME-4/17/99-06-MO-09	34S 36E	Surface	GC	PL, FG	1
ME-4/17/99-07-MO-01	36S 32E	Surface	AB	FG	1
ME-4/17/99-07-MO-02	36S 32E	Surface	BA	FG	8
ME-4/17/99-07-MO-03	36S 32E	Surface	SN	CO, FG	1
ME-4/17/99-07-MO-04	36S 32E	Surface	CH	PL	16
ME-4/17/99-07-MO-05	36S 32E	Surface	LI	CA	1
ME-4/17/99-07-MO-06	36S 32E	Surface	MU	UM, FG	7

Metini #	Unit #	Level	Taxa	Diagnostic Element	Counts
ME-4/17/99-07-MO-07	36S 32E	Surface	UN	FG	0
ME-4/17/99-08-MO-01	39S 37E	Surface	CH	PI	1
ME-4/17/99-08-MO-02	39S 37E	Surface	MU	FG	1
ME-4/17/99-08-MO-04	39S 37E	Surface	UN	FG	0
ME-4/17/99-08-MO-05	39S 37E	Surface	SN	CO	1
ME-4/17/99-08-MO-06	39S 37E	Surface	SN	FG	1
ME-4/17/99-09-MO-01	40S 26E	Surface	AB	WO	1
ME-4/17/99-09-MO-02	40S 26E	Surface	CH	PL	1
ME-4/17/99-09-MO-03	40S 26E	Surface	MU	UM, FG	1
ME-4/17/99-10-MO-01	36S 22E	Surface	BA	FG	3
ME-4/17/99-10-MO-02	36S 22E	Surface	OL	WH	2
ME-4/17/99-10-MO-03	36S 22E	Surface	SN	CO, FG	1
ME-4/17/99-10-MO-04	36S 22E	Surface	SN	WH, FG	2
ME-4/17/99-10-MO-05	36S 22E	Surface	AB	FG	1
ME-4/17/99-10-MO-06	36S 22E	Surface	CH	PL	11
ME-4/17/99-10-MO-07	36S 22E	Surface	MU	UM	3
ME-4/17/99-10-MO-08	36S 22E	Surface	ND	FG	1
ME-4/21/99-01-MO-01	1N 35E	Surface	CH	PL	15
ME-4/21/99-01-MO-02	1N 35E	Surface	BA	FG	20
ME-4/21/99-01-MO-03	1N 35E	Surface	SN	WH, FG	1
ME-4/21/99-01-MO-04	1N 35E	Surface	SN	CO, WH, FG	4
ME-4/21/99-01-MO-05	1N 35E	Surface	AB	FG	1
ME-4/21/99-01-MO-06	1N 35E	Surface	MU	UM	15
ME-4/21/99-01-MO-07	1N 35E	Surface	ND	FG	1
ME-4/21/99-02-MO-01	5N 38E	Surface	LI	CA	1
ME-4/21/99-02-MO-02	5N 38E	Surface	SN	CO, FG	2
ME-4/21/99-02-MO-03	5N 38E	Surface	AB	FG	1
ME-4/21/99-02-MO-04	5N 38E	Surface	CH	PL	29
ME-4/21/99-02-MO-05	5N 38E	Surface	BA	FG	17
ME-4/21/99-02-MO-06	5N 38E	Surface	WH	WH	1
ME-4/21/99-02-MO-07	5N 38E	Surface	MU	UM, FG	25
ME-4/21/99-02-MO-08	5N 38E	Surface	ND	FG	1
ME-4/21/99-02-MO-09	5N 38E	Surface	GC	PL, FG	1.5
ME-4/21/99-03-MO-01	0N 28E	Surface	AB	FG	1
ME-4/29/99-01-MO-01	6S 43E	Surface	OL	WH, CO, AP	3
ME-4/29/99-01-MO-02	6S 43E	Surface	LI	CA, FG	1
ME-4/29/99-01-MO-03	6S 43E	Surface	SN	WH, CO, FG	5
ME-4/29/99-01-MO-04	6S 43E	Surface	SN	WH, FG	1
ME-4/29/99-01-MO-05	6S 43E	Surface	BA	FG	8
ME-4/29/99-01-MO-06	6S 43E	Surface	CH	PL, FG	12

184

Metini #	Unit #	Level	Taxa	Diagnostic Element	Counts
ME-4/29/99-01-MO-07	6S 43E	Surface	GC	PL, FG	5
ME-4/29/99-01-MO-08	6S 43E	Surface	AB	FG	1
ME-4/29/99-01-MO-09	6S 43E	Surface	MU	UM, FG	10
ME-4/29/99-01-MO-10	6S 43E	Surface	ND	FG	1
ME-4/29/99-02-MO-01	11S 41E	Surface	SN	WH, FG	3
ME-4/29/99-02-MO-02	11S 41E	Surface	SN	WH, CO, FG	11
ME-4/29/99-02-MO-03	11S 41E	Surface	BA	FG	68
ME-4/29/99-02-MO-04	11S 41E	Surface	AB	FG	1
ME-4/29/99-02-MO-05	11S 41E	Surface	LI	CA, FG	1
ME-4/29/99-02-MO-06	11S 41E	Surface	GC	PL, FG	2
ME-4/29/99-02-MO-07	11S 41E	Surface	CH	PL	36.5
ME-4/29/99-02-MO-08	11S 41E	Surface	MU	UM, FG	76
ME-4/29/99-02-MO-09	11S 41E	Surface	ND	FG	0
ME-4/29/99-02-MO-10	11S 41E	Surface	WH	WH	1
ME-4/29/99-03-MO-01	20S 21E	Surface	UN	FG	1
ME-4/29/99-07-MO-01	1N 40E	Surface	LI	CA, FG	1
ME-4/29/99-07-MO-02	1N 40E	Surface	SN	WH, FG	2
ME-4/29/99-07-MO-03	1N 40E	Surface	AB	FG	1
ME-4/29/99-07-MO-04	1N 40E	Surface	BA	FG	66
ME-4/29/99-07-MO-05	1N 40E	Surface	GC	PL, FG	1
ME-4/29/99-07-MO-06	1N 40E	Surface	CH	PL	29.5
ME-4/29/99-07-MO-07	1N 40E	Surface	SN	WH, CO, FG	6
ME-4/29/99-07-MO-08	1N 40E	Surface	MU	UM, FG	61
ME-4/29/99-07-MO-09	1N 40E	Surface	ND	FG	1
ME-4/30/99-02-MO-01	19S 43E	Surface	AB	FG	1
ME-4/30/99-02-MO-02	19S 43E	Surface	SN	FG	1
ME-4/30/99-02-MO-03	19S 43E	Surface	BA	FG	4
ME-4/30/99-02-MO-04	19S 43E	Surface	MU	UM, FG	2
ME-4/30/99-02-MO-05	19S 43E	Surface	CH	PL	7.5
ME-4/30/99-02-MO-06	19S 43E	Surface	GC	PL, FG	1
ME-4/30/99-02-MO-07	19S 43E	Surface	ND	FG	1
ME-4/30/99-03-MO-01	27S 42E	Surface	SN	FG	1
ME-4/30/99-03-MO-02	27S 42E	Surface	CH	PL, FG	3
ME-4/30/99-03-MO-03	27S 42E	Surface	AB	FG	1
ME-4/30/99-03-MO-04	27S 42E	Surface	UN	FG	1
ME-4/30/99-04-MO-01	4S 40E	Surface	AB	FG	1
ME-4/30/99-04-MO-02	4S 40E	Surface	CH	PL	7
ME-4/30/99-04-MO-03	4S 40E	Surface	MU	UM, FG	2
ME-4/30/99-04-MO-04	4S 40E	Surface	GC	FG	1
ME-4/30/99-04-MO-05	4S 40E	Surface	SN	CO, FG	2

Metini #	Unit #	Level	Taxa	Diagnostic Element	Counts
ME-4/30/99-04-MO-06	4S 40E	Surface	UN	FG	1
ME-4/30/99-05-MO-01	35S 43E	Surface	SN	AP, FG	1
ME-4/30/99-05-MO-02	35S 43E	Surface	MU	UM	1
ME-4/30/99-05-MO-03	35S 43E	Surface	SN	FG	1
ME-4/30/99-05-MO-04	35S 43E	Surface	CH	PL	9
ME-4/30/99-05-MO-05	35S 43E	Surface	UN	FG	1
ME-4/30/99-06-MO-01	38S 41E	Surface	AB	FG	1
ME-4/30/99-06-MO-02	38S 41E	Surface	MU	UM, FG	2
ME-4/30/99-06-MO-03	38S 41E	Surface	BA	FG	2
ME-4/30/99-06-MO-04	38S 41E	Surface	CH	PL	3
ME-4/30/99-06-MO-05	38S 41E	Surface	UN	FG	1
ME-4/30/99-06-MO-06	38S 41E	Surface	SN	FG	1
ME-4/30/99-06-MO-07	38S 41E	Surface	SN	CO	2
ME-4/30/99-06-MO-08	38S 41E	Surface	GC	PL, FG	1
ME-4/30/99-09-MO-01	6N 41E	Surface	LI	CA	4
ME-4/30/99-09-MO-02	6N 41E	Surface	SN	WH, CO, FG	3
ME-4/30/99-09-MO-03	6N 41E	Surface	SN	CO, FG	4
ME-4/30/99-09-MO-04	6N 41E	Surface	AB	FG	1
ME-4/30/99-09-MO-05	6N 41E	Surface	CH	PL	3.5
ME-4/30/99-09-MO-06	6N 41E	Surface	BA	FG	5
ME-4/30/99-09-MO-07	6N 41E	Surface	MU	UM, FG	4
ME-4/30/99-09-MO-08	6N 41E	Surface	UN	FG	1
ME-4/30/99-09-MO-09	6N 41E	Surface	GC	PL, FG	0.5
ME-5/01/99-01-MO-01	22N 38E	Surface	UN	FG	1
ME-6/18/98-07-MO-01	6S 6E	Surface	UN	FG	1
ME-6/20/98-01-MO-01	5S 16E	Surface	UN	FG	1
ME-6/20/98-02-MO-01	13S 14E	Surface	AB	FG	1
ME-6/20/98-02-MO-02	13S 14E	Surface	BA	FG	11
ME-6/20/98-02-MO-03	13S 14E	Surface	LI	CA	3
ME-6/20/98-02-MO-04	13S 14E	Surface	SN	CO, FG	4
ME-6/20/98-02-MO-05	13S 14E	Surface	GC	PL, FG	1
ME-6/20/98-02-MO-06	13S 14E	Surface	CH	PL	19
ME-6/20/98-02-MO-07	13S 14E	Surface	CL	UM	1
ME-6/20/98-02-MO-08	13S 14E	Surface	MU	UM	27
ME-6/20/98-02-MO-09	13S 14E	Surface	ND	FG	1
ME-6/20/98-03-MO-01	10S 14E	Surface	CH	PL	1
ME-6/20/98-03-MO-02	10S 14E	Surface	GC	FG	1
ME-6/20/98-03-MO-03	10S 14E	Surface	MU	FG	1
ME-6/20/98-04-MO-01	12S 17E	Surface	CH	PL	60
ME-6/20/98-04-MO-02	12S 17E	Surface	BA	FG	78

Metini #	Unit #	Level	Taxa	Diagnostic Element	Counts
ME-6/20/98-04-MO-03	12S 17E	Surface	MU	UM, FG	114
ME-6/20/98-04-MO-04	12S 17E	Surface	AB	FG	1
ME-6/20/98-04-MO-05	12S 17E	Surface	SN	CO, WH, FG	17
ME-6/20/98-04-MO-06	12S 17E	Surface	GC	PL, FG	0.5
ME-6/20/98-04-MO-07	12S 17E	Surface	ND	FG	1
ME-6/20/98-04-MO-08	12S 17E	Surface	UN	FG	1
ME-6/20/98-04-MO-09	12S 17E	Surface	LI	CA, FG	5
ME-6/20/98-04-MO-10	12S 17E	Surface	OL	WH	1
ME-6/20/98-05-MO-01	17S 14E	Surface	BA	FG	1
ME-6/20/98-05-MO-02	17S 14E	Surface	MU	UM	2
ME-6/20/98-05-MO-03	17S 14E	Surface	LI	CA	1
ME-6/20/98-05-MO-04	17S 14E	Surface	ND	FG	1
ME-6/20/98-05-MO-05	17S 14E	Surface	GC	PL, FG	1
ME-6/20/98-06-MO-01	6S 18E	Surface	AB	FG	1
ME-6/20/98-06-MO-02	6S 18E	Surface	MU	UM, FG	3
ME-6/20/98-06-MO-03	6S 18E	Surface	CH	PL, FG	3
ME-6/20/98-06-MO-04	6S 18E	Surface	BA	FG	1
ME-6/20/98-06-MO-05	6S 18E	Surface	SN	CO, WH, FG	2
ME-6/20/98-06-MO-06	6S 18E	Surface	ND	FG	1
ME-6/20/98-07-MO-01	17S 16E	Surface	AB	FG	1
ME-6/20/98-07-MO-02	17S 16E	Surface	SN	CO, FG	2
ME-6/20/98-07-MO-03	17S 16E	Surface	BA	FG	7
ME-6/20/98-07-MO-04	17S 16E	Surface	CH	PL	0.5
ME-6/20/98-07-MO-05	17S 16E	Surface	MU	UM	16
ME-6/20/98-07-MO-06	17S 16E	Surface	CH	PL	15.5
ME-6/20/98-07-MO-07	17S 16E	Surface	GC	PL, FG	5
ME-6/20/98-07-MO-08	17S 16E	Surface	ND	FG	1
ME-6/20/98-07-MO-09	17S 16E	Surface	LI	CA	1
ME-6/23/98-02-MO-01	22S 6E	Surface	MU	UM, FG	5
ME-6/23/98-02-MO-02	22S 6E	Surface	CH	PL	8
ME-6/23/98-02-MO-03	22S 6E	Surface	OL	WH	2
ME-6/23/98-02-MO-04	22S 6E	Surface	SN	CO, FG	1
ME-6/23/98-02-MO-05	22S 6E	Surface	BA	FG	1
ME-6/23/98-02-MO-06	22S 6E	Surface	ND	FG	1
ME-6/23/98-02-MO-07	22S 6E	Surface	GC	PL, FG	0.5
ME-6/23/98-02-MO-08	22S 6E	Surface	LI	CA	1
ME-6/23/98-04-MO-01	25S 11E	Surface	UN	FG	1
ME-6/23/98-04-MO-02	25S 11E	Surface	SN	WH	3
ME-6/24/98-02-MO-01	22S 19E	Surface	CH	PL	3
ME-6/24/98-02-MO-02	22S 19E	Surface	SN	CO	1

Metini #	Unit #	Level	Taxa	Diagnostic Element	Counts
ME-6/24/98-02-MO-03	22S 19E	Surface	AB	FG	1
ME-6/24/98-02-MO-04	22S 19E	Surface	MU	FG	1
ME-6/24/98-06-MO-01	36S 18E	Surface	CH	PL	1
ME-6/24/98-06-MO-02	36S 18E	Surface	MU	FG	1
ME-6/24/98-06-MO-03	36S 18E	Surface	SN	CO	1
ME-6/24/98-06-MO-04	36S 18E	Surface	UN	FG	1
ME-6/26/98-01-MO-01	5S 24E	Surface	MU	UM	1
ME-6/26/98-01-MO-02	5S 24E	Surface	AB	FG	1
ME-6/26/98-01-MO-03	5S 24E	Surface	UN	FG	1
ME-6/26/98-03-MO-01	8S 22E	Surface	AB	FG	1
ME-6/26/98-03-MO-02	8S 22E	Surface	BA	FG	6
ME-6/26/98-03-MO-03	8S 22E	Surface	GC	PL, FG	1
ME-6/26/98-03-MO-04	8S 22E	Surface	CH	PL	16
ME-6/26/98-03-MO-05	8S 22E	Surface	SN	CO, FG	3
ME-6/26/98-03-MO-06	8S 22E	Surface	MU	UM	15
ME-6/26/98-03-MO-07	8S 22E	Surface	ND	FG	1
ME-6/26/98-03-MO-08	8S 22E	Surface	OL	FG	1
ME-6/26/98-04-MO-01	7S 27E	Surface	GC	PL, FG	1.5
ME-6/26/98-04-MO-02	7S 27E	Surface	CH	PL	10
ME-6/26/98-04-MO-03	7S 27E	Surface	BA	FG	9
ME-6/26/98-04-MO-04	7S 27E	Surface	AB	FG	1
ME-6/26/98-04-MO-05	7S 27E	Surface	MU	UM, FG	6
ME-6/26/98-04-MO-06	7S 27E	Surface	SN	CO, WH, FG	6
ME-6/26/98-04-MO-07	7S 27E	Surface	ND	FG	1
ME-6/26/98-04-MO-08	7S 27E	Surface	OL	WH	1
ME-6/26/98-04-MO-09	7S 27E	Surface	LI	CA	2
ME-6/26/98-05-MO-01	5S 33E	Surface	AB	WO, FG	1
ME-6/26/98-05-MO-02	5S 33E	Surface	SN	CO, WH, FG	3
ME-6/26/98-05-MO-03	5S 33E	Surface	MU	UM, FG	3
ME-6/26/98-05-MO-04	5S 33E	Surface	BA	FG	4
ME-6/26/98-05-MO-05	5S 33E	Surface	CH	PL	18
ME-6/26/98-05-MO-06	5S 33E	Surface	GC	PL, FG	2
ME-6/26/98-05-MO-07	5S 33E	Surface	ND	FG	1
ME-6/26/98-06-MO-01	5S 36E	Surface	MU	UM, FG	7
ME-6/26/98-06-MO-02	5S 36E	Surface	SN	CO, WH, FG	4
ME-6/26/98-06-MO-03	5S 36E	Surface	BA	FG	8
ME-6/26/98-06-MO-04	5S 36E	Surface	CH	PL	6
ME-6/26/98-06-MO-05	5S 36E	Surface	ND	FG	1
ME-6/26/98-06-MO-06	5S 36E	Surface	GC	FG	1
ME-6/26/98-06-MO-07	5S 36E	Surface	AB	WO	1

Metini #	Unit #	Level	Taxa	Diagnostic Element	Counts
ME-6/26/98-07-MO-01	7S 30E	Surface	GC	PL	0.5
ME-6/26/98-07-MO-02	7S 30E	Surface	MU	UM, FG	3
ME-6/26/98-07-MO-03	7S 30E	Surface	AB	FG	1
ME-6/26/98-07-MO-04	7S 30E	Surface	SN	CO	1
ME-6/26/98-07-MO-05	7S 30E	Surface	ND	FG	1
ME-6/26/98-08-MO-01	10S 37E	Surface	MU	UM, FG	3
ME-6/26/98-08-MO-02	10S 37E	Surface	CH	PL	9
ME-6/26/98-08-MO-03	10S 37E	Surface	LI	CA	1
ME-6/26/98-08-MO-04	10S 37E	Surface	BA	FG	11
ME-6/26/98-08-MO-05	10S 37E	Surface	AB	FG	1
ME-6/26/98-08-MO-06	10S 37E	Surface	SN	CO, FG	1
ME-6/26/98-08-MO-07	10S 37E	Surface	ND	FG	1
ME-6/26/98-08-MO-08	10S 37E	Surface	GC	PL, FG	0.5
ME-6/26/98-08-MO-09	10S 37E	Surface	OL	WH	2
ME-6/26/98-09-MO-01	18S 22E	Surface	MU	UM, FG	7
ME-6/26/98-09-MO-02	18S 22E	Surface	CH	PL	18
ME-6/26/98-09-MO-03	18S 22E	Surface	ND	FG	1
ME-6/26/98-09-MO-04	18S 22E	Surface	SN	WH, CO, FG	8
ME-6/26/98-09-MO-05	18S 22E	Surface	BA	FG	6
ME-6/26/98-09-MO-06	18S 22E	Surface	GC	PL	0.5
ME-6/26/98-10-MO-01	16S 26E	Surface	BA	FG	4
ME-6/26/98-10-MO-02	16S 26E	Surface	MU	UM	8
ME-6/26/98-10-MO-03	16S 26E	Surface	CH	PL	7
ME-6/26/98-10-MO-04	16S 26E	Surface	AB	FG	1
ME-6/26/98-10-MO-05	16S 26E	Surface	SN	CO	1
ME-6/26/98-10-MO-06	16S 26E	Surface	ND	FG	1
ME-6/26/98-11-MO-01	20S 30E	Surface	BA	FG	10
ME-6/26/98-11-MO-02	20S 30E	Surface	CH	PL	7
ME-6/26/98-11-MO-03	20S 30E	Surface	AB	FG	1
ME-6/26/98-11-MO-04	20S 30E	Surface	SN	FG	1
ME-6/26/98-11-MO-05	20S 30E	Surface	ND	FG	1
ME-6/26/98-11-MO-06	20S 30E	Surface	MU	UM, FG	5
ME-6/26/98-11-MO-07	20S 30E	Surface	GC	PL, FG	1
ME-6/26/98-11-MO-08	20S 30E	Surface	OL	WH	1
ME-6/26/98-12-MO-01	19S 38E	Surface	MU	UM, FG	30
ME-6/26/98-12-MO-02	19S 38E	Surface	CH	PL	15
ME-6/26/98-12-MO-03	19S 38E	Surface	LI	CA	1
ME-6/26/98-12-MO-04	19S 38E	Surface	AB	FG	1
ME-6/26/98-12-MO-05	19S 38E	Surface	GC	PL, FG	1
ME-6/26/98-12-MO-06	19S 38E	Surface	BA	FG	36

Metini #	Unit #	Level	Taxa	Diagnostic Element	Counts
ME-6/26/98-12-MO-07	19S 38E	Surface	ND	FG	1
ME-6/26/98-12-MO-08	19S 38E	Surface	SN	CO, FG	2
ME-9/12/98-03-MO-01	15S 21E	Surface	LI	CA	1
ME-9/12/98-03-MO-02	15S 21E	Surface	CH	PL	19
ME-9/12/98-03-MO-03	15S 21E	Surface	GC	FG	1
ME-9/12/98-03-MO-04	15S 21E	Surface	SN	WH, CO, FG	9
ME-9/12/98-03-MO-05	15S 21E	Surface	AB	FG	1
ME-9/12/98-03-MO-06	15S 21E	Surface	BA	FG	9
ME-9/12/98-03-MO-07	15S 21E	Surface	MU	UM, FG	17
ME-9/12/98-03-MO-08	15S 21E	Surface	ND	FG	1
ME-9/12/98-03-MO-09	15S 21E	Surface	OL	WH	1
ME-9/12/98-03-MO-10	15S 21E	Surface	WH	WH	1
ME-9/12/98-04-MO-01	11S 28E	Surface	MU	UM, FG	14
ME-9/12/98-04-MO-02	11S 28E	Surface	CH	PL	9
ME-9/12/98-04-MO-03	11S 28E	Surface	AB	FG	1
ME-9/12/98-04-MO-04	11S 28E	Surface	SN	CO	1
ME-9/12/98-04-MO-05	11S 28E	Surface	ND	FG	1
ME-9/12/98-05-MO-01	12S 33E	Surface	AB	FG	1
ME-9/12/98-05-MO-02	12S 33E	Surface	LI	CA	1
ME-9/12/98-05-MO-03	12S 33E	Surface	CH	PL	13
ME-9/12/98-05-MO-04	12S 33E	Surface	GC	PL	1
ME-9/12/98-05-MO-05	12S 33E	Surface	BA	FG	3
ME-9/12/98-05-MO-06	12S 33E	Surface	SN	CO, FG	1
ME-9/12/98-05-MO-07	12S 33E	Surface	MU	UM, FG	3
ME-9/12/98-05-MO-08	12S 33E	Surface	ND	FG	1
ME-9/12/98-06-MO-01	13S 36E	Surface	BA	FG	9
ME-9/12/98-06-MO-02	13S 36E	Surface	SN	FG	1
ME-9/12/98-06-MO-03	13S 36E	Surface	AB	FG	1
ME-9/12/98-06-MO-04	13S 36E	Surface	MU	UM, FG	4
ME-9/12/98-06-MO-05	13S 36E	Surface	CH	PL	7
ME-9/12/98-06-MO-06	13S 36E	Surface	GC	FG	1
ME-9/12/98-06-MO-07	13S 36E	Surface	ND	FG	1

KEY TO CODES

Appendix 10: Shellfish Assemblage

Taxa:

AB=Abalone	BA=Barnacle	CL=Clam	CH=Chiton
GC=Gumboot Chiton	LI=Limpet	HS=Horned Slipper Shell	MU=California Mussel
TU=Turban Snail	DW=Dog Whelk	TS=Terrestrial Snail	OL=Olivella Shell
UN=Unidentifiable	ND=Not Diagnostic		

Diagnostic Element:

CA=Cap	AP=Shell Aperture	CO=Columellae	
UM=Umbo	PL=Plate	WH=Whorl	FG=Fragment

Appendix 11: Worked Shell Artifacts

Metini #	Species	Modification Type	Artifact Classification	Count	Weight (g)	Bennyhoff and Hughes (1987) Type	Max. Length (mm)	Max Width (mm)	Perforation Diameter (mm)	Thickness (mm)
ME-6/26/98-08-MO-09A	OBP	HT, WW	WS	1	1.8	-	22.83	13.13	-	11.22
ME-6/26/98-08-MO-09B	OBP	HT, GR, WW	BE	1	2.21	A1c	21.4	12.5	5.36	10.85
ME-6/26/98-11-MO-08	OBP	HT, GR	BE	1	1.64	A1c	19.26	11.56	2.01	10.18
ME-9/12/98-03-MO-09	OBP	HT	WS	1	0.97	-	19.44	10.94	-	9.23
ME-4/17/99-02-MO-06	OBP	HT, WW	BE	1	3.21	A1c	24.67	14.06	2.33	12.53
ME-4/17/99-04-MO-01	OBP	HT	BE	1	2.36	A1c	21.61	13.67	5.29-6.03	12.26
ME-4/17/99-10-MO-02A	OBP	HT, GR	BE	1	2.14	A1c	20.5	12.3	2.46	10.46
ME-4/17/99-10-MO-02B	OBP	HT	BE	1	1.77	A1c	21.05	12.34	5.03	11.37
ME-4/29/99-01-MO-01A	OBP	HT	BE	1	1.88	A1c	20.84	12.78	4.15	11.29
ME-4/29/99-01-MO-01B	OBP	HT	DT/BEF	1	0.16	-	12.44	7.32	2.24	6.72
ME-4/29/99-01-MO-01C	OBP	HT	DT	1	0.35	-	17.23	9.71	-	0.65
ME-4/29/99-06-MO-01	OBP	HT	BE	1	1.66	A1c	19.24	11.45	4.51-5.09	10.58

KEY TO CODES

Appendix 11: Worked Shell Artifacts

Species: OBP=*Olivella biplicata*

Modification Type: HT=Heat Treated   GR=Ground
                                      WW=Water Worn

Artifact Classification: WS=Worked Shell   BE=Bead
                                      DT=Detritus   DT/BEF=Detritus, Bead Fragment

Appendix 12: Vertebrate Faunal Assemblage / page 1

Cat#3	Unit	Level	Taxon	Cf	Element	Part	Side	Age	Burn	Cut	Gnaw	Worked	Weight (g)	Count	AR	BT	C/O	LR	Mam	Mlrg	Mlg	Mmed	MC	OH	OT	SC	SE	UN	Comments
ME6/20/98-05-FA-01	17S 14E	Surface	Artiodactyla		Tooth	Fragment							0.94	1	1	.	.	.	.	.	.	.	.	.	.	.	.	.	cf Bos taurus
ME4/06/99-06-FA-01	29S 36E	Surface	Bos taurus		Rib	Fragment		J					13.19	1	.	1	.	.	.	.	.	.	.	.	.	.	.	.	
ME4/07/99-08-FA-01	39S 37E	Surface	Bos taurus		Tooth, molar	Lwr, pos1, most	L						8.6	3	.	3	.	.	.	.	.	.	.	.	.	.	.	.	
ME4/16/99-01-FA-01	23S 23E	Surface	Mammalia		Indeterminate	Fragment							0.46	3	.	.	.	.	3	.	.	.	.	.	.	.	.	.	
ME4/16/99-02-FA-01	21S 29E	Surface	Bos taurus		Mandible	Horizntl ramus	R			C			15.36	1	.	1	.	.	.	.	.	.	.	.	.	.	.	.	
ME4/16/99-02-FA-01	21S 29E	Surface	Mammalia, lg		Indeterminate	Fragment				C		W	0.7	1	.	.	.	.	.	1	.	.	.	.	.	.	.	.	Artifact
ME4/16/99-02-FA-01	21S 29E	Surface	Mammalia, lg		Indeterminate	Fragment							3.08	3	.	.	.	.	.	3	.	.	.	.	.	.	.	.	
ME4/16/99-02-FA-01	22S 32E	Surface	Mammalia, lg		Vertebrae	Fragment							1.26	1	.	.	.	.	.	1	.	.	.	.	.	.	.	.	
ME4/16/99-03-FA-01	22S 32E	Surface	Mammalia, lg		Limb	Shaft, frag							2.18	1	.	.	.	.	.	1	.	.	.	.	.	.	.	.	
ME4/16/99-03-FA-01	22S 32E	Surface	Mammalia, lg		Indeterminate	Fragment							1.73	1	.	.	.	.	.	1	.	.	.	.	.	.	.	.	
ME4/16/99-03-FA-01	23S 38E	Surface	Bos taurus		Vert, cervical	Fragment							7.59	1	.	1	.	.	.	.	.	.	.	.	.	.	.	.	Weathered
ME4/16/99-04-FA-01	23S 38E	Surface	Mammalia, lg		Indeterminate	Fragment							1.92	1	.	.	.	.	.	1	.	.	.	.	.	.	.	.	
ME4/16/99-04-FA-01	23S 38E	Surface	Mammalia, lg		Rib	Shaft, frag	R						2.22	1	.	1	.	.	.	.	.	.	.	.	.	.	.	.	Weathered
ME4/16/99-04-FA-01	23S 38E	Surface	Odocoileus hemionus		Patella	Fragment	R						1.79	1	.	.	.	.	.	.	.	.	.	1	.	.	.	.	
ME4/16/99-04-FA-02	23S 38E	Surface	Bos taurus	Cf	Tooth	Fragment				C			3.7	1	.	1	.	.	.	.	.	.	.	.	.	.	.	.	Scapula or vertebrae sawed
ME4/16/99-05-FA-01	26S 28E	Surface	Bos taurus		Tooth	Fragment							10.08	1	.	1	.	.	.	.	.	.	.	.	.	.	.	.	
ME4/16/99-06-FA-01	29S 36E	Surface	Mammalia, lg		Vertebrae	Fragment							3.31	1	.	.	.	.	.	1	.	.	.	.	.	.	.	.	Weathered
ME4/17/99-01-FA-01	29S 21E	Surface	Artiodactyla		Vert, cervical	Process	A						1.75	1	1	.	.	.	.	.	.	.	.	.	.	.	.	.	Lateral process
ME4/17/99-01-FA-01	29S 21E	Surface	Capra/Ovis sp	Cf	Vert, atlas	Fragment	A	A					8.42	2	.	.	2	.	.	.	.	.	.	.	.	.	.	.	
ME4/17/99-01-FA-01	29S 21E	Surface	Mammalia, lg		Indeterminate	Fragment							4.26	9	.	.	.	.	.	9	.	.	.	.	.	.	.	.	
ME4/17/99-01-FA-01	29S 21E	Surface	Mammalia, lg		Indeterminate	Fragment							6.06	2	.	.	.	.	.	2	.	.	.	.	.	.	.	.	Flat bone
ME4/17/99-01-FA-01	29S 21E	Surface	Mammalia, lg		Indeterminate	Fragment							15.07	1	.	.	.	.	.	1	.	.	.	.	.	.	.	.	Not sea mammal cow size
ME4/17/99-01-FA-01	29S 21E	Surface	Mammalia, lg		Limb	Shaft, frag							4.04	3	.	.	.	.	.	3	.	.	.	.	.	.	.	.	
ME4/17/99-01-FA-01	29S 21E	Surface	Mammalia, lg		Indeterminate	Fragment							0.49	1	.	.	.	.	.	1	.	.	.	.	.	.	.	.	
ME4/17/99-01-FA-01	29S 21E	Surface	Mammalia, lg		Indeterminate	Fragment							0.59	1	.	.	.	.	.	1	.	.	.	.	.	.	.	.	
ME4/17/99-02-FA-01	30S 34E	Surface	Artiodactyla		Tooth	Fragment							0.56	1	1	.	.	.	.	.	.	.	.	.	.	.	.	.	
ME4/17/99-02-FA-01	30S 34E	Surface	Mammalia, lg		Indeterminate	Fragment							2.09	2	.	.	.	.	.	2	.	.	.	.	.	.	.	.	
ME4/17/99-03-FA-01	31S 33E	Surface	Mammalia, lg		Indeterminate	Fragment							4.11	2	.	.	.	.	.	2	.	.	.	.	.	.	.	.	
ME4/17/99-03-FA-01	31S 33E	Surface	Mammalia, lg		Limb	Shaft, frag			B				5.9	2	.	.	.	.	.	2	.	.	.	.	.	.	.	.	
ME4/17/99-04-FA-01	35S 21E	Surface	Mammalia, lg		Indeterminate	Fragment							1.57	1	.	.	.	.	.	1	.	.	.	.	.	.	.	.	
ME4/17/99-05-FA-01	35S 28E	Surface	Artiodactyla		Radius	Distal	L						3.88	1	1	.	.	.	.	.	.	.	.	.	.	.	.	.	
ME4/17/99-05-FA-01	35S 28E	Surface	Mammalia, lg		Indeterminate	Fragment							2.11	2	.	.	.	.	.	2	.	.	.	.	.	.	.	.	Cancellous
ME4/17/99-06-FA-01	34S 36E	Surface	Mammalia, lg		Limb	Fragment							6.61	5	.	.	.	.	.	5	.	.	.	.	.	.	.	.	Cow size
ME4/17/99-06-FA-01	34S 36E	Surface	Mammalia, lg		Limb	Shaft, frag							2.17	1	.	.	.	.	.	1	.	.	.	.	.	.	.	.	
ME4/17/99-06-FA-02	34S 36E	Surface	Bos taurus	Cf	Tooth, molar	Fragment			B				3.11	2	.	2	.	.	.	.	.	.	.	.	.	.	.	.	2 pieces, conjoined
ME4/17/99-07-FA-01	36S 32E	Surface	Mammalia, lg		Rib	Shaft, frag							3.93	1	.	.	.	.	.	1	.	.	.	.	.	.	.	.	Cow size, weathered, green stain
ME4/17/99-07-FA-02	36S 32E	Surface	Mammalia, lg		Indeterminate	Fragment							3.88	6	.	.	.	.	.	6	.	.	.	.	.	.	.	.	
ME4/17/99-07-FA-03	36S 32E	Surface	Mammalia, lg		Indeterminate	Fragment			B				0.4	1	.	.	.	.	.	1	.	.	.	.	.	.	.	.	
ME4/17/99-10-FA-01	36S 32E	Surface	Bos taurus		Metapodial	Distal epiph		J					9.77	2	.	2	.	.	.	.	.	.	.	.	.	.	.	.	
ME4/17/99-10-FA-01	36S 32E	Surface	Mammalia		Indeterminate	Fragment			B				1.08	1	.	.	.	.	1	.	.	.	.	.	.	.	.	.	Calcined
ME4/17/99-10-FA-01	36S 32E	Surface	Mammalia		Indeterminate	Fragment							0.88	3	.	.	.	.	3	.	.	.	.	.	.	.	.	.	
ME4/17/99-10-FA-01	36S 32E	Surface	Mammalia, lg		Indeterminate	Fragment							0.71	1	.	.	.	.	.	1	.	.	.	.	.	.	.	.	
ME4/17/99-10-FA-02	36S 32E	Surface	Bos taurus		Vertebrae	Articular surface	A			C			3.23	1	.	1	.	.	.	.	.	.	.	.	.	.	.	.	
ME4/21/99-01-FA-01	1N 35S	Surface	Bos taurus	Cf	Indeterminate	Fragment							9.75	1	.	1	.	.	.	.	.	.	.	.	.	.	.	.	

Cat#3	Unit	Level	Taxon	Cf	Element	Part	Side	Age	Burn	Cut	Gnaw	Worked	Weight (g)	Count	AR	BT	C/O	LR	Mam	Mlrg	Mmed	MC	OH	OT	SC	SE	UN	Comments
ME-4/21/99-01-FA01	1N 35S	Surface	Mammalia, lg		Indeterminate	Fragment							1.1	1						1								
ME-4/21/99-02-FA01	5N 38E	Surface	Mammalia, lg		Indeterminate	Fragment							5.12	13						13								
ME-4/21/99-02-FA01	5N 38E	Surface	Mammalia, lg		Limb	Shaft, frag							1.46	1						1								
ME-4/21/99-02-FA01	5N 38E	Surface	Mammalia, lg		Vert,lumbar	Fragment	A						2.92	1						1								Zygopophysis cow size
ME-4/21/99-02-FA01	5N 38E	Surface	Odocoileus hemionus	Cf	Phalanx	Proximal							1.15	1					1									
ME-4/21/99-01-FA01	5N 38E	Surface	Vertebrata		Indeterminate	Fragment			B				0.02	1													1	Calceined
ME-4/29/99-01-FA01	6S 43E	Surface	Mammalia		Indeterminate	Fragment							0.45	4					4									
ME-4/29/99-01-FA01	6S 43E	Surface	Mammalia, lg		Indeterminate	Fragment			B				0.42	1						1								
ME-4/29/99-02-FA01	11S 41E	Surface	Microtus californicus		Mandible	Most	L						0.09	1								1						
ME-4/29/99-02-FA01	11S 41E	Surface	Odocoileus hemionus		Metatarsal	Proximal frag	L	A					36.18	1									1					
ME-4/29/99-02-FA01	11S 41E	Surface	Odocoileus hemionus		Tooth, premolar	Upr, pos3, complt	R	A					0.88	1									1					
ME-4/29/99-07-FA01	1N 40E	Surface	Lynx rufus		Tarsal, calcaneus	Complete	L	A					2.46	1				1										
ME-4/29/99-07-FA03	1N 40E	Surface	Odocoileus hemionus		Phalanx, 2nd	Complete							2.19	1									1					
ME-4/29/99-07-FA03	1N 40E	Surface	Scorpaenichthys marmoratus		Rib	Complete	L						0.47	1											1			
ME-4/30/99-02-FA01	19S 43E	Surface	Bos taurus		Tooth, premolar	Lwr, pos2, complt	L	A					2	2		2												2 pieces, conjoined
ME-4/30/99-03-FA01	27S 42E	Surface	Mammalia, lg		Indeterminate	Fragment							0.76	1						1								
ME-4/30/99-03-FA01	27S 42E	Surface	Mammalia, lg		Indeterminate	Articlr surface							1.18	1						1								
ME-4/30/99-04-FA01	4S 40E	Surface	Mammalia, lg		Indeterminate	Fragment							1.58	2						2								
ME-4/30/99-09-FA01	6N 41E	Surface	Mammalia, lg		Vertebrae	Process	A						0.88	2						2								
ME-4/30/99-09-FA01	6N 41E	Surface	Mammalia, lg		Indeterminate	Fragment							0.61	1						1								Deer size; 2 pieces, conjoined
ME-4/30/99-09-FA01	6N 41E	Surface	Mammalia, lg		Vert, lumbar	Fragment							0.42	1						1								
ME-6/06/98-09-FA01	18S 22E	Surface	Bos taurus		Vert, lumbar	Articlr surface	A	J					1.14	1		1												Cancellous
ME-6/18/98-04-FA01	8S 4E	Surface	Mammalia, lg		Indeterminate	Fragment							0.42	1						1								Posterior
ME-6/20/98-02-FA01	13S 14E	Surface	Mammalia, lg		Indeterminate	Fragment					G		0.35	1						1								
ME-6/20/98-02-FA01	13S 14E	Surface	Mammalia, lg		Indeterminate	Fragment							0.88	1						1								
ME-6/20/98-02-FA01	13S 14E	Surface	Odocoileus hemionus		Metatarsal	Shaft, frag	A						1.75	1										1				
ME-6/20/98-04-FA01	12S 17E	Surface	Artiodactyla	Cf	Tooth	Fragment							0.38	1	1													
ME-6/20/98-04-FA01	12S 17E	Surface	Bos taurus	Cf	Rib	Shaft, frag			B		G		14.24	1		1												
ME-6/20/98-04-FA01	12S 17E	Surface	Capra/Ovis sp		Tarsal, astraglus	Complete	L	A	B				6.87	1			1											
ME-6/20/98-04-FA01	12S 17E	Surface	Mammalia		Indeterminate	Fragment							0.34	3					3									
ME-6/20/98-04-FA01	12S 17E	Surface	Mammalia, lg		Limb	Shaft, frag							1.66	1						1								
ME-6/20/98-04-FA01	12S 17E	Surface	Mammalia, lg		Indeterminate	Fragment							9.23	1						1								
ME-6/20/98-04-FA01	12S 17E	Surface	Odocoileus hemionus		Mandible	Fragment	R						3.66	2									2					Tooth, molar; lower Mm1 or M2; complete tooth fits in mandible
ME-6/20/98-04-FA02	12S 17E	Surface	Bos taurus		Tooth, incisor	Complete							2.04	1		1												Worn
ME-6/20/98-04-FA02	12S 17E	Surface	Capra/Ovis sp		Tibia	Shaft, frag	L						4.8	1			1											
ME-6/20/98-05-FA01	17S 14E	Surface	Mammalia, lg		Indeterminate	Fragment							4.87	7						7								
ME-6/20/98-06-FA01	6S 18E	Surface	Mammalia, lg		Indeterminate	Fragment							4.18	4						4								Cow size

Appendix 12: Vertebrate Faunal Assemblage / page 3

Cat#3	Unit	Level	Taxon	Cf	Element	Part	Side	Age	Burn	Cut	Gnaw	Worked	Weight (g)	Count	AR	BT	C/O	LR	Mam	Mfrg	Mmed	MC	OH	OT	SC	SE	UN	Comments
ME-6/20/9806-FA-01	6S 18E	Surface	Mammalia, md		Rib	Vertebral end		J					0.61	1							1							
ME-6/20/9807-FA-01	17S 16E	Surface	Artiodactyla		Tooth	Root							1.47	1	1													Cow size
ME-6/20/9807-FA-01	17S 16E	Surface	Mammalia, lg		Indeterminate	Fragment							2.58	4						4								
ME-6/20/9807-FA-03	17S 16E	Surface	Odocoileus hemionus		Sesamoid	Complete		A					0.22	1									1					Foot
ME-6/23/9802-FA-01	22S 6E	Surface	Mammalia, lg		Indeterminate	Fragment			B				0.3	1						1								
ME-6/23/9802-FA-01	22S 6E	Surface	Mammalia, lg		Indeterminate	Fragment							5.47	4						4								
ME-6/26/9801-FA-01	5S 24E	Surface	Bos taurus	Cf	Tooth, incisor	Fragment							0.33	1		1												
ME-6/26/9801-FA-01	5S 24E	Surface	Bos taurus		Tooth	Most							4.02	1		1												
ME-6/26/9801-FA-01	5S 24E	Surface	Bos taurus		Rib	Fragment							6.37	1		1												
ME-6/26/9801-FA-01	5S 24E	Surface	Odocoileus hemionus		Tooth	Fragment	R						1.67	1									1					
ME-6/26/9803-FA-01	8S 22E	Surface	Mammalia, lg		Indeterminate	Fragment							0.93	2						2								
ME-6/26/9803-FA-01	8S 22E	Surface	Mammalia, lg		Indeterminate	Fragment			B				0.76	1						1								
ME-6/26/9803-FA-01	8S 22E	Surface	Odocoileus hemionus		Radius	Distal epiph	R	J					3.8	1									1					
ME-6/26/9804-FA-01	7S 27E	Surface	Bos taurus		Carpal	Complete	R	A					14.03	1		1												Level-surface; Element - radial carpal
ME-6/26/9804-FA-01	7S 27E	Surface	Bos taurus		Sesamoid	Complete							2.74	1		1												Level-surface
ME-6/26/9804-FA-01	7S 27E	Surface	Mammalia, lg		Limb	Shaft							1.28	1						1								Level-surface
ME-6/26/9804-FA-01	7S 27E	Surface	Mammalia, lg		Tooth	Fragment							0.28	1						1								Level-surface cf Bos taurus
ME-6/26/9804-FA-01	7S 27E	Surface	Mammalia, lg		Indeterminate	Fragment				C			0.66	1						1								Level-surface
ME-6/26/9804-FA-01	7S 27E	Surface	Mammalia, lg		Indeterminate	Fragment							8.27	6						6								Level-surface
ME-6/26/9804-FA-01	7S 27E	Surface	Odocoileus hemionus		Tarsal	Complete	R	A					1.6	1									1					Level-surface trapezoid magnum tarsal
ME-6/26/9804-FA-01	7S 27E	Surface	Odocoileus hemionus		Fibula	Distal	R						0.81	1									1					Level-surface, complete distal end
ME-6/26/9804-FA-01	7S 27E	Surface	Sebastes sp		Vertebrae	Most		A					0.2	1														
ME-6/26/9805-FA-01	5S 33E	Surface	Mammalia, lg		Limb	Shaft, frag							2.81	1						1								
ME-6/26/9805-FA-01	5S 33E	Surface	Mammalia, lg		Indeterminate	Fragment							0.99	1						1								Possible cranial weathered
ME-6/26/9805-FA-01	5S 33E	Surface	Mammalia, lg		Indeterminate	Fragment							1.49	4						4								
ME-6/26/9805-FA-01	5S 36E	Surface	Odocoileus hemionus		Carpal, scaphoid	Complete	L	A					1.61	1									1					
ME-6/26/9805-FA-01	5S 36E	Surface	Odocoileus hemionus		Tars, navclrcubd	Complete	R	A	B				6.19	1									1					
ME-6/26/9806-FA-01	5S 36E	Surface	Bos taurus		Rib	Articular surface							5.28	1		1												Rib (sternal)
ME-6/26/9808-FA-01	10S 37E	Surface	Mammalia, lg		Indeterminate	Fragment							3.08	2						2						1			
ME-6/26/9809-FA-01	18S 22E	Surface	Mammalia		Indeterminate	Fragment			B				0.18	2				2										Calcined
ME-6/26/9809-FA-01	18S 22E	Surface	Mammalia, lg		Indeterminate	Fragment							5.25	2						2								Flat bone
ME-6/26/9809-FA-01	18S 22E	Surface	Mammalia, lg		Indeterminate	Fragment							5.64	14						14								
ME-6/26/9809-FA-01	18S 22E	Surface	Mammalia, lg		Femur	Head							1.93	1						1								Deer/sheep sized
ME-6/26/9809-FA-02	18S 22E	Surface	Bos taurus		Carpal	Complete							3.99	1		1												Accessory carpal
ME-6/26/9811-FA-01	20S 30E	Surface	Artiodactyla		Mandible	Fragment	R						1.91	1	1													Weathered
ME-6/26/9811-FA-01	20S 30E	Surface	Bos taurus		Femur	Shaft, frag							31.23	1		1												Weathered
ME-6/26/9811-FA-01	20S 30E	Surface	Mammalia, lg		Limb	Shaft							1.84	1						1								Cow size, weathered
ME-6/26/9811-FA-01	20S 30E	Surface	Microtus californicus		Mandible	Complete	L	A					0.11	1								1						Plus teeth
ME-6/26/9812-FA-01	19S 38E	Surface	Bos taurus		Rib	Fragment							1.89	1		1												

194

Appendix 12: Vertebrate Faunal Assemblage / *page 4*

Cat#3	Unit	Level	Taxon	Cf	Element	Part	Side	Age	Burn	Cut	Gnaw	Worked	Weight (g)	Count	AR	BT	C/O	LR	Mam	Mfrg	Mned	MC	OH	OT	SC	SE	UN	Comments
ME-6/26/98-12-FA01	19S 38E	Surface	Mammalia, lg		Indeterminate	Fragment				C			1.69	1						1								
ME-6/26/98-12-FA01	19S 38E	Surface	Mammalia, lg		Indeterminate	Fragment							4.78	5						5								1 piece cancellous
ME-6/28/98-07-FA01	7S 30E	Surface	Bos taurus		Cranial	Occipital condyle	R						14.63	1		1												
ME-6/28/98-07-FA01	7S 30E	Surface	Mammalia, lg		Indeterminate	Fragment							0.31	1						1								
ME-9/12/98-03-FA01	15S 21E	Surface	Bos taurus		Carpal, trapezoid	Fragment			B				6.63	1		1												Trapazoid-magnum
ME-9/12/98-03-FA01	15S 21E	Surface	Bos taurus		Tooth	Most		A					4.43	1		1												Worn
ME-9/12/98-03-FA01	15S 21E	Surface	Mammalia, lg		Indeterminate	Fragment							1.29	1						1								
ME-9/12/98-03-FA01	15S 21E	Surface	Mammalia, lg		Indeterminate	Fragment							1.01	1						1								
ME-9/12/98-03-FA01	15S 21E	Surface	Otariidae		Tarsal	Fragment	L						4.67	1										1				
ME-9/12/98-04-FA01	11S 28E	Surface	Mammalia, lg		Indeterminate	Fragment							0.17	1						1								
ME-9/12/98-04-FA01	11S 28E	Surface	Mammalia, lg		Indeterminate	Fragment							3.86	5						5								
ME-9/12/98-05-FA01	12S 33E	Surface	Mammalia, lg		Indeterminate	Fragment							0.23	1						1								
ME-9/12/98-05-FA01	12S 33E	Surface	Mammalia, lg		Indeterminate	Fragment							3.75	1						1								
ME-9/12/98-05-FA01	12S 33E	Surface	Odocoileus hemionus		Metacarpal	Proximal, shaft	L						14.27	1									1					
ME-5/01/99-02-FA01	15S 4E	1 (0-10 CM)	Mammalia		Indeterminate	Fragment			B				0.49	5					5									Calcined
ME-5/01/99-02-FA01	15S 4E	1 (0-10 CM)	Mammalia, lg		Limb	Shaft, frag			B				0.61	1						1								Calcined
ME-5/01/99-11-FA01	15S 4E	2 (10-20 CM)	Bos taurus	Cf	Limb	Shaft, frag							10.93	1		1												
ME-5/01/99-11-FA01	15S 4E	2 (10-20 CM)	Mammalia, lg		Indeterminate	Fragment			B				0.51	4						4								Calcined
ME-5/01/99-11-FA01	15S 4E	2 (10-20 CM)	Mammalia, lg		Indeterminate	Fragment							1.83	1						1								
ME-5/02/99-03-FA01	15S 4E	2 (20-25 CM)	Mammalia		Indeterminate	Fragment			B				0.13	3					3									
ME-5/02/99-03-FA01	15S 4E	2 (20-25 CM)	Mammalia		Indeterminate	Fragment							0.48	4					4									
ME-5/02/99-01-FA01	15S 4E	3 (20-27 CM)	Mammalia		Indeterminate	Fragment			B				0.24	4					4									Unit NW 1/4 of unit near feature 2
ME-5/02/99-01-FA01	15S 4E	3 (20-27 CM)	Mammalia, lg		Indeterminate	Fragment							0.58	5						5								Unit NW 1/4 of unit near feature 2
ME-5/02/99-06-FA01	15S 4E	WEST WALL	Mammalia, lg		Indeterminate	Fragment							0.63	3						3								
ME-5/02/99-06-FA01	15S 4E	WEST WALL	Odocoileus hemionus	Cf	Radius	Proximal	L						1.12	1									1					Cf radius
ME-5/02/99-12-FA01	15S 4E	N/A	Mammalia, lg		Indeterminate	Fragment							0.45	1						1								South wall, fell out of wall near southwest corner
ME-4/29/99-03-FA01	20S 21E	Surface	Mammalia, lg		Indeterminate	Fragment							1.29	1						1								cf deer, femur head, cancellous
ME-4/29/99-03-FA01	20S 21E	Surface	Mammalia, lg		Indeterminate	Fragment							0.7	2						2								Cancellous
ME-4/29/99-04-FA01	20S 21E	1 (0-10 CM)	Artiodactyla		Indeterminate	Fragment							0.33	1	1													
ME-4/29/99-04-FA01	20S 21E	1 (0-10 CM)	Bos taurus		Tooth, premolar	Upr, pos2, complt	L						3.28	1		1												Worn
ME-4/29/99-04-FA01	20S 21E	1 (0-10 CM)	Mammalia		Indeterminate	Fragment							0.06	1					1									
ME-4/29/99-04-FA01	20S 21E	1 (0-10 CM)	Mammalia, lg		Indeterminate	Fragment			B				1.07	3						3								Calcined
ME-4/29/99-04-FA01	20S 21E	1 (0-10 CM)	Mammalia, lg		Indeterminate	Fragment			B				1.31	1						1								
ME-4/29/99-04-FA01	20S 21E	1 (0-10 CM)	Mammalia, lg		Femur	Head							1.21	1						1								Deer sized
ME-4/29/99-06-FA01	20S 21E	2 (10-20 CM)	Artiodactyla		Tooth, incisor	Complete		A					0.21	1	1													
ME-4/29/99-06-FA01	20S 21E	2 (10-20 CM)	Bos taurus		Tooth, molar	Fragment							8.88	1		1												Upper position?

Appendix 12: Vertebrate Faunal Assemblage / page 5

Cat#3	Unit	Level	Taxon	Cf	Element	Part	Side	Age	Burn	Cut	Gnaw	Worked	Weight (g)	Count	AR	BT	C/O	LR	Mam	Mlrg	Mmed	MC	OH	OT	SC	SE	UN	Comments
ME-4/29/99Q6-FA-01	20S 21E	2 (10-20 CM)	Bos taurus	Cf	Innominate	Fragment							5.2	1		1												
ME-4/29/99Q6-FA-01	20S 21E	2 (10-20 CM)	Mammalia		Indeterminate	Fragment			B				1.54	4					4									3 pieces, calcined
ME-4/29/99Q6-FA-01	20S 21E	2 (10-20 CM)	Mammalia, lg		Indeterminate	Fragment							9.36	27						27								
ME-4/29/99Q6-FA-01	20S 21E	2 (10-20 CM)	Mammalia, lg		Indeterminate	Shaft, frag							3.07	2						2								Rib or vertebrae
ME-4/29/99Q6-FA-01	20S 21E	2 (10-20 CM)	Mammalia, lg		Limb	Shaft, frag							12.91	4						4								Cow sized
ME-4/29/99Q6-FA-01	20S 21E	2 (10-20 CM)	Mammalia, lg		Indeterminate	Fragment							0.29	1						1								
ME-4/29/99Q6-FA-01	20S 21E	2 (10-20 CM)	Microtus californicus		Mandible	Most	R	A					0.09	2								2						
ME-4/29/99Q6-FA-01	20S 21E	2 (10-20 CM)	Odocoileus hemionus		Carpal, trapezoid	Complete	L	A					1.22	1									1					Carpal magnum
ME-4/30/99-12-FA-02	20S 21E	3 (20-30 CM)	Bos taurus		Tibia	Distal	L	A					50.03	3		3												3 pieces, conjoined
ME-4/30/99-12-FA-02	20S 21E	3 (20-30 CM)	Bos taurus		Fibula	Distal	R	A					5.12	1		1												
ME-4/30/99-12-FA-01	20S 21E	3 (20-30 CM)	Mammalia, lg		Indeterminate	Fragment							2.24	1						1								
ME-4/30/99-12-FA-02	20S 21E	3 (20-30 CM)	Mammalia, lg		Indeterminate	Fragment							3.29	1						1								Cow size, cancellous
TOTAL												Σ		329	9	37	4	1	37	215	1	4	18	1	1	1	1	

KEY TO CODES

Appendix 12: Vertebrate Faunal Assemblage (above)

Mammal/Fish Codes:
- BT=Domestic Cow
- C/O=Goat/Sheep
- OH=Black-Tailed Deer
- LR=Bobcat
- MC=California Vole
- OT=Eared Seal
- SC=Cabezon
- SE=Rockfish
- Mlrg=Large Mammal
- Mmed=Medium Mammal
- MA=Mammal
- AR=Artiodactyl
- UN=Unidentified

Appendix 13: Plant Material Absolute Counts and Weights

Plant Material Absolute Counts and Weights (g) for the Analyzed Soil Samples from Metini Village (CA-SON-175), Sonoma County, California

Unit	0N 10W			15S 4E					20S 21E			
Level	1	2	3	1	2	Feature 1	East of Feature 1	3	1	2	3	4
Depth (cm)	0-10	10-25	25-40	0-15	15-30	20-25	20-25	40-60	0-10	10-20	20-30	30-40
EB Number	4084	4085	4086	4087	4088	4089	4090	4091	4092	4093	4094	4095
TYPE												
SEEDS												
Caryophyllaceae cf.		1									2	
Eschscholzia sp. cf.					1							
Fabaceae										3		1
Hordeum vulgare cf.						1						
Poa sp. cf.											7	
Poaceae										3		
Polygonum/Rumex sp.						1						
Pulse frag. cf.									3			
Rosaceae cf.											4	
Solanaceae cf.										1		
Triticum spp.							1					
Umbellularia californicab				0.002					0.004		0.006	
Unidentifiable seeds		1	1	1					2	7	7	
Seed Total[a]	0	2	1	0	2	6	1	0	5	14	20	1
PLANT PARTS												
Wood[b]			<0.01	0.67	0.38	1.68	1.98	P	0.4	0.99	1.34	0.09
Amorphous[b]						0.14	0.84		0.03	0.04		0.02
Nutshell/seedcoat[b]						0.004			0.006	0.009	0.007	
Conifer cone frag.										3	6	2

[a] Seed total includes unidentifiable seeds and fragments. P indicates presence in fractions < 2.0 mm.

[b] Weight in grams.

197

Appendix 14: Plant Material Densities

Plant Material Densities (counts/liter or grams/liter) for the Samples from Metini Village (CA-SON-175), Sonoma County, California.

Unit	ON 10W			15S 4E					20S 21E			
Level	1	2	3	1	2	Feature 1	East of Feature 1	3	1	2	3	4
Depth (cm)	0-10	10-25	25-40	0-15	15-30	20-25	20-25	20-25	0-10	10-20	20-30	30-40
EB Number	4084	4085	4086	4087	4088	4089	4090	4091	4092	4093	4094	4095
TYPE												
SEEDS												
Caryophyllaceae cf.		0.25									0.25	
Eschscholzia sp. cf.					0.29							
Fabaceae										0.6		0.42
Hordeum vulgare cf.						0.33						
Poa sp. cf.											0.88	
Poaceae										0.6		
Polygonum/Rumex sp.						0.33						
Pulse frag. cf.									0.79			
Rosaceae cf.											0.5	
Solanaceae cf.										0.2		
Triticum spp.						1.33	0.36					
Umbellularia californicab				0.0006					0.001		0.0008	
Unidentifiable seeds		0.25	0.27		0.29				0.53	1.4	0.88	
Seed Total[a]	0	0.5	0.27	0	0.59	2	0.36	0	1.32	2.8	2.5	0.42
PLANT PARTS												
Wood[b]			<0.01	0.209	0.113	0.56	0.72	P	0.105	0.1 98	0.168	0.038
Amorphous[b]						0.047	0.305		0.008	0.008		0.008
Nutshell/seedcoat[b]						0.0013			0.002	0.0018	0.0009	
Conifer cone frag.										0.6	0.75	0.83

[a] Seed density total includes unidentifiable seeds and fragments.

[b] Density in grams/liter.

P indicates presence in fractions < 2.0 mm.

Appendix 15: Wood Charcoal Absolute Counts and Weights

Wood Charcoal Absolute Counts and Weights (g) for the Samples from Metini Village (CA-SON-175), Sonoma County, California

Unit	0N 10W				15S 4E						20S 21E							
Level	2		1		2		Feature 1		East of Feature 1		1		2		3		4	
Depth (cm)	25-40		0-15		15-30		20-25		20-25		0-10		10-20		20-30		30-40	
EB Number	4086		4087		4088		4089		4090		4092		4093		4094		4095	
TYPE	Ct.	Wt.	Ct.	Wt.	Ct.	Wt.	Ct.	Wt.	Ct.	Wt.	Ct.	Wt.	Ct.	Wt.	Ct.	Wt.	Ct.	Wt.
Amorphous											2	0.03	2	0.02				
Asteraceae cf.	2	<0.01	1	0.02									3	0.05				
Conifer			6	0.13	6	0.12	2	0.04	3	0.07	5	0.05	7	0.23	6	0.11	4	0.09
Conifer cone frag.					1	0.01									4	0.07		
Diffuse porous					2	0.07	3	0.04			3	0.04						
Pinus sp.			4	0.11	2	0.04	8	0.58	1	0.02	6	0.16	5	0.11	3	0.23		
Salix sp. cf.					1	0.01			3	0.13								
Sequoia sempervirens			8	0.13	8	0.08	7	0.24	13	0.56			3	0.09	5	0.18		
Type A			1	0.02														
Umbellularia californica															1	0.01		
Total Identified	2	<0.01	20	0.41	20	0.33	20	0.9	20	0.78	16	0.28	20	0.5	19	0.6	4	0.09
Total Charcoal				0.67		0.38		1.68		1.98		0.4		0.99		1.34		0.09

199